Paramedic Chief

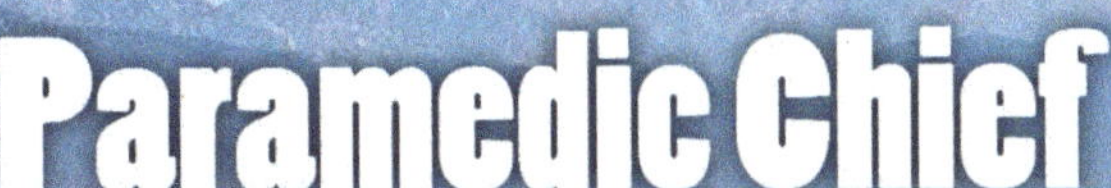

Extraordinary Experiences from the Streets of Los Angeles

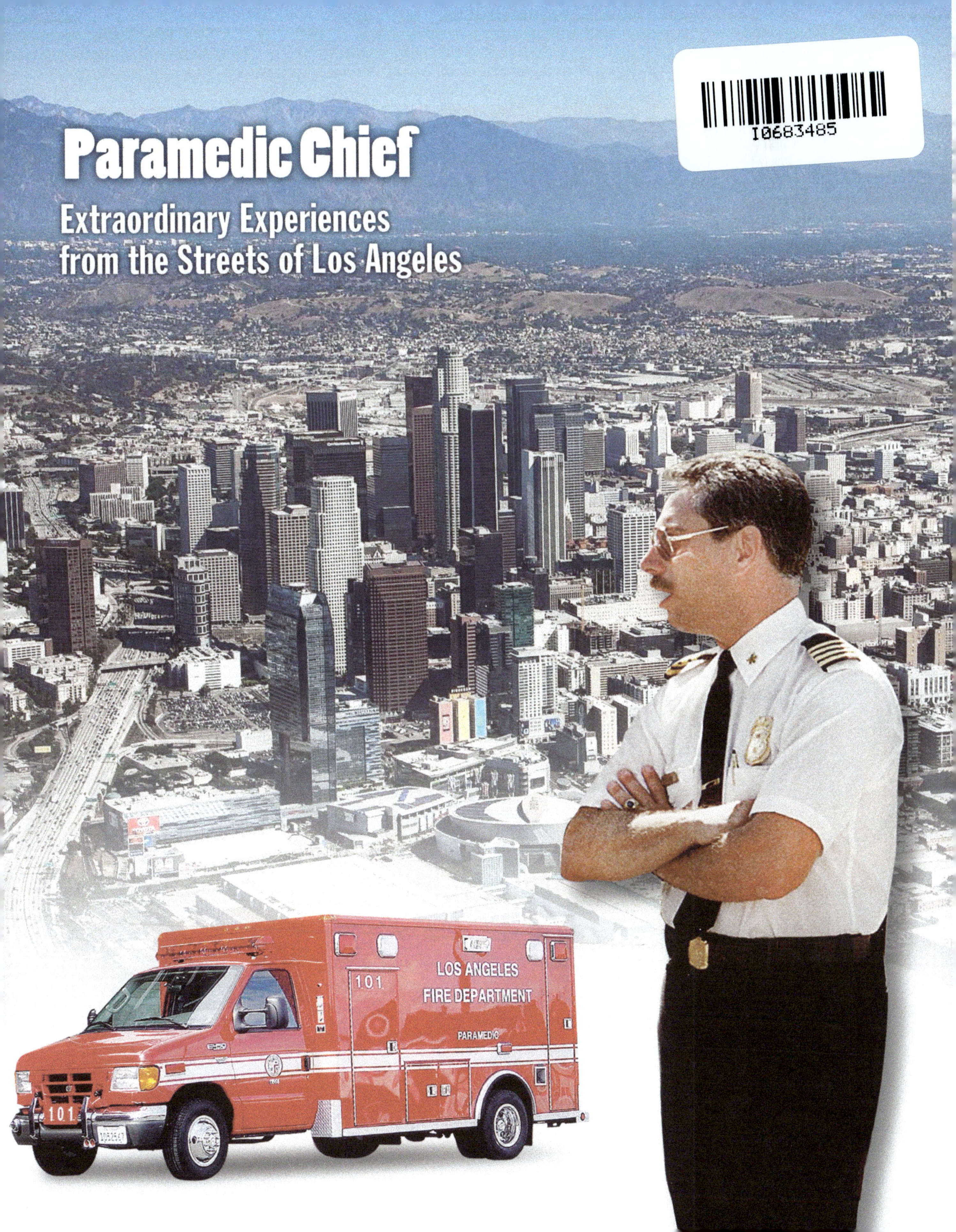

Chief Alan Cowen

Born in Santa Monica, CA, Alan Cowen grew up in Southern California.
He earned his B.A. in Speech from California State University, Northridge.
Later he obtained a B.S. in Biology
and a Masters Degree in Education with a specialty in Counseling and Guidance.
Concurrently he was continuing his work in the field of Emergency Medical Services.
In 1974, just 4 years after the Los Angeles City Fire Department took over
the Los Angeles Receiving Hospital System,
Alan became one of the first field paramedics.
He rapidly rose to Lead Paramedic and in 1980 was promoted to Paramedic Supervisor (Captain).
In 1985 he became Assistant Commander of the Bureau of Emergency Medical Services
and in 1987 he was appointed Chief Paramedic
and Commander of the Bureau of Emergency Medical Services.
In 1995 he was promoted to Fire Deputy Chief.
Alan also obtained a DC Degree (Doctor of Chiropractic),
he continues to be licensed as a MICP (Mobile Intensive Care Paramedic),
as he has for the last 49 years,
and is currently a Professor of Fire Technology at Los Angeles Valley College.

Design and Layout: McMac Publications, Mammoth Lakes & Borrego Springs, CA

Dedication

This book is dedicated to the memory of my mother and father,
Pauline and Joseph Cowen, who gave me this life to live.
And to my grandparents, who helped me grow up, Sarah and Fred Actor.

To Dolly Cowen, my dedicated wife, and my three children, Aron, Robby and Kate,
is this book affectionately dedicated.

To all my EMT students - past, present, and future -
who make it all worthwhile as we all try to do the job better.

Also, for my Los Angeles Valley College family, who work so hard day after day to train
our students and test them on their learned skills and where I had a second home
for more than 23 years. You know who you are. Eileen Brodsky, Phil Gibson, Martin Givens,
Matt Jones, Deresa Kenney, Ken Krupnik, Keith Scott, Arthur Sorrentino, Victor Vasquez,
Jose Banuelos, Michael Debesirian, Jeremy Sonenschein, Rick Erquiaga
and others along the way. What a journey indeed!

A special thank you to Eileen Brodsky, who has assisted in the formulation and organizing
of this collection of stories and exciting adventures of
a Paramedic Chief and Deputy Fire Chief for the Los Angeles Fire Department,
where I had the pleasure of working for nearly 32 years before retirement.

Finally, a thank you to Dr. Max Silvernail, who, long ago, introduced me to the wonders
of Zoology and Biology, and Dr. Ronald Stewart and Dr. Charles McElroy
who encouraged me to pursue those wonders.

Many thanks to our City's great photographers of the last century.
Their contributions to this book cannot be understated.
Additionally, my colleagues, Joe Ortiz and Richard McClure,
provided a substantial number of on-scene photos from the 1990s.

America is a place where if you fall down, there are people who will respond, treat,
and transport you for medical help.

FOREWORD

By Donald O. Manning
Retired Fire Chief
Los Angeles City Fire Department

During my nearly forty year career with the Los Angeles City Fire Department (LAFD), I had the opportunity to work alongside Deputy Chief Alan R. Cowen for much of my tenure as the Fire Chief. I came to know Chief Cowen in the early 1970s when he came to the Department from the City's separate ambulance service which was running out of the Los Angeles Central Receiving Hospital located in the Westlake District of the City. This was the first step towards the Department becoming fully integrated as a dual-function Department, whereas, both Fire/Rescue and EMS services would be under the umbrella of the Fire Department. Decades later the Los Angeles Fire Department became the second largest pre-hospital care system in the United States.

Chief Cowen and I have always enjoyed a strong friendship which grew ever-stronger when I appointed him to the rank of Deputy Chief and placed him in charge of the Bureau of Emergency Medical Services where he forged the path for the Department having a pre-hospital care system which is now a model for the fire service. Chief Cowen's intellect coupled with his vision caused the Department to take a quantum leap into the world of providing pre-hospital basic life support (BLS) and advanced life support (ALS) to the residents of Los Angeles.

Chief Cowen has drawn from his nearly four decade fire service career, serving the four million residents of the second largest city in the country, to share his vast experience and take the reader on a journey through some very tumultuous periods of time. Chief Cowen's unique perspective provides a deep look into the stresses, dangers, and rewards of giving care to those in medical distress. *Paramedic Chief - Extraordinary Experiences from the Streets of Los Angeles* shines a bright light on delivering EMS services at the ground level.

Chief Cowen's recounting of his personal experiences will undoubtedly elicit emotions from the reader similar to that of a first responder who faces tragedy on a daily basis. Chief Cowen provides graphic detail of life and death, giving the reader a real feel for what it's like to save lives on the streets of Los Angeles.

Chief Cowen always seemed to be in the right place at the right time. Clearly, he was the best person to transition the LAFD into becoming a premier pre-hospital care provider. Once again Chief Cowen finds himself in the right place at the right time to enlighten others about the rigors of being a first-responder. *Paramedic Chief - Extraordinary Experiences from the Streets of Los Angeles* is a unique and exhilarating read and Chief Cowen is clearly the most qualified to tell this story.

I am as honored to be asked to write this Foreword as I am to call Chief Cowen my friend, exceptional Chief Officer, and now author. Prepare yourself to be taken on a rollercoaster ride of emotions as *Paramedic Chief - Extraordinary Experiences from the Streets of Los Angeles* will most certainly enlighten and entertain all readers.

Table of Contents

A DATE WITH DESTINY

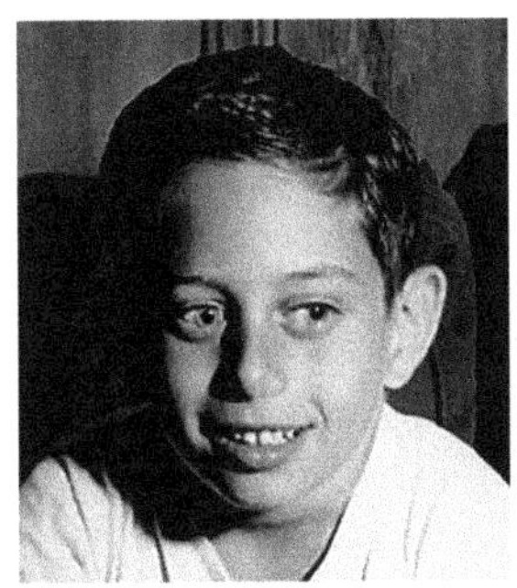
Alan Cowen at age 10

Even as a child, I could identify an approaching fire engine, police car or ambulance by the sound of its siren. By the time I was 10, I had memorized the pitch and depth of sound for each vehicle. For most people, that would be overkill, but it wasn't enough for me.

I got to know all of the drivers and knew each one's peculiarities. For example, Floyd "Pappy" Fair, driver of G-14 out of the Venice Police Station, always kept the ambulance siren at its highest pitch and frequency for a long time before he let it drop. At the time, I didn't realize I wanted to be like Pappy. My skill at identifying sirens was just a game. That all changed when I was 10.

I was playing outside with my black mixed terrier, Candy, when I saw his ears perk up at the sound of a tremendous crash, and I imagined shattered glass and mangled debris on the railroad tracks. It took only a moment to lock Candy in the house and race toward the sound. I was afraid of what I was going to see, but an inner force propelled me on.

A light rain had made the sidewalk slippery, and I took extra care to not lose my footing. At the end of the first long block, I could hear the distant siren of a fire engine approaching. The low-pitched siren was a "growler" – my name for the Culver City fire engines. I wanted to beat it to the scene. As I passed Washington Blvd. my side ached but I couldn't stop. The same morbid curiosity that causes people to stop at crash sites carried me along too.

The crash had happened on the railroad track at the corner of Culver Blvd. and Berryman Ave. - about two blocks south of my house. I had lived there my whole 10 years and liked watching the trains go by. Sometimes I put a penny on the track and let the train run over it so I knew how much destruction a train could create.

I arrived at the accident site just ahead of the fire truck. A police car was already on scene, and people stood around talking and pointing to the crash. No one knew what to do. It was my first time seeing the helplessness of hysterical bystanders. Years later, as a paramedic, I saw it often. I called it the "hands-on-head syndrome." But that day, I was one of those bystanders.

An eastbound freight train with a gigantic wooden bumper had struck a car, leaving several passengers trapped and critically injured – some of them actually under the train. The vehicle was a piece of twisted wreckage and only shreds of wood remained of the train's bumper, but the train seemed to be untouched.

I stood frozen to the spot and wished my dad was there. He was always so calm, and I thought he could make things OK. I suddenly realized that I didn't know what to do either, and watching the adults lose control of the situation made me terribly afraid. Then, the heroes came. I watched in awe as the firemen rode up, standing on the back bumper of the engine in their heavy turnout coats, big boots and traditional helmets. As they passed me with their emergency equipment, they looked so tall and strong. But more important, they brought order to the chaos. The assembled crowd moved aside to let the firefighters through to the shattered vehicle, where they used oversized crowbars to extricate the victims.

**I was impressed by his sense of calm.
As I watched him and his partner place a rubber splint on a patient's leg,
I knew I wanted to be just like them.**

It was no surprise when the brown Los Angeles City Receiving Hospital Ambulance arrived. I had already recognized the approaching siren. Two men got out wearing police-like uniforms with shoulder patches that identified them as "Emergency Medical Los Angeles." As a frantic woman screamed, "Hurry up; hurry up, quick!" the ambulance driver looked her in the eyes, snapped his fingers and said, "Take it easy lady. One thing at a time." Even as a kid, I was impressed by his sense of calm. As I watched him and his partner place a rubber splint on a patient's leg, I knew I wanted to be just like them. I stayed until the last tow truck was gone, deeply affected by what had happened.

For this 10-year-old kid, the last hour had been life-altering. I thought about the accident for days. How could I become one of those rescuers? How could I learn to do what they did so I could ride on a city ambulance? The seed had been planted - a few years later, it would start to grow.

Entry into the System

Long after the train accident, thoughts about being an ambulance driver filled my head. I knew where the fire station was because my dad had been a Reserve Police Officer since 1939. He occasionally took me to the fire station in Culver City, but I knew the ambulance I had seen did not come from there. I learned that it was a City police ambulance from the Venice Police Station. After that, I rode my bike down to the Venice station and sat there studying the ambulance. It was an infamous "Brown Bomber." The vehicles were brown in color, with a small, two-foot glass window on each side, emblazoned with a red cross. I'd look at it, then approach it, peer through the window at the mysterious equipment, and pray for a chance to ride in it. Sometimes I rode my bike as fast as I could, chasing the ambulance as red lights glowed and the siren screamed.

During those early teenage years, whenever I heard a siren stop in my neighborhood, I instantly hopped on my bike and pedaled off to see what had happened. As time went on, I wasn't going for the chance to see blood and gore, but rather to watch the ambulance crew; always a driver and an attendant. The gray-haired attendants frequently seemed much older and had far more authority than the drivers. In contrast, the drivers looked young and fresh-faced.

Sometimes the door of the ambulance would be left open when the crew entered a home, which only increased my curiosity. A look inside revealed whether the gurney or stretcher was gone. If I leaned close enough in, I could hear an anonymous female voice on the radio dispatching other ambulances throughout the city. I'd stay there listening while waiting to watch the men come out with their patient. Looking at their faces, which may have appeared stoic to other onlookers, I could read how serious the situation was. As time went on, I was getting to know the crews and they didn't even know it. At traffic collisions I watched them examine patients, bandage, splint and give oxygen. Without ever having touched a patient, I was no longer merely a "hands on head" bystander.

The ambulance attendants seemed to emanate a sense of professionalism and confidence. There was no question that they knew what they were doing. Even though some of them looked older than my dad (in their 40s or 50s) and seemed old to me, I was convinced they were better than doctors. They saw patients from the street perspective. This was the epitome of handling emergencies and I knew ambulance work was for me. Ironically, I would work with some of these same men a decade later.

While in high school I enrolled in a Red Cross emergency first aid training class and, at age 16, worked as an orderly at Washington Hospital. It was a small private facility located in Culver City and I found myself happily mopping the floors of the emergency room. To my delight, some of the doctors would allow me to watch as they sutured patients' wounds. I'd put the broom down, don a surgical mask, and stand there hypnotized by their movements. Hospital smells became familiar: alcohol, antiseptics, and sterilizer machines - nothing bothered me. I also worked in the kitchen, offering interns iced tea for a chance to talk to them about what they were learning. I didn't know it then but my career was on the right track. Still, it wasn't until I started classes at Santa Monica College in 1963 that my dreams turned to action.

"Hi. My name is Alan Cowen and I want to work on this ambulance."
"You do, do you? Well, come on in."

Just after turning 18, I finally found a way to work on an ambulance. Although still living at home with my parents in Culver City, I decided to try my luck in Malibu because I learned that in Los Angeles County, ambulance employees could be hired at 18. Los Angeles City required ambulance drivers and attendants to be 21 years old at that time. This was a way around that.

After some research, I found out that Frank Morgan and Dan Johnson owned the local ambulance company in Malibu. They worked out of their apartments, but I didn't have their address. Undaunted, I set out for Malibu one day. After hours of driving around, I followed my intuition and headed down near the Malibu Pier; there, to my astonishment, at 22816 Pacific Coast Highway, I found a Morgan-Johnson ambulance parked in front of a yellow beachfront apartment complex. "This is it. I'm going to work here," I thought. Everything about it felt right.

Guessing which door to approach, I climbed to the top of a long wooden staircase of a rustic beachfront apartment while gazing at the pounding surf below. Gathering up my courage, I knocked on the door of what turned out to be Frank Morgan's apartment. A tall Troy Donahue look-alike answered. Swallowing hard, I decided to go for broke.

"Hi. My name is Alan Cowen and I want to work on this ambulance."

"You do, do you? Well, come on in."

Entering the room, what I saw fascinated me. Sea shells and spiny fish lined the room and a slender, 10-foot piece of mottled driftwood caught my eye where it leaned up against the window. Behind it, the view took my breath away. His window framed a picture of the beach and coastline looking south as far as the eye could see. The apartment itself stood on stilts and waves crashed in against it. "This guy has the world by the tail," I thought. "This is heaven. I've entered heaven."

"Why do you want to work on an ambulance," Frank asked me. For the first time, I really looked at him. Frank had the bronzed appearance of a beach bum and his home only added to that mystique.

"Because I want to help people."

We talked for a few minutes as he sized me up. Then he said the four words I had been waiting all my life to hear.

"When can you start?"

"When do you want me?"

"Friday night. And, by the way, you get that apartment over there to live in plus a salary. That's our ambulance quarters. Yours is the apartment in the middle. Come on over and I'll show your apartment to you."

First day on the job

As we entered the nearby apartment, the on-duty attendant sat watching television in the living room. Taking in the surroundings, I became more and more thrilled with my newfound fortune. This apartment was on stilts as well and I could hear the surf as it pounded in. Every 15 to 20 seconds waves crashed under the house. Sand came up against the front door, entering the room with us as we walked in.

The apartment contained two bedrooms, old weather-worn furniture and a railing outside that stood over the water. There was nothing special about the place but, to me, it couldn't have been more beautiful. It represented career, acceptance, and independence - much more than the sum of its contents. And one other attraction - girls walked up and down the beach in bikinis!

"I'll see you next Friday," I said, pumping Frank's hand in gratitude. "Thanks very much."

"Just wear a pair of black pants and a white shirt - and we wear white smocks here," Frank told me matter-of-factly, not knowing how thrilled I was.

On my drive home back to Culver City in my Anthracite 1963 Volkswagen bug, I grinned all the way. I sang. I pounded the steering wheel. I waved at passersby. I was on my way - finally.

I arrived at the apartment on Friday night with a bag of groceries and some clothes. For the next three years I lived there with several other ambulance attendants who seemed to come and go with the seasons. That was fine with me. I made friends easily and stayed busy. I believed I could handle anything to be able to fulfill my dream. As I soon learned, only my deep love for what I was doing could carry me through the rough parts.

On my very first call, I literally shivered from fear and cold huddled against the ambulance as Frank opened the door for me. Climbing into the attendant's seat of the ambulance, I wondered about what I'd gotten myself into. It was Friday night and other kids my age were out having fun. Was this what I had waited for?

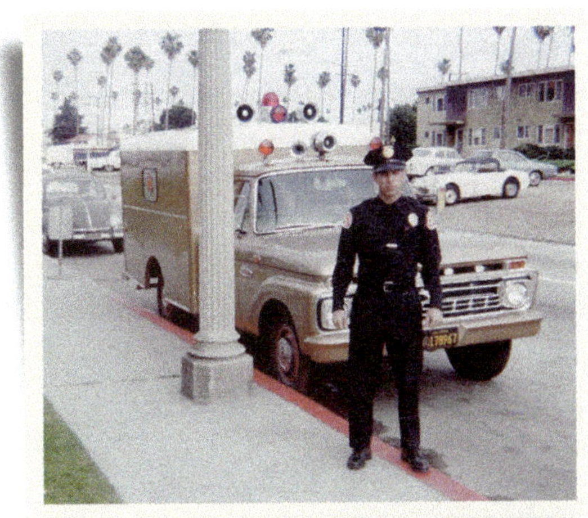

On the job in Venice, CA, 1967

Frank started the engine, pulled out onto the Pacific Coast Highway, turned to me and said, "Well, let's get going and see what we've got." Just then, he reached down under the dashboard and pulled two levers, one of them initiating the red revolving beacon ray atop the ambulance; the other activating the two steady-burning red forward lights and two amber flashing lights in the rear.

As we flew past store fronts along the beach, I could see the red lights in their reflection. I saw my face as well. Here I was, racing to the scene of God knows what, but this time I wasn't on my bike. Instead, I was behind the red lights and siren. Perhaps somewhere, some boy was listening to the siren as we rushed to help someone. This was the fun part. My career had begun.

We arrived at a trailer park high in the Malibu Hills. As a result of a domestic dispute, a man had knocked his wife down and driven over her with his car. The impact had torn her clothes away leaving clear tire marks on her chest and stomach. We placed her on a backboard and flat stretcher (which holds the board) and lifted her into the ambulance as she slipped in and out of consciousness. I gently placed an oxygen mask on her bruised and bleeding face and thought, "Oh my God. Don't die." I was petrified.

As we sped toward Santa Monica hospital I thought to myself, "Well, here I am in the back of an ambulance being the caregiver of a terribly injured woman. This doesn't feel like I thought it would." I watched the flashing red lights from the ambulance reflect off the mountains as we traveled down Topanga Canyon Boulevard toward the beach. I was judging the irony of the situation. This, after all, is what I had wanted. This is what I had worked for, wasn't it? I wanted to feel confident but I didn't. I wanted to feel in control but I didn't. I wanted to help this poor lady but I couldn't. Cars were maneuvering out of our way as we snaked along the Pacific Coast Highway toward Santa Monica, the wail of the siren filling my ears.

Finally, after what seemed like an hour, we arrived at Santa Monica Hospital. Wheeling my patient into the hospital on the gurney, I wondered whether there would be any sign of approval from the other ambulance drivers and attendants standing around - but they didn't acknowledge me. It was all just routine for them as they stood smoking cigarettes in the alley where the Santa Monica Hospital ambulance ramp used to be. We dropped off our patient, restocked our equipment, and began the long trip back to Malibu. I felt shaken and exhilarated waiting for any kind of reaction from Frank. Finally, it came.

"You did a good job," Frank told me as we drove back in the darkness. "Your best work will be in the back with the patient."

His words touched my heart. I had found my niche, content to be with the patient in the back of the ambulance. Frank's praise validated every wish I had made since that day on the train tracks in Culver City when I was 10. My confidence started building even after that first call. These were exciting times for me. They helped shape and prepare me to become the Chief of Paramedics 24 years in the future. Although I would need vast amounts of training, this was a beginning.

A Career Begins

Classes at Santa Monica City College filled the week days. After classes, and on weekends from Friday night to Monday morning, I'd be on call. I soon discovered that the work was grueling and often gruesome. Worse yet, apprehension filled me with fear on every call.

Still, learning by doing speeded my progress. There was no such thing as formal ambulance training yet. Most of my training, like everyone else's at that time, was on the job and in the streets. In the middle of the night, not long after I had been hired, the phone's shrill ring startled me awake. I picked up the receiver while clearing my head and eyes of sleep and said, "Ambulance." A voice from the sheriff's department reported that there was a traffic collision on the Pacific Coast Highway near Zuma Beach. That's all I needed to hear.

Adrenalin kick-started my movements and in less than a minute I was dressed and sitting in the passenger seat of the ambulance. We put on the thick ambulance seat belts and took off, red lights and siren blaring. It was almost everything I ever wanted - except that my knees wouldn't stop shaking.

We drove 75 or 80 miles per hour in the 1959 International and in the distance we could see only red lights and flares from many Fire Department and sheriff's cars. As we drove up, everyone was waving us in at the site of an auto accident.

When I saw the sheriff's department stopping traffic so that we could drive in, I was suddenly struck by the idea that they were doing this so an 18-year-old kid could come in as if he had some special talent. For the first time in my life I felt important, needed. I also felt frightened and inexperienced.

I got out of the ambulance and took a first aid kit. I had watched the city ambulance guys for years, so I knew how to act. I knew the lingo. Several people were injured and I heard the sound of a woman moaning from inside the car. In a very confident voice I told her, "Take it easy, ma'am. What seems to be the problem?" I was using my voice for control because inside, I was in pieces.

After Frank bandaged the other accident victims on scene, we put the woman on a stretcher and placed her into the ambulance. While administering oxygen to my patient, I held her hand and confidently said, "You're going to be just fine. We're on the way to the hospital. You're in good hands now. " I naturally seemed to know what to say.

Within that first year, there were more crashes and deaths than I could have anticipated. Out on the streets, one learned from experienced partners. They showed me how to lift, how to work the gurney, how to bandage, administer oxygen, and resuscitate. One thing they didn't teach me, though, was how to turn off my emotions.

A blonde, blue-eyed, 16-year-old "Gidget," a surfer girl from back east had come out to join the Malibu crowd of the 1960s. She was lovely. She was dying.

By the end of my first year on the streets, I had dealt with a death that continues to haunt me. On a hot August day in 1964, we received a call of a pedestrian struck by a car. In the mid-afternoon, we arrived at the scene just south of the Malibu Pier, less than a block from where the ambulance was stationed.

A blonde, blue-eyed, 16-year-old "Gidget," a surfer girl from back east had come out to join the Malibu crowd of the 1960s. She was lovely. She was dying. A car traveling 50-60 mph had struck her, tearing her body open. Both her legs and arms were fractured, bones protruded in each direction. Her abdomen and side were ripped open with blood spurting everywhere. When I reached her, she lay on the hot pavement gasping for air. As she looked at me, her skin slightly blue from a lack of oxygen, her eyes told me what she couldn't say, "Can you save me?"

I tried to put her back together but I had trouble even getting her on the gurney. She was so broken, her legs were nearly severed. I placed a cardboard splint under her legs and tried to secure it; then I worked with her arms. We eased a board and flat under her. We lifted her up and into the ambulance. I felt despondent looking at this broken girl, twisted and destroyed. This was the first time I felt a controlled panic. I tapped on the window between the driver and patient compartment.

"You better hurry up on this one," I called to Frank.

I knew she would probably die and wasn't surprised when she stopped breathing in the ambulance; her eyes just started to glaze over. In desperation, I decided to try something new; something I had read about but hadn't seen done. I put her head back, pinched her nose, lifted her neck, placed my mouth over her mouth, and blew air into her mouth. As air entered her lungs, her chest expanded. I kept breathing for her all the way to the hospital. She didn't respond, but I kept on.

We arrived at Malibu Medical and Emergency, screeched to a stop and rushed her in to Dr. Tom Hodges, who ran the emergency facility. He looked at her for a second and went right to work. I watched Dr. Hodges blow the last breath of air into her life. When he did, she vomited and blood spilled all over. He looked at the clock and said, "Let's call it," and they pronounced her dead. I would later learn that her name was Toby.

I walked outside. Numbness overcame me. Outside, I leaned up against a pole and started to cry. "Why? How could this happen?" I wondered.

Back at the station, I thought about the phone call her parents would receive. I knew they would never know what actually happened in those final minutes of her life. I hoped for years that I might have the chance to meet her family and explain to them what really happened and what the scene looked like. I wanted to let them know how I had tried to save their daughter's life.

The good times helped offset those tough, soul-wrenching moments. From 1963 to 1966, in the summer months, we put the emergency phone out on a table to listen for calls while we played volleyball in the sand. During the day, we barbecued and flirted with the girls that came by. At night, we lit torches and drove them into the sand to continue the party on the beach.

Whether working or playing, we were constantly on the move. My off hours took on the theme of a constant party. Girls would crowd around our volleyball games and I had more dates than I had ever imagined. Work, nonetheless, always stayed top priority.

By 1964, I rendered emergency first aid on the streets, transported patients to the hospital, and, if time permitted, became part of the emergency room team at Malibu Medical and Emergency. Occasionally, we delivered two or three patients at a time which overwhelmed the hospital staff. Because of this, I helped out by taking vital signs and assisted in bandaging. I soon graduated to preparing medications and solutions for the doctor and learned to give injections, take X-rays, and draw blood - all at 19. As a result, Dr. Tom Hodges, for whom I had tremendous admiration, offered me a part-time job.

From 1964 to 1966, I continued to work for Morgan-Johnson Ambulance Service in Malibu, dividing my time between the ambulance, medical center and college. But through it all, my ultimate goal was to get a job with the Los Angeles City Receiving Ambulance system.

On one occasion, a young man was brought in by his friends after being struck in the flank by his surfboard. He looked pale and shocky and I knew at once that something was seriously wrong. I took his vital signs and realized he had a very low blood pressure and rapid pulse. As oxygen was being administered to him, Dr. Hodges began a careful assessment of his injuries.

Dr. Hodges' persistence in working to diagnose the young man's condition fascinated me. He methodically first inspected, then palpated, all four quadrants of the man's abdomen. I watched in total surprise as Dr. Hodges then punctured each quadrant of the man's belly with a 20-gauge needle. Two of the punctures yielded nothing but the fourth needle diagnosed the problem. Blood poured out the end of the needle, indicating an internal hemorrhage.

Dr. Hodges' nurse was on the phone instantly with a nurse at Santa Monica Hospital, making the necessary arrangements to accept the patient for surgery. As a result, my hat changed again from hospital worker to ambulance attendant, and my partner and I transported the patient to the hospital. I was learning to adapt to whatever the situation needed me to be. Adapting became a never-ending process.

Dreams and Demons and Death

In 1965, on a Thursday afternoon in January, Frank and I responded to reports of a car having plummeted off Malibu Canyon and down a steep canyon. Firefighters had tied a rope to the front of the fire engine and were using it for support to back down the 150' incline. Frank stayed at the top with the equipment while I joined the firefighters in their rescue effort.

For more than 20 minutes, we carefully edged our way down. Any misstep could have meant serious injury or even death. This was the first time I truly understood the inherent dangers of rescue work and began to appreciate the courage and dedication of the firefighters. Once we reached the rocky bottom, we could see that the car had landed upside down and was half buried in the undergrowth. As we approached the demolished vehicle, I hoped we would find it abandoned. It wasn't.

We carefully peered through the shattered windows. A surge of relief overwhelmed me. "Thank God, it's only dolls inside," I thought. But, a moment later, the truth struck me with a wave of nausea. The two middle-aged women inside the car appeared to be dolls, perfectly still and silent. Both occupants had died instantly upon impact. The women were local residents who had been missing since the night before. Whatever the cause, their car left the highway airborne and their lives ended in an instant. Firefighter Jackson turned to me, gesturing for my help, and my instincts snapped me back to reality. The nausea subsided as soon as we began carrying both victims back up the cliff toward the highway. Planning to make two trips, we each took a hold on the flat stretcher with one hand and held onto the rope with the other hand. At the other end, more firefighters slowly backed up the fire engine to pull us up.

2 Women Die In Crash At Topanga

The author and other firefighters struggle up the side of Malibu Canyon with the body of one of two women killed when their auto reportedly plunged 150 feet down an embankment.

Once at the top with both victims, we placed them on the side of the highway and covered them with clean white sheets. I couldn't help wondering what those poor women went through during that last 30 seconds. This would not be the last time we scaled the steep cliffs and dangerous drop-offs through the steep canyons.

The accidents, drownings, injuries, and sicknesses continued to fill my nights and weekends while Santa Monica City College filled my days. In early 1965, a friend told me about applying for full-time summer work as a firefighter for the federal government, so we both applied. One day in May of 1965, a letter of acceptance arrived for me with a start date. I would report to the Mill Creek Ranger Station in the San Bernardino National Forest within two weeks. In order to accept this employment and satisfy my curiosity, I took a short hiatus from my ambulance and emergency department duties.

The Forest Service trained me as a "hotshot," a firefighter who is flown in to large-scale brush and forest fires to fight them, clear brush and create fire breaks. Some of the best "hotshots" I worked with were Native Americans who lived on local reservations. Unlike the other firefighters, they strode into fires wearing bandanas over their faces. This innovation covered everything except their eyes to shield them from the heat and smoke. They amazed me with their skills and ability to tackle huge forest fires. More than once, I saw them go up against 100' walls of fire; at times I thought the whole forest was aglow. I've never met a group of harder working, committed firefighters. They taught me how to properly use brush hooks, pulaskis, and how to care for the tools after their use. More importantly, these men showed me unabashed bravery and professionalism under the most difficult conditions.

Toward the end of that summer, I worked on an engine company in Yucaipa, California on a local reservation. It was so hot that we would work 30 minutes and have to rest for an hour. During many hours of the day, we sat in an old water tank, drinking lemonade to keep cool. Although the tank probably provided our drinking water, we were desperate enough that we didn't care.

Although the sun burned us by day, there were thunderstorms every night. We would sit on a mountain peak and watch for lightning strikes. Often a fire would result and off we'd go to find and extinguish it. Some nights we put out as many as four, using the 500 gallon water tank we had bathed in earlier. This routine continued throughout the summer whenever lightning struck, yet my heart yearned to be back running emergency calls at the beach.

HOTSHOTS

Some of our nation's very best "hotshots" were Native Americans that lived on the local Reservations of California.

Returning to Malibu in the fall, I settled down to a routine of college classes while maintaining my job duties at the medical center. I continued to live in the Malibu beach apartment and was on call nights and weekends. My schedule continued to be tough, with little time for sleep, but I still enjoyed the pace – and the constant adrenalin rush.

Special Delivery

On one particular call, we found ourselves en route to an emergency obstetrical case. As we approached the home, the husband met us in the street, completely hysterical, pulling on my arm to hurry me. We grabbed our first aid kit and supplies and entered their sprawling beach estate. He led us to the upstairs bedroom and into the bathroom where I heard his wife before I saw her. She was sitting on the toilet, screaming that her baby was coming. "Do something!" she pleaded with us.

"Ma'am, take it easy, everything's going to be just fine," I assured her, trembling.

We quickly laid her down on the bathroom floor and, while my partner tried to make her comfortable, I gloved up and realized my hands were shaking. My heart was pounding. I had never delivered a baby before but my first aid class had talked about the various stages of labor. Not wanting to look like a novice, I tried to imagine how the Los Angeles City Ambulance attendants would have handled this scenario.

"Ma'am, take it easy, everything's going to be just fine," I assured her, trembling.

All at once, the baby's head began to emerge from the birth canal. Thank goodness nature was doing all the work with the mother. In the next minute, the shoulders emerged and finally, I had a newborn baby girl in my hands. To my relief, she was crying already, so I carefully wrapped a blanket around the infant and handed the precious bundle to her mother.

By this time, the firefighters had arrived and were observing my actions. They had brought in the gurney and were talking to the baby's father to determine where we would be transporting. Without warning, the mother delivered the placenta, something I had read about but never witnessed. I placed two umbilical clamps on the cord, and with a special sterile scissors, cut the cord. For me, this represented the transition from the baby's internal environment to the external environment, completing the birth process.

One of the firefighters said, "You did a great job. We're glad you didn't need any help because we've never done this before." Little did they know. The father approached me, reaching out to shake my hand. "Hold on a moment," I said, and removed my glove. He took my hand and thanked me profusely, but I felt grateful, as well, for the experience. I held onto that special feeling of knowing I had made a difference and my efforts had been appreciated. That knowledge kept me going.

For three years I continued working for Morgan-Johnson Ambulance Service in Malibu, dividing my time between the ambulance, medical center, and college. In the back of my mind, though, my goal had never changed - the Los Angeles City ambulance system. I never stopped thinking about working there and wondered how to make that transition. Without knowing it, my intuition moved me in the right direction.

In 1966, I applied for a job as an ambulance driver with Goodhew Ambulance Service. I wanted to be closer to downtown L.A. where the action was and they were located in the heart of the city. Goodhew hired me immediately and for the next six months I worked with a wide variety of partners.

Working there, it seemed that everyone I spoke with had visions of working for the City of L.A., as I did. Although we responded to some emergency calls, most of our work centered around inter-facility transports. I soon longed for the days back in Malibu, where every call for service meant red lights, siren and action.

One of the employees I met was Doug Brown, who worked part-time at Goodhew, but spent his nights working as an ambulance attendant for the City of L.A. on the "Brown Bombers." He worked on the "G-Units," city ambulances affectionately named for Georgia Street Receiving Hospital, where they were previously assigned. Doug and I not only became friends, but would work occasionally as a team, both at Central Receiving and later at the L.A. Fire Department. Doug's stories of working for the city fueled my daydreams. I had to try to get in - but was I ready? I decided to find out.

I'm Gonna Be An Ambulance Driver!

In late 1966 I took the written examination for the position of Ambulance Driver with the City of Los Angeles. The day I arrived to take the test, I was flabbergasted by the huge number of applicants taking the exam with me at Hollywood High School. Lines of hopeful city drivers formed around the block. Many were strangers to me, but there were plenty of faces I recognized, fellows who worked for different ambulance companies in the area. The test was tough, but I felt I had done as well as I possibly could have.

Not long afterward, I was notified by mail that I had ranked number 6 out of all those who had taken the test. Re-reading the letter to make sure it was true, I dialed the number listed. An unknown voice at the other end told me a date to report to Central Receiving Hospital at 1401 W. Sixth Street, ready for work. Someone I had never met and didn't know was telling me my wish had come true. I had worked for this since age 10 and I was 22 years old. I felt numb with happiness.

For days, I barely ate or slept. When March 17 came, I drove to the Central Receiving Hospital wearing civilian clothes. Walking up to the front door, I was taken aback at the sight of the multiple brown ambulances parked out in front. There were so many, and they represented not only transportation to emergencies, but an entrance to the world I had long waited to be a part of.

I walked in the front door of the hospital and saw a number of guys in police uniforms wearing a patch that said, "Emergency Medical Los Angeles," with a spoke, a wheel and a cadueces. The attendants, the ones in the back with the patients, had a silver band on their hat; the rest of them had a regular black band. I immediately noticed the class distinctions. The men with the silver bands had the authority.

I pulled back my shoulders, took in a breath of air, and entered through the front doors. To my dismay, everyone seemed a head taller than my five-foot-seven-inch frame.

"Yeah, what do you need?" a blustery attendant asked.

“I'm here to see the boss."

"Oh, in that room."

An old man sat behind one of two desks in the next room. He seemed an old hard-boiled egg of a guy, short and squatty, with a round face.

"What can I do for you?" he asked, in a gravely voice.

"Yes, sir, I‘m here to see Harold Patton, the Chief Ambulance Attendant."

I was almost standing on my tiptoes, I had drawn my shoulders up so high, and lowered my voice to have some sort of commanding presence in that room.

"I was told to report here."

”What's your name," he asked, rifling through a list, amid a tipping pile of paperwork.

”Alan Cowen."

"Oh, yeah, You need to go get your uniform. I'm going to start you tonight, for your orientation ride."

My heart was pounding in my chest. ”Okay. Where do I go?"

"Uniforms Incorporated at Olympic and Fedora."

I didn't know where Olympic was and I sure as hell didn't know where Fedora was. So, I got in my car and looked at the map. Fortunately, it was very close.

Once there, I walked in and announced proudly, "I‘m an ambulance driver for the city, and I'm here to get uniforms."

No one seemed impressed but I felt sure they must know what a special occasion this was. They simply hid it well.

Obligingly, they fitted me for the traditional police uniform, the dark, dark blue that I would wear each day. Uniforms and patches in hand, I reported back at the hospital about 4 p.m. I was in seventh heaven.

They assigned me to G-18 for an orientation ride and then in Venice the next day. This was a Godsend for me. I was still a student, continuing at San Fernando Valley State College, and going to school during the day. They were kind enough to put me on the 3-to-11 shift to accommodate my school schedule. I would be working with a man named Dan Cesarotti, but my first night I rode along with David Eisenman and Bob Dougherty.

I was thrilled about being in the ambulance but I didn't let anyone know how excited I was. I didn't tell them that my heart was beating a mile a minute.

That night, I was in the big time. Putting my uniform on I felt like a million dollars. I was proud and felt important. This was the fulfillment of a goal. In 1963, Dan Johnson had told me, "You want to work for the city? Those guys are like doctors, they're so good." So, here I was, fitting the description of being SO GOOD, when in reality, I was scared to death.

I was thrilled about being in the ambulance but I didn't let anyone know how excited I was. I didn't tell them that my heart was beating a mile a minute, that I was full of pride looking at those uniforms - that I still looked up at them although I was soon going to be their equal.

David Eisenman was the attendant, with probably 20 years experience at the time. Bob Dougherty was a young kid with a crewcut, probably in his late 30s, who worked that night as the driver. This was my introduction to my future. I climbed in the back of the ambulance and away we went - call after call after call.

We flew through downtown L.A. in a 1963 Dodge which had a huge engine. It was a rocket on wheels. Although it was exciting, I thought these rugged ambulance drivers from the city drove like maniacs. Dougherty drove up to 60 and 70 mph on city streets and back down in the passing gear, up and down, braking like he didn't care about the equipment. I thought the driving was terrible. In retrospect, I realize they were pretty good drivers; I was just in the back getting thrown all over.

I found it odd, though, that they didn't speak to one another. They had obviously developed a code to replace actual conversation. David Eisenman knew the city well, and when we were in a part of the city the driver didn't know, Eisenman would take his call book in his right hand and hit his left hand. That meant a left turn. Or he'd put it in the opposite hand and hit his right hand for a right turn. That's how they communicated instead of talking. It was weird, but I had other things on which to concentrate.

That night, my job was to carry the big black first aid kit and when the attendant said give me a lap pad, I just slapped it in his hand. He was in complete charge of that ambulance.

We worked until 1 AM that morning and on one call I almost started crying. We went to a fleabag hotel where an elderly woman had died. Both the woman and her husband appeared to be in their 80s. They were obviously destitute, living in only one room together. The attendant pronounced the woman dead and they were ready to leave, when the husband started saying, "What will I do? What will I do?"

...and I was thinking to myself, "Alan, you're supposed to be hardened to this. You're in the big time now. You're in the city ambulance corps."

I was struck by the sadness of this old man and I was thinking to myself, "Alan, you're supposed to be hardened to this. You're in the big time now. You're in the city ambulance corps. These guys are rough and tumble. They don't worry about that." Still, I was touched by how sad I was inside and, in comparison, by the callousness of the ambulance people. They had been doing this for so long that they had developed a type of hardness and a barrier. My sensitivities told me to stay human, even back then, and yet I wanted to be hardened, to be like them. It was a very strange paradox.

The final straw came when the old man opened his refrigerator and there was dog food in there, but it wasn't for a dog. The elderly couple had been eating dog food because it was cheap. I couldn't believe it. We stayed until the police came and took a report and I was emotionally a wreck at the end of that one shift. Still, I was completely energized when the shift ended. I went home that night and couldn't sleep.

The next day I reported to G-14 at the Venice Division. I knew right where it was because for so many days, I had stationed myself out there in front - on my bicycle. Now I was there to work. Halfway up the long staircase to the office I met a young Hispanic fellow, probably six to eight years my senior, dressed in a uniform like mine. We exchanged greetings and he introduced himself as Pete Segura. We would become friends even though he worked the day shift and I worked the evenings. For the next six months, he was the day driver that I relieved when our shifts changed.

Upstairs, my partner, Dan Cesarotti, came in about 15 minutes later.

"Hi, I'm Alan Cowen," I said, extending my hand.

He just looked at me. He wouldn't talk to me. He made me feel minimal, as though I didn't deserve to wear the same uniform he did. Not talking to me was akin to shunning me and felt intimidating.

That first day we had one or two calls. Thank God I knew where they were because he wouldn't speak to me or acknowledge me. It took probably close to a week for him to even talk to me. Fortunately, I understood that's the way the old-timers treated the new kids and I knew I was with the group that was breaking the ice. No one had been hired on the Central Receiving system for many years because the drivers and attendants already hired would stay until they died or retired. Breaking in was a major thing.

I soon fell into a pattern with Cesarotti. I would drive him on an emergency and we'd get there and take appropriate action. I'd open the kit and hand him what he needed. He'd tell me what he wanted, but other than that we had no discussion. I was very upset with that. It didn't bother me that he wouldn't talk to me, but I wanted to pick his brain and find out some of his experiences. I wanted to make friends with this man and I couldn't. He wasn't alone in this hazing ritual. Some of the old codgers wouldn't tell you how to get to a house. They would rather you were 10 minutes late than for them to have to tell you. You were just supposed to know where you were going, if you didn't they wouldn't help you. There was no team spirit.

Still, I was more impressed to have the opportunity to work with these old-timers than I was with the fact that I was actually working there. On one of the first calls I ever went out on with Cesarotti, a call came out at the 4300 block of Berryman Avenue, my parents' street. I knew exactly where it was and pulled up right at the house. I got out and I looked around to see if anyone, particularly my parents, had come out to see, but they hadn't. I desperately wanted to be seen as a city ambulance driver. In those days, working for the city ambulance was like being accepted to medical school today. It was such a triumph. But, like all childhood dreams, it wasn't the same as I had imagined it as a kid.

As a 10-year-old, I hadn't known that there was an intense rivalry between the attendants and the drivers. Also, the attendant was completely in charge of the ambulance, driver, equipment, decisions. He even chose whether or not you were going to go red lights and siren to a hospital. If he wanted you to go red lights and siren, he'd say, "Go ahead and take it in." The words "take it in" meant Code 3, red lights and siren, and he would reserve that for the most serious emergencies.

Cesarotti was extremely confident in his own abilities. He had studied the human body enough to earn a doctorate degree as a chiropractor. No matter how many times I watched him, sometimes his inherent skill in diagnosing a medical problem still surprised me. The Venice Police station on Venice Boulevard at Shell where we were located was then known as Pacific division of the LAPD. In those days, they maintained a jail there and when they booked people in we handled the medical treatment. We also routinely performed medical treatment for the prisoners in the jail. If someone was injured or sick, we'd go back and I would watch Cesarotti administer the medical care.

By today's standards, he couldn't compete with what modern paramedics can do, but he did pretty well, as did his contemporaries. Looking back, those old-timers knew their stuff. They were technically proficient at applying bandages such as spirals, recurrent turns, figure-eights, spicas, four-tails, and pressure dressings. I learned how to do it all from them, including the use of muslin binders, which are still widely used to this day.

At the beginning of 1968, I started working at a relief station. That meant I worked three days at one station, three days at another and then enjoyed three days off. I wasn't assigned to Venice all the time because it was a very sought-after station. I wasn't the only one who enjoyed its trendy location and infrequent calls. Since I had to work elsewhere to fill in my schedule, I took an assignment at a relief station nobody else wanted. So I worked Venice/Wilshire relief for the next year and liked it a lot.

Climbing the Career Ladder

I was promoted January 1, 1969, becoming the youngest ambulance attendant within the city ambulance system. All of the other attendants were in their 40s and 50s. I wasn't yet 24. My scores on the test had been so high they had to promote me, but they didn't want to. I found out later that there were a lot of bad feelings about promoting a 23-year-old to ambulance attendant. It was unheard of. But I was ecstatic. I desired it. I had earned it and I wanted to go to the top. Never did I dream at that time that I would end up in my own system as the Chief Paramedic. By those standards, I would have been Chief Ambulance Attendant Patton at that time.

When I passed the test and was promoted, I moved from driver to the attendant spot, assuming many more responsibilities and making more money. In 1967, I began working for the City of Los Angeles as an ambulance driver for $525 a month. As an attendant, I made $715 a month. Rent cost was $79 a month.

Upward Mobility

In November 1968 my interview was conducted for the position of City of Los Angeles Receiving Hospital Ambulance Attendant. From my perspective it was a coveted position that I had worked toward since the train incident 13 years prior. I had studied maps, first aid textbooks and attended many lectures and presentations offered by the physicians at Central Receiving Hospital, all of which helped me as I raced toward the finish line. My preparation was second to none and I even practiced in a mirror to ensure good eye contact, at least that was what the interview books I obtained said to do.

From my perspective it was a coveted position that I had worked toward since the train incident 13 years prior.

This time the interview process was more formal; a panel of 5 or 6 people who grilled the candidates, each with an expertise. While I had expected to see a Senior Ambulance Attendant or the Chief Ambulance Attendant on the board it was not to be so. All were strangers to me and I was fearful, due to my young age, in an era where field experience and tenure as an ambulance driver would be paramount. The list of names outside the Personnel Office were totally unknown to me and a couple of them had MD after the names. While fear overcame me, I also had a sense that no one would have an advantage over anyone else and ambulance drivers would be selected on their merit. A gentleman walked out and introduced himself to me and we shook hands. He simply said, "Please follow me."

I was wearing a dark suit, white shirt and tie, polished shoes and recent haircut when I entered the room. A chill went through me as I eyed each person trying to wear a smile that I did not feel. The lead or chair of the panel asked me to sit down and relax for a moment and I thought to myself, "right, try and relax". He re-stated that this was a City of Los Angeles Promotion Examination for the Ambulance Attendant position and was a Supervisory position and then asked me to tell the panel a little about myself. I realized that too much was not good and too little was probably worse, so I began by telling them where I was born and grew up, how I got my first job on an ambulance at 18 years of age and worked the Emergency Ambulance in Malibu while working my way through college. I added that I was to receive my Bachelor's Degree in June 1969. They all listened intently and as I spoke my eyes scanned each person back and forth, not maintaining a gaze at any one interviewer. I reiterated how this was an important opportunity to me and that my history as ambulance driver led me to this very minute in time.

The next question was more of a personnel issue and how to handle it, followed by several others in the same general arena. So far I felt good with my anxiety reduced and my comfort level was increasing. The two physicians peppered me with emergency care issues and I felt well prepared. Another board member asked me about laws relating to driving of emergency ambulances with respect to safety and operational issues. While answering questions, a voice in the back of my mind was worried that a question might be asked that I did not know the answer to. Sure enough, one interviewer asked a question about the downtown area and how to read a Thomas Brothers Map. My stomach churned in an instant, but I managed to listen to the entire question and then answer it. Many questions were asked and many I don't recall, but the interview was approximately 45 minutes to 1 hour in length. The last question was, "Is there anything else you would like to share with the board to help us rate you for the position you are seeking?" I had anticipated that particular question and had an outline in my mind as to how I would answer. It was short and sweet. I first thanked each member of the interview board and looked at each one eyes to eyes. Then I stated, "I am physically fit, mentally alert and resourceful. If I don't know something, I will look up the answer and not forget it. And I will help new ambulance drivers learn the job duties and responsibilities."

"Is there anything else you would like to share with the board to help us rate you for the position you are seeking?"

My interview was over yet my anxiety lingered. As I walked out of the Personnel Offices, I saw some of the numerous ambulance drivers waiting for their interviews and couldn't help but think of how old and experienced they looked; how many more emergencies they had experienced than I had and why they would be promoted. It was hard to shake the negative feeling that had been branded in me by the likes of a few ambulance attendants who simply were arrogant and sour. I had just vowed to help future ambulance drivers that were not even hired yet based on my own negative contact with some of the current attendants who did just the opposite to me. That thought filled my head and gave me some relief.

In December a letter arrived that stated, "Congratulations" and gave me my score and where I landed on the new list for Ambulance Attendant.

The Promotion

My promotion was to take effect on January 1, 1969. I was so happy to have been promoted and it was the icing on the cake. All that study and hard work had paid off at last. There was, however, sadness involved as well since I would be leaving Willie Wilson and the Venice/Wilshire Relief for good and would be transferred somewhere else in the huge, 464 square miles of the City of Los Angeles. A whole new set of concerns overwhelmed me but I knew that in the long run this was meant to be. How did I know that? Simple: it was happening.

Willie was overjoyed for me and told me how proud he was that I had been promoted and was the youngest ambulance attendant in Los Angeles history. I just smiled and tried to take it all in. It has always been an issue for me to accept accolades and compliments. There is the deep feeling that somehow I don't deserve the recognition and that I did not earn it. While this has plagued me for a lifetime, it gradually was abating from my subconscious. I knew that college had helped me, since my Bachelor's Degree would be in Speech, and I was comfortable talking to groups, thus rationalizing that my oral interview board went well due to my presentation.

What I knew for sure was that I would be an excellent ambulance attendant, treat people with respect and help new ambulance drivers learn their job duties. The time had come to take that extra step as a supervisor of an ambulance and driver. I was ready for the challenge.

In December I was informed that my new assignment would be G-17, in the 3000 block of South LaBrea Avenue in South Los Angeles and, amazingly, the only G-unit in the city stationed at a Funeral Home. It was called Spaulding Mortuary Funeral Home. It is hard to imagine today that ambulance services would work out of a funeral home but in the 1940s and 1950s it was quite common throughout the country for this type of arrangement. Still, it rubbed me the wrong way when I reported to that location in January, 1969. My partner was a new driver, who reminded me of myself two years prior. We had an office within the building and parked our brown ambulance, G-17, right outside the door. It was an unusual arrangement but we got the job done.

The driver was Fred McCuistian, a young eager-beaver, who I was to find out was an excellent ambulance driver. In my experience, some drivers can go 60-70 miles per hour and I felt safe, while others could do 30-40 miles per hour and scare the wits out of me. Some ambulance drivers could be traveling Code 3 and I was comfortable enough to read the newspaper; they were smooth and cautious, others careless, bordering on reckless. I considered myself lucky to have a competent driver who did what he was told, without having to repeat it.

Our first call was a dead body found in an alley near Adams Boulevard and LaBrea. Upon arrival, we found a nude, approximately 25-year-old female, who had received gunshot wounds to her face and torso. We immediately called for the police and secured the scene. Shortly thereafter, detectives from the Wilshire Division responded to our location and took over the investigation. Our job consisted of determining if death had occurred and pronouncing the patient dead at the scene. Additionally, we secured the scene and made mental notes of everything we saw and did. I did a cursory examination of the deceased but was very careful to not contaminate the area; that included keeping track of where we walked and what we touched or did not touch. We cleared the scene after leaving the detectives the copy of the Emergency Medical Report.

I helped her up and she asked me if I wanted a drink of wine and told us she was "blitzed". It was hard to keep a straight face but we helped her up just as a police car arrived on scene.

Immediately, we received a radio call for an unconscious female on the street on Crenshaw Blvd. This time it was me helping my driver get to the location since he did not know where it was. My working of Venice/Wilshire Relief meant that half of my shifts were done in this area so I was quite familiar with the Wilshire Division. Within two to three minutes we arrived on scene of Crenshaw near Venice Boulevard to find a crowd of people around the patient. It was amazing to hear comments from community members such as, "Get out of their way", "Let them through" and some even praying out loud. Fred carried the First Aid Box and opened it for me and stood ready to assist as directed. I first determined that she was not unconscious but apparently under the influence of alcohol - in fact, under her was a bottle of wine, nearly gone. I helped her up and she asked me if I wanted a drink of wine and told us she was "blitzed". It was hard to keep a straight face but we helped her up just as a police car arrived on scene. She did not have any apparent injuries and answered all of my questions so she was turned over to the police officers for disposition. I left them the copy of the Emergency Medical Report and we cleared the scene.

I lifted the microphone and said, G-17 clear and Eugie, the dispatcher, said, “G-17 handle an auto vs. pedestrian at Olympic and Fedora”. I wrote in the time of alarm on my report book, which the attendant filled out, and Fred asked me where we were going. I repeated the address and said just go straight up Crenshaw to Olympic and turn right. At that time, a flood of emotion came over me and I could not help but to relive the scenario in Hollywood Division, G-6, when working with George Antonelli and how he embarrassed me by not helping me with an address. I felt empowered to be able to assist Fred in getting to the address without an issue. After all, the reason I remembered where Fedora was is that it was the location I visited to be sized for my uniforms when I was first hired. At Olympic and Fedora was Uniforms, Incorporated.

Five minutes later we arrived and found a man who had been struck by a hit and run vehicle. He was unconscious and barely breathing, in critical condition. I wasted no time in examining, splinting his fracture and placing him on the gurney. I placed an airway in his throat to ensure that he could breathe and told Fred to "take it in", our code word for Code 3 transport to the hospital. I began using the Elder Valve Resuscitator to breathe for the patient when he could not on his own. I had made the decision to bypass Central Receiving Hospital in favor of Los Angeles County General Hospital due to his condition and probable need for surgery. It took a few minutes longer but his chance of survival would be enhanced. In retrospect, it was similar to today, where in severe trauma one bypasses smaller hospitals to transport to a Trauma Center. Of course in 1969, there were no trauma centers; that would not occur until 1983, a full 14 years later when California Hospital became the first trauma center in Los Angeles County. Unfortunately, it was the first to close its doors a year or so later.

Our first day was busy and rewarding as we had about 10 calls. Fred was a good partner and we got along well. I also found out how difficult it was to guide a new driver to a hospital while rendering aid in the patient compartment. I had responsibility to supervise the activities of the ambulance, driver, and the patient, not to mention all patient records and journal at the station. I relished my job as an attendant and felt pangs of pride in what I was doing. I was 24 years old and had the world by the tail or so I thought.

During the rest of 1969 my duties and responsibilities were that of Ambulance Attendant. Being low on the seniority list of Ambulance Attendants, I floated to various police areas and worked with a horde of different ambulance drivers. Each one had their particular eccentricities and habits which intrigued me. While I did not have to drive anymore, I still kept a sharp eye on where we were going and the locations of the hospitals. Toward that end, I learned more day after day about the geography of the City of Los Angeles and realized that some areas were indeed complex like the Hollywood Hills, Highland Park and East Los Angeles. Even downtown Los Angeles could be tricky if one was not a Bill McCraken.

Only once did I have the opportunity to work G-18, the ambulance that was stationed out of Central Receiving Hospital, with veteran Ambulance Driver Bill McCraken. He had been on the job for well over 25 years when he drove me and had the reputation of not carrying a map book in the ambulance. This amazed me but even more startling was his ability to tell you what color house we were headed to. What a joy it was to be driven by Bill; he would go through alleys, back streets and unusual byways but always show up in front of the location in record time. I finally asked him how he did it and he replied, "I was a mailman for many years." It all began to make sense when he informed me that the downtown area was his during the period he was a Federal Employee delivering the U.S. mail. He not only knew all the streets but the colors of the houses. I thought it a rumor that no map book was in the ambulance, but he acknowledged it to be true. I dreaded having been given a call outside our normal area and having him not know the location. Thankfully that never occurred during the one time we worked together.

My confidence was increasing at a remarkable rate when I was functioning as an Ambulance Attendant. Being able to be the primary treatment person allowed me to refine my bandaging skills, which I had learned from the best, splinting and patient care so that I felt comfortable handling anything. And we did just that, from boys falling out of trees, to falling off horses, from traffic accidents involving cars and motorcycles, planes and helicopter crashes, burns, falls, strokes, heart attacks, poisonings, shock, fractures, and just about anything else. We did it all. It was common to deal with sick calls, headaches, nosebleeds, fights, stabbings, knife wounds and car crashes.

I spent several weeks doing vacation relief; that is covering for other Ambulance Attendants who were on vacation or other leaves, vacancies and a host of other reasons. I worked the Lincoln Heights area, Playa del Rey area, airport, East Los Angeles, West Los Angeles, and even sometimes G-15, a roving ambulance. When an ambulance took a meal break (Code-7), G-15 would drive toward that area to cover any calls that might occur during the Code-7. It was called a roving ambulance and the individuals picked to work on it usually had lots of experience both in terms of knowing the city as well as medical knowledge. To my surprise, several times I was selected to cover the PM watch (5:00PM to 1:00AM) which was quite busy. We would find ourselves in Hollywood and an hour later in the Wilshire area, then Venice and maybe back downtown. It was a fast-paced ambulance and everyone wanted to work it for the action that went along with always being busy.

He looked me right in the eye and said, "Good job, let's go back in."

Once while working G-14 (Venice), covering for Willie Wilson, who was on vacation, the phone rang and my driver answered it and said, "Traffic accident Venice and Overland." I immediately headed out to the ambulance and came face-to-face with D.V. Harris, one of three Ambulance Attendant Supervisors. He had a stop watch in his hand and had counted the time it took for us to get to the ambulance. He looked me right in the eye and said, "Good job, let's go back in." D.V. Harris was a very senior ambulance attendant, who had been on the job for well over 30 years and was well known for his immaculate uniforms, shined shoes, and impeccable standards. He looked sharp as a tack all the time and was somewhat feared by most of the ambulance personnel. His physical appearance, however, from my 24-years of age perspective made him look like an elderly grandpa. He was all business and took his job seriously. He drove a brown sedan with red lights on top and amber lights to the rear. Everyone knew that when that particular car showed up a boss was prowling around.

Whether one liked D.V. Harris or not, you had to respect him and the image he represented. He was one of three field supervisors who could show up at any time and there was no question who would be in charge. The other Supervisor was Paul Clum, who had the same persona. They were older than most of the ambulance attendants and had many years of experience in the field. The third supervisor was the second in command of the whole organization and his name was Senior Ambulance Attendant James Logan. His boss and the head of the organization was Chief Ambulance Attendant Harold Patton.

It was Harold Patton who hired me on March 17, 1967 in his office at 1401 West 6th Street, the Ambulance Headquarters. Other members of the upper management of the Receiving Hospital were: Assistant Superintendent F. K. Sauer M.D., and his boss, Superintendent M.X. Anderson. The Executive Director was C.T. Hill.

Prior to the noted supervisors, particularly in the 1950s, the Assistant Chief was Gaston, the Chief Ambulance Attendant was H.G. Roberts and the Superintendent was C.F. Sebastian.

From 1963 to 1970, a revolution was occurring in Ireland, starting with the J. F. Pantrige Paper and the beginning of the paramedic program in Florida. In fact, the day I began with the City of Los Angeles as an ambulance driver (March 17, 1967) was the day in Florida that the first mobile intensive care unit defibrillated a patient and saved his life. That's how far ahead this program was in Florida. It was to take another three years to come to fruition in LA.

The promotion from ambulance driver to ambulance attendant created positive, significant changes in my life. But far bigger changes were yet to come.

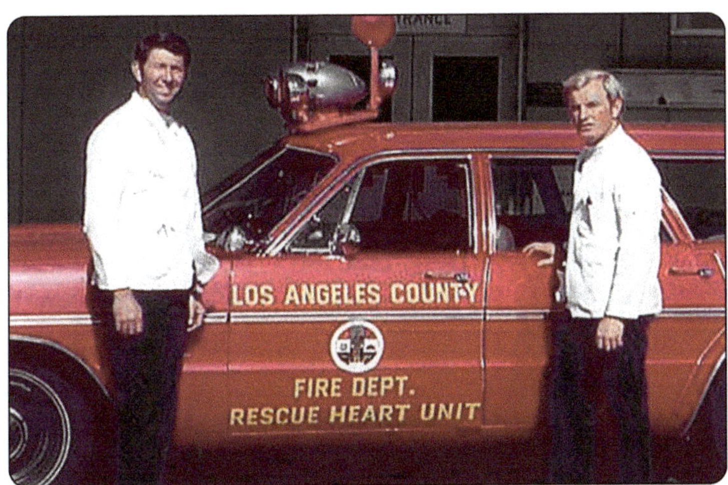

Paramedics Dale Cauble and Rocky Doke pose in front of the first ALS vehicle, a green Plymouth station wagon repainted red and labelled Rescue Heart Unit.

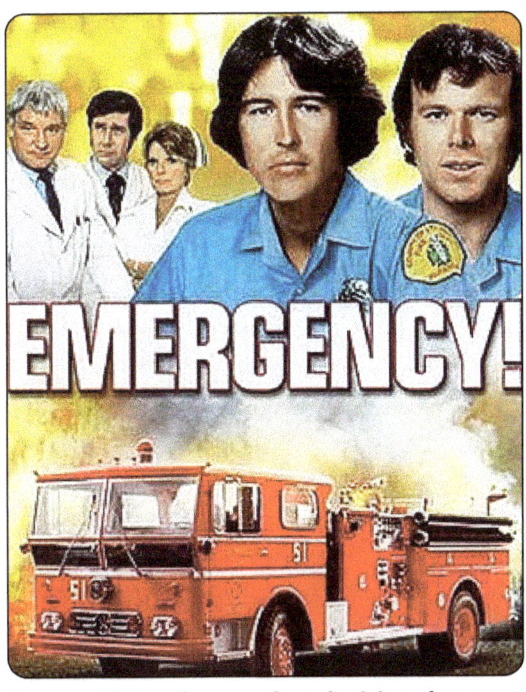

January 1972: The popular television show *Emergency!* was an unexpected, valuable tool for the expansion of Paramedic programs nationwide.

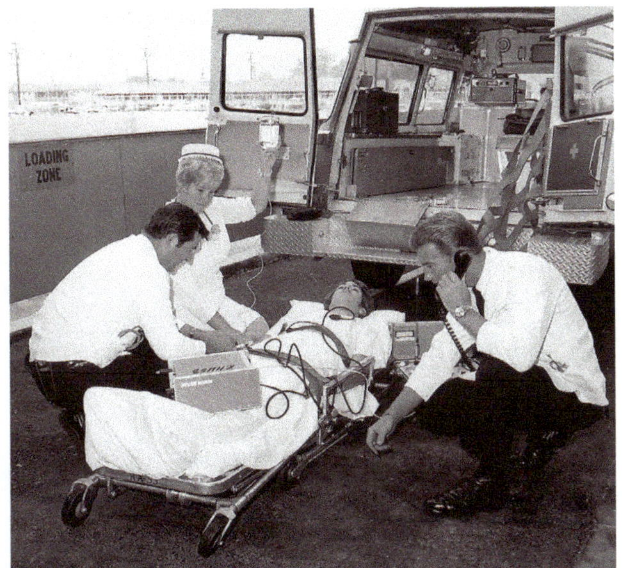

Rescue 53: LAFD's first Paramedic Rescue team, 1970.

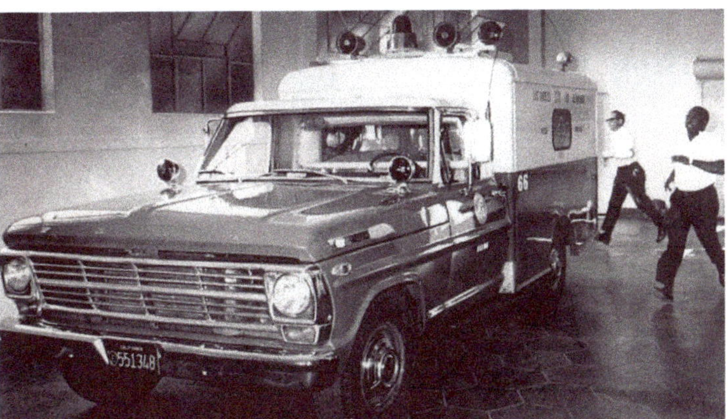

LAFD Ambulance Driver Jim Watkins and Ambulance Attendant Rick Woods sprint from their unfinished dinners to Rescue 66 for an emergency response to a traffic accident in 1971.

An exterior view of the first police and fire department building built by the City of Los Angeles in Hollywood. On the left is the Fire Station 27 and on the right is the Los Angeles Police Department. Note the ambulance on the police side. (circa 1927)

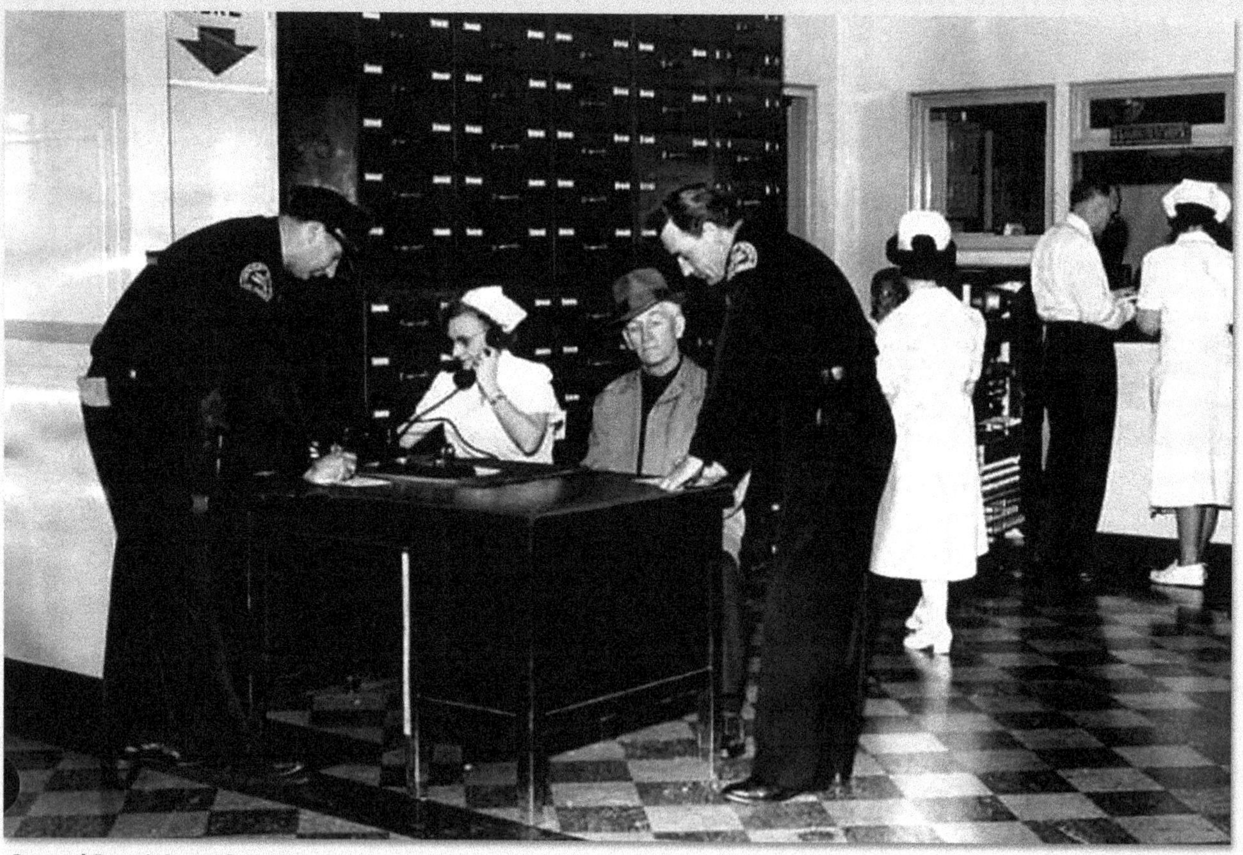

Central Receiving admissions

AMBULANCE & HOSPITAL HISTORY
City of Los Angeles

Amoskeag Pumper and Horse Cart

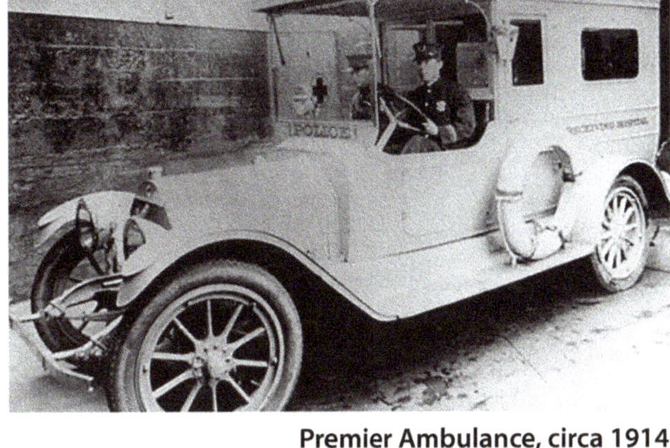

Premier Ambulance, circa 1914

Engine House 18

Auborn 851 Coach-Built Ambulance, circa 1936

Central Receiving Ambulance, circa 1948

Construction of Central Receiving Hospital, 1956

Los Angeles...the Early Days

Pueblo de Los Angeles

Founded in 1781, Los Angeles began as a small pueblo under the auspices of the King of Spain, as a farming and agricultural community. Adobe and tile made up the buildings that were practical and more resistant to fire. Nevertheless, large fires resulted from very hazardous conditions such as large quantities of hay. Neighboring farms would respond to assist in the saving of property by forming "volunteer bucket brigades" using three-gallon leather buckets assisted by Native Americans. No fire alarms or fire bells existed so a person who discovered fire would shoot a pistol into the air repeatedly to warn the town. This system was common into the late 1800s.

In 1850, the City Council was authorized to create a Fire Department but no formal action was taken until 1871 when the volunteer fire department was organized. Prior to 1871, Los Angeles did not have a fire house, fire department, or firefighters. In November of 1869, during a meeting at Buffums' Saloon, an informal volunteer organization was created, made up generally of young businessmen and civic leaders.

The volunteer fire department worked for many years and had many difficulties obtaining support from the city council. For example, in March 1874, city council agreed to authorize two horses to pull a hand-drawn piece of equipment. The council reconsidered the request due to other needs for the money and as a result the volunteer fire company disbanded in anger. The problem was resolved in 1875 when city council voted funds to purchase a pair of horses to pull the engine.

The first fire house erected adjacent to City Hall on Spring Street was an adobe structure which remained in service until 1884. The cost was $665.00. The apparatus was a Amoskeag Pumper and hose cart, manufactured in Massachusetts and shipped to San Francisco by train. Since a railway did not exist between San Francisco and Los Angeles, the Amoskeag was transported by boat along the California coast.

Los Angeles volunteer firefighters, 1871 to 1885

AMBULANCE & HOSPITAL HISTORY

City of Los Angeles

In the late 1850s, the City of Los Angeles initiated a paid police force. At that time if citizens became sick or injured, they were cared for by a friend or family member or taken to the hospital or the local doctor. Occasionally, a doctor would make a home visit or would transport the patient by buggy or a buckboard. As time passed, police officers on patrol loaded patients into a horse-drawn wagon and take them to the nearest place of care.

Later, when the department had enclosed patrol wagons, the police officers would transport the sick and injured. Early in the 1900s, the department was using a 1908 electric patrol ambulance which had no brakes. As a result, when it rolled up to a call the wheels needed to be blocked to keep it from rolling away.

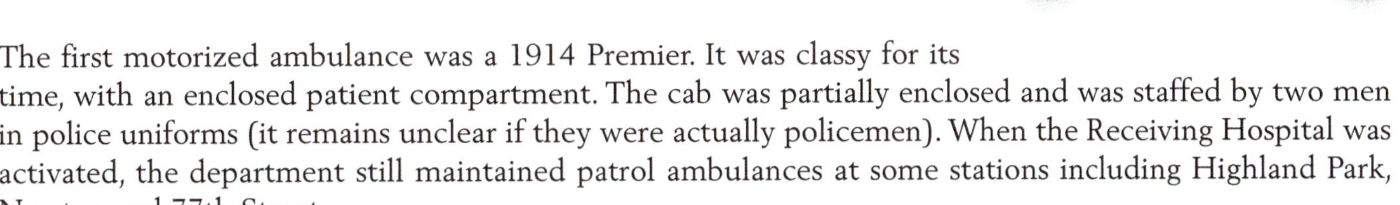

The first City Receiving Hospital first opened in 1868. It provided emergency care for victims of small pox. Located in Chavez Ravine, the hospital rapidly increased its scope of practice admitting patients with other contagious diseases. Central Receiving Hospital was Los Angeles's first public hospital.

The first motorized ambulance was a 1914 Premier. It was classy for its time, with an enclosed patient compartment. The cab was partially enclosed and was staffed by two men in police uniforms (it remains unclear if they were actually policemen). When the Receiving Hospital was activated, the department still maintained patrol ambulances at some stations including Highland Park, Newton and 77th Street.

In the early 1900s, the police department was using Ford, Studebaker, Pierce Arrow and a few other models. In some areas of the city a doctor was picked up to ride on the ambulance with two police officers, a practice that become rather common later on. In 1927, some nurses responded with an officer. Sometime in the late 1920s or 1930s, the officers were taken off the ambulances and replaced with an ambulance driver and either a doctor or nurse. Later, the doctors were replaced with ambulance attendants. From then on, it became standard practice to have a driver and attendant on each ambulance which was housed at a police station or the Receiving Hospital.

For the next 40 years, the driver and attendant system worked very well.

On July 1, 1970, by City Council action, the Los Angeles Fire Department took control of all city ambulance services and dispatched them from fire stations. They remained on an 8-hour shift, with three working shifts per 24 hours until years later when they adopted the Fire Department's 24-hour shift.

At about the same time, the paramedic program that initially began in Ireland, had migrated to Florida, then spread to Los Angeles and across the country. The television show ***Emergency!*** was responsible for explosive growth in the paramedic program nationally.

Georgia Street Receiving Hospital

In 1907 the Georgia Street Receiving Hospital began. Emergency cases prior to the Receiving Hospital were treated by trusties (prisoners given special privileges) in the jail. Of course by today's standards we would not allow prisoners to treat people but in the early 1900s that was frequently done as the public did not know the difference.

In the same year the City of Los Angeles had matured enough to sustain an emergency hospital. The first hospital was constructed at 326 West First Street and was supervised by Dr. Sumner J. Quint as well as three assistant surgeons. The staff consisted of two male nurses who were constantly on duty without days off or any vacations.. The shifts were both 8 and 16 hours; sometimes double shifts were the norm. The nurses earned $75.00 per month.

At that time the ambulance was operated by horse-drawn wagons. There were 3 shifts of horses that worked 8 hours each.

In September 1908, Mr. Charles Whitehead (appointed to Chief Nurse in 1916) filled the position due to the demand for an additional nurse. Mr. Whitehead stayed in his position well into the 1930s.

At that time the ambulance was operated by horse-drawn wagons. There were 3 shifts of horses that worked 8 hours each. When an emergency call came in the horses responded similarly to the old fire horses and upon hearing the sound of the bell, which was used as a siren, they would quicken their pace.

Police officers manned the ambulances and all those in the area knew something was wrong when Officer Jack Hill, Bill Plischke or Jack Mart came galloping through the streets sitting on the wagon and ringing the bell.

The ambulance was also used as a police patrol wagon for transporting intoxicated individuals to the jail. When the ambulance was out on one of its missions, the City of Los Angeles was left uncovered as far as emergency transportation was concerned. The problem was resolved by use of the private ambulance from the old emergency and general hospital, later known as Golden State Hospital. Rumor had it the private ambulance team was faster than the City team. Old timers recall sometimes the two ambulances would race one another. Nurse Grace Phillips, an emergency room nurse of that era, claimed she could tell how serious an emergency was, noting the amount of froth on the horses mouths. If the froth was thick and heavy the sterilizer began to boil in preparation for the injured patient.

Mr. Whitehead recalled an incident at which the ambulance was summoned to Gladys Avenue, at that time a very exclusive neighborhood, for a woman who had cut her throat. When the police officer pulled his horses up to the door and entered the dwelling, he discovered that the woman had severed the jugular vein. He quickly pinched the bleeding vessel and held it tightly all the way to the hospital. The officer saved the woman's life but his fingers were numb and had to be pried off the woman's neck.

By 1910 the work load had increased so much that a new hospital was built at First and Hill Streets. There were many more rooms, lots more equipment, and as modern as could be at that time. As a result, female nurses Ethel Crall and Alina Parker were added to the staff. Ethel Crall was a supervising nurse at the City Hall and worked well into the 1930s.

In 1914, and at the beginning of the First World War, an automobile was purchased to replace the horses. The Premier was the first model and was the "crown jewel" of the staff. It was "on duty" for 8 hours, was put up every night for repairs and to be washed. It would be several years later that the horses would be put out to pasture at various farms to live out the rest of their natural lives.

All the nurses were still working 12-hour shifts with no days off. In 1916 the chief nurse did not have any days off either but for the initiative to establish such an impossible (at the time) thing as days off. At that time Mr. Whitehead's salary was raised to $80.00 per month. This was monumental at the time as the war inflated very high prices.

Dr. Goodrich entered the scene about 1921 as the Chief Surgeon and soon made history by adding additional ambulances and placing them in outlining districts. More nurses were added to the staff and improved equipment and supplies were added as well. Dr. Goodrich served the City of Los Angeles as a well respected and esteemed surgeon until his death in 1928.

Soon after Dr. Wallace Dodge was appointed to succeed Dr. Goodrich and took over as Chief Surgeon. He continued the good work of his predecessor and developed an extensive network of hospitals to cover the entire city. When the old Hill Street quarters became too small, a new hospital was built in 1927 on Georgia Street. A small receiving hospital on Pasadena Avenue in 1928 - a complete unit in itself - was built to serve the east end of the City of Los Angeles. In 1930 the Hollywood area also received a stand-alone small emergency hospital as well. The same year, San Pedro also received an emergency hospital.

As of 1932, there were 9 ambulances from Georgia Street Receiving Hospital and 5 operating from more remote regions of the City. This was an amazing transformation from when the City's first receiving hospital was originated. In 1932 the City of Los Angeles covered an area of 400 square miles. Mr. Whitehead had seen the development of growth for 25 years and was responsible for much of the improvement of emergency medical services.

The staff at Georgia Street Receiving Hospital consisted of Dr. Edwin Goodrich, Chief Surgeon, assisted by Doctors Dunsmoor, Dorn, Sebastian, Lepizich and Saverin, Chief Nurse Charlie Whitehead and Supervising Nurse W. J. Pearce. In 1932 there were 3,631 patients seen at Georgia Street Receiving Hospital in the month of July alone.

In 1933 when the earthquake hit the Los Angeles and Long Beach areas, there were 136 patients seen in 12 hours and 91 ambulance calls were also handled in that time frame.

On February 5, 1941 Chief Nurse Charlie Whitehead retired at the age of 67 with service to the city of more than 32 years.

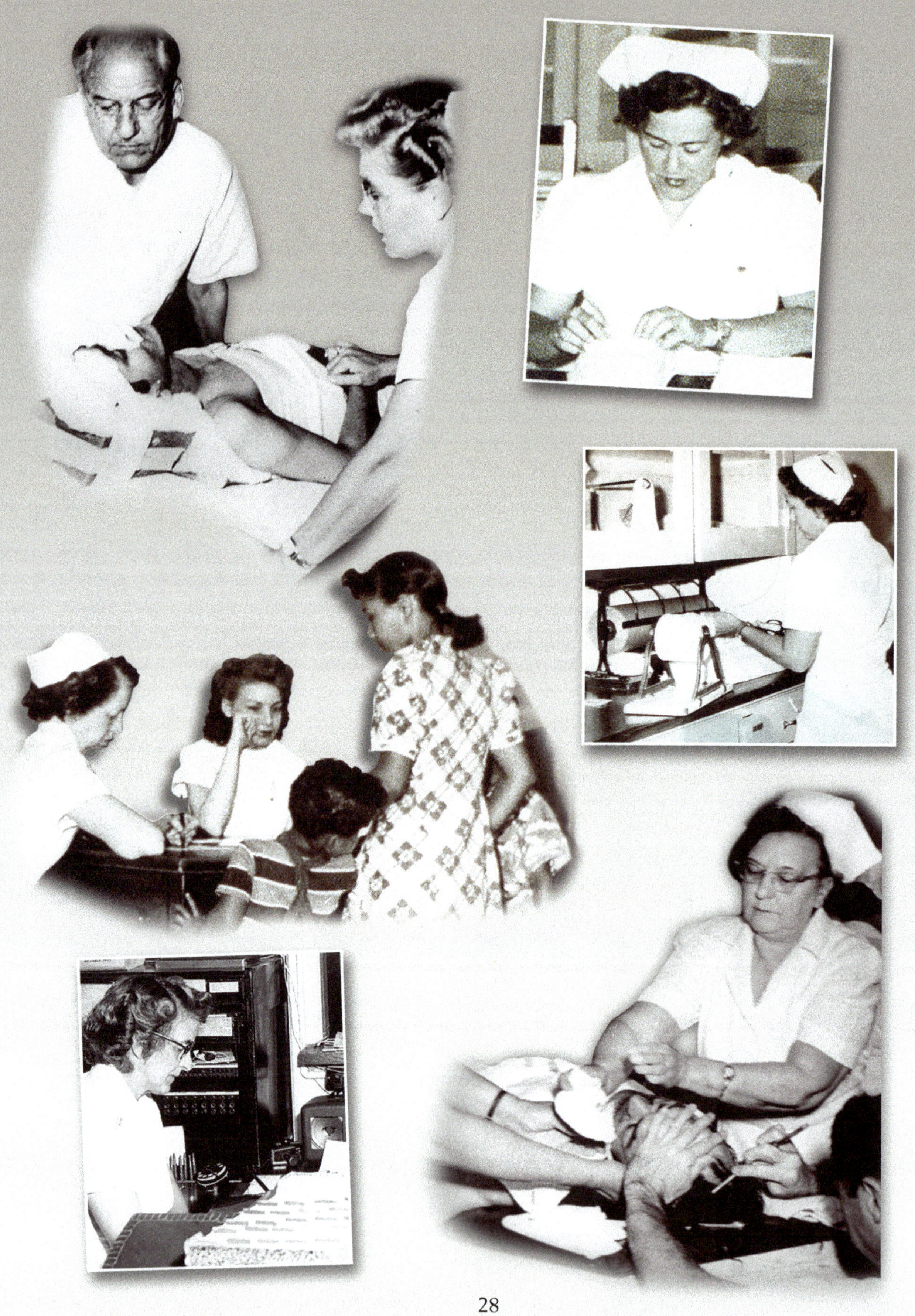

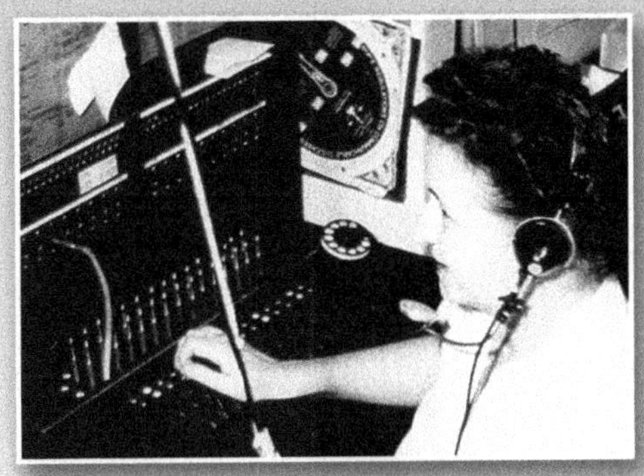

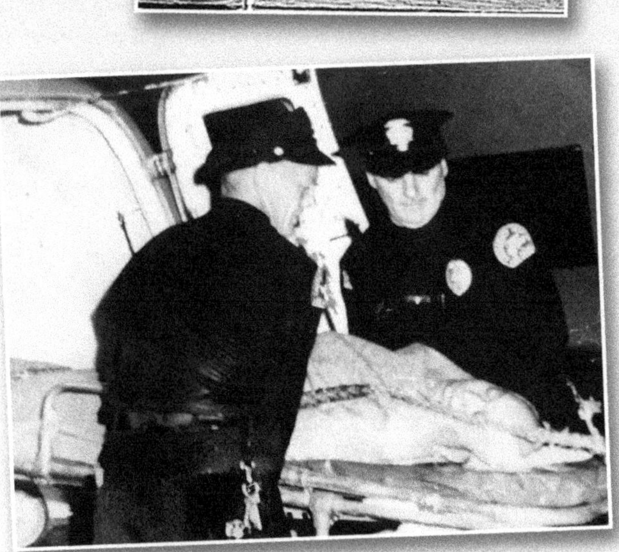

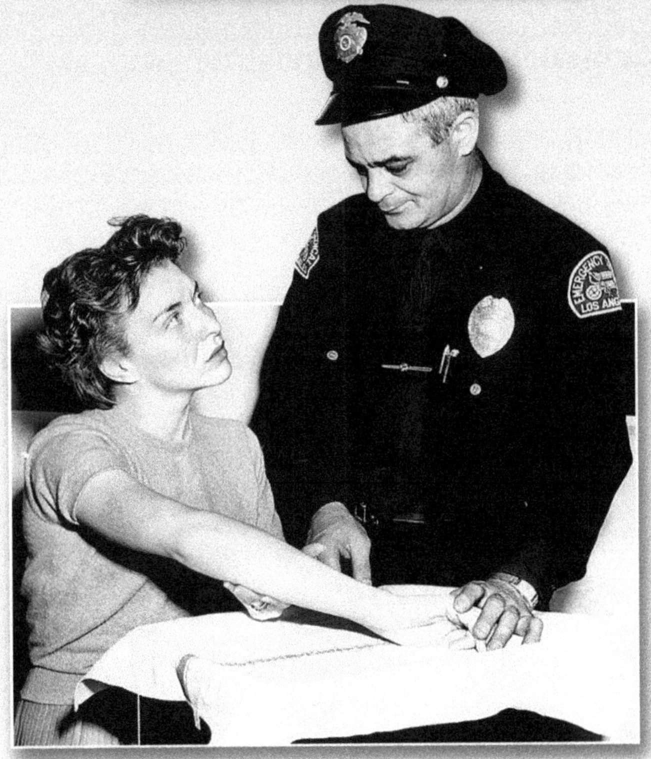
EMERGENCY

In the years of 1945 and 1947 the scope of the receiving hospital expanded to include medical or surgical care to both active and retired police, firemen, and members of the police reserve corps, when medical service was required as a result of performance of their official duties.

Ambulances became known as "The Brown Bombers" (because they were light brown in color) and worked out of Central Receiving Hospital with many units assigned to police stations. All ambulances were known as "G-Units" (because the original ambulances were assigned to Georgia Street Receiving Hospital from 1927 to 1957) with a corresponding number of the police station jurisdictions. Examples include G-7 (Wilshire Police Division), G-14 (Venice Police Division), G-12 (77th Street Division), G-6 (Hollywood Police Division) and G-18 (assigned to Central Receiving Hospital).

New Ordinance

In 1949 a new ordinance was passed bringing the Receiving Hospital in the control of a Superintendent. In 1957 when the Receiving Hospital made its move from Georgia Street to its new location, 1401 West 6th Street, the staff consisted of Superintendent Dr. Charles Sebastian, Chief Nurse Vera Cooper, RN, Principal Nurse John Stickles, RN, and Chief Ambulance Attendant Harold Patton.

During 1956 and up until June 1957 (when the hospital relocated) there had been 107,990 patients seen at the Receiving Hospital.

In 1960 there was a change in the Ambulance Department and the staff included: Chief Ambulance Attendant Harold Patton, Assistant Chief Ambulance Attendant James Logan, with senior Ambulance Attendants D.V. Harris and Paul Clum.

Central Receiving Hospital

Central Receiving Hospital officially opened on June 27, 1957 after moving from the original Georgia Street Receiving Hospital. Many early police officers and firefighters owe their lives to both facilities as it was THE hospital for them since 1927 when Georgia Street Receiving was located on the third floor of the Georgia Street Police Station. Georgia Street Receiving was the fourth hospital since the inception of the City hospital system.

Central Receiving Hospital was located in a two-story structure at 1401 West 6th Street in Los Angeles. It was at 6th and Loma Drive, just west of downtown, and was the hospital's fifth location. The cost was $1.5 million and was a 37,000 square foot building that replaced Georgia Street Hospital.

The year 1968 is remembered vividly by this author as a year that commemorated the 100th Anniversary of the opening of the first City Hospital: Central Receiving Hospital. In addition to giving examinations to police and firefighters, the hospital also accommodated 20 patients in their police and fire ward on the second floor. On the first floor there were 6 emergency treatment rooms and 6 with a 15-bed capacity. From January to June 1968 there were 50,850 patients seen at the Central Receiving Hospital.

The famous and historic Central Receiving Hospital was demolished in October 2005. It was Central Receiving Hospital that provided emergency care and ambulance services to the City of Los Angeles for 115 years.

It was my pleasure to work as an Ambulance Driver and Ambulance Attendant out of Central Receiving Hospital in 1967 as I began my City service. The memories of those wonderful early days, and experiencing the birth of the Emergency Medical Program, began here.

Those who staffed the hospital are those who helped create what today are Los Angeles' Emergency Medical Services. Here are some of them:

- **Robert "Bob" Roberts** began his career with the City as an ambulance driver in 1928. He moved up the ladder to become Chief Ambulance Attendant for some 20 years. He retired in 1957 after almost 30 years of service.
- **Superintendent M.X. Anderson** began working at the hospital at the age of 25 and eventually ran Central Receiving in 1950s.
- **Leon Boudreay**
  was Anderson's Executive Officer
- **Dr. Kearney Sauer**
  was Anderson's Assistant Superintendent
- **Dr. Bazilauskas**
- **Dr. Rooney**
- **Dr. Swain**
- **Dr. Hands**
- **Dr. Soskin**
- **Dr. Saverin**
- **Dr. Douglas Arterberry**
- **Dr. Famillaro**

The most famous person treated at Central Receiving Hospital occurred in the early morning hours of June 5, 1968 when then Senator Robert Kennedy had been shot at the Ambassador Hotel after winning the California Presidential Primary.

On duty was Ambulance Driver Bob Hulsman and Ambulance Attendant Max Behrmann.

Robert Kennedy, Ambassador Hotel, 1968

SPLENDID RECORD OF ACHIEVEMENT. Kearney Sauer, M.D., Senior Supervising Surgeon, Central Receiving Hospital, and Councilman Gilbert W. Lindsay, 9th District, Chairman, Public Health and Welfare Committee, in foreground, discuss the superior services rendered by the staff to citizens of the City. In the background are five of the highly trained ambulance drivers standing by two modern ambulances equipped to meet emergency requirements, at the Central Receiving Hospital, 1401 West Sixth St. The City also maintains Receiving Hospitals in Hollywood, Lincoln Heights and Van Nuys, a First Aid Division in City Hall, and an Infirmary at the Central Jail. (Photo by Charles "Chuck" Williams.

September 1968

City's Receiving Hospital Founded 100 Years Ago, Saluted for Superior Service

By BOB HOLLEY
Receiving Hospital

By BOB HOLLEY
Receiving Hospital

During September 1868, the City of Los Angeles had its first major Smallpox Epidemic and the local government realized its responsibility to help the citizens of the area. A hospital was built in Chavez Ravine for the treatment of these people. Dr. Henry S. Orme was City Health Officer at this time.

One year later, in 1869, after working day and night caring for the people in and around the City of Los Angeles, Dr. Orme resigned. The following is a resolution given to Dr. Orme by the City Board of Health: "To Dr. H. S. Orme. Sir: I am instructed by the Board of Health of the City of Los Angeles to return to you from the Board of Health, their warmest thanks for the efficient manner in which you discharged your duties as Health Officer and attending Physician at the City Smallpox Hospital. Respectfully, W. G. Dryden, Secretary." (Taken from the book "Medical Profession of Southern California, 1910 Edition).

Accident Cases

Through the years this hospital continued to operate with Smallpox victims and other cases coming in. Sometime between 1868 and 1889 accident cases started to be taken to the "Central Police Station" at 326 West First Street, possibly because it was closer than Chavez Ravine.

In the year 1889 there were 562 cases treated at the "Central Police Station," Dr. Granville MacGowan, Health Officer and Chief Police Surgeon, along with his assistant, Dr. Earnest A. Bryant, realized that to serve the public better, they should have a well equipped Emergency First Aid and Operating Room at the Police Station. Their wish was granted by the City Council and work began on the converting of an emergency power battery room into the much needed facility. The Chief Police Surgeon and his staff moved into the building in 1890.

From December 1, 1889 to November 30, 1890 there were 3,515 patients treated at the "Central Police Station." The population at this time was 65,000. In 1891 Dr. Ernest A. Bryant became Chief Police Surgeon. He was to hold this position until 1896. During the time Dr. Ernest A. Bryant was Chief Police Surgeon, the Emergency First Aid and Operating Room was moved to a building on Hill Street near the corner of First Street.

Between the years of 1896 and 1927 the hospital functioned under various heads of staff. It was in 1908 that Charles "Charley" Whitehead was hired on a temporary basis as Police Nurse along with two other nurses. In 1907 the Police Department used patrol wagons drawn by horses as ambulances. Some of the officers on this duty were Jack Hills, Bill Plischke and Jack Mart.

Hospital Becomes Dept.

On December 14, 1910 the Receiving Hospital became a department for the medical and surgical treatment of all persons brought to the City Jail or Receiving Hospital and for the medical and surgical treatment of all policemen and firemen.

In 1914 the first motor driven ambulance owned by the City of Los Angeles was a Premier. In 1916 Charley Whitehead was appointed Chief Police Nurse. Between 1916 and 1927 the hospital continued to give aid to those persons in need of it.

In the period from 1920 to 1921 there were 29,957 patients seen, and by 1926 the number of patients seen had climbed to 67,210. It was clear to Chief Surgeon Edwin G. Goodrich that a larger and better equipped facility was needed. And so it was in the year of 1927 that Georgia Street Receiving Hospital at 1337 Georgia Street opened its doors. The first patient treated there was Baby Fausto Bustus, 3-year-old son of Mrs. E. Bustus.

Georgia St. Hospital

The staff at Georgia Street Receiving Hospital at that time consisted of Dr. Edwin G. Goodrich, Chief Surgeon, assisted by Doctors Dunsmoor, Dorn, Sebastian, Lopizich and Saverein, Chief Nurse, Charley Whitehead and Supervising Nurse, W. J. Pearce. In the year of 1932 there were 3,631 patients seen at Georgia Street Receiving Hospital in the month of July alone! In 1933 when an Earthquake struck the Los Angeles and Long Beach areas there were 136 patients seen in 12 hours and 91 ambulance calls were answered in 12 hours. In 1940 Chief Nurse Charles (Charley) Whitehead took leave of absence. He retired on February 5, 1941 at the age of 67 years with a service to the City of Los Angeles of more than 32 years.

Nurse J. W. Pearce took over the duties of Chief Nurse. The ambulance department was under the supervision of Mr. Robert (Bob) Roberts with John Gaston as Senior Ambulance Attendant. In the years of 1945 and 1947 the scope of the Receiving Hospital was enlarged to include furnishing of hospital and medical or surgical care to both active and pensioned firemen, policemen, and members of police reserve corps, when services were required as a result of the performance of official duties.

New Ordinance

In 1949 a new ordinance was passed, bringing the Receiving Hospital under the control of a Superintendent. In 1957 when the Receiving Hospital made its move from Georgia Street to its present location at 1401 West 6th Street, the staff consisted of Dr. Charles F. Sebastian, Superintendent, Chief Nurse, Vera Cooper, R.N., Principal Nurse, John Stickles, R.N., Chief Ambulance Attendant Ambulance Attendant, Harold B. (Pat) Patton.

During 1956 to 1957 and from January to June, 1957, (when the hospital moved) there had been 107,990 patients seen at the Receiving Hospital. In 1960 there was a change in the Ambulance Department and the staff included; Chief Ambulance Attendant, Harold B. (Pat) Patton, Assistant Chief Ambulance Attendant,

(Continued on Page 9)

(Continued from Page 8)

James A. Logan, with D. V. Harris and Paul Clum as Senior Ambulance Attendants.

100th Anniversary

This year is 1968, one hundred years after the first City Hospital opened. The hospital opened in 1957 is still the home of "Central Receiving Hospital." There are three (3) branch hospitals: Lincoln Heights Receiving, Hollywood Receiving and Van Nuys Receiving.

The Central Receiving Hospital, in addition to giving physical examinations to police and firemen, can accommodate twenty (20) police and/or firemen in their inpatient Police and Fire Ward in the second floor. On the first floor there are six (6) emergency treatment rooms and six (6) rooms with 15 beds.

Outstanding Staff

The Receiving Hospital System is headed by Superintendent, M. X. Anderson, M.D., Executive Officer. Leon J. Boudreau, Assistant Superintendent, Kearney Sauer, M.D., Police and Fire Medical Director, C. Harry Lindsley, M.D., Chief Nurse, Vera Cooper, R.N., Principal Nurse, John Stickles, R.N. The Ambulance Department consists of James A. Logan, Chief Ambulance Attendant, and Senior Ambulance Attendants — D. V. Harris, Paul Clum, and Charles W. Gilbert, Lee Jackson, Supervising Orderly.

Some of the Doctors on the staff with Doctors Anderson, Linsley and Sauer are Doctors Bazilauskas, Grisdale, Swain, Rooney, Hands, Soskin, Arterberry and a name from the past, Saverin.

In this year of 1968 from the month of January, up to and including the month of June, there have been 50,850 patients seen at Central Receiving Hospital, alone.

Over the years there have been many, many dedicated persons who have worked and who are still working for the City of Los Angeles in the Receiving Hospital System and Ambulance Service. I wish that I could mention them all; they certainly deserve it, but space and time will not permit. But to them, I would like to say "Thanks for giving up part of your lives to help the people of the City of Los Angeles."

Groundbreaking for Central Receiving Hospital, 1956

THE RECEIVING HOSPITAL

One of the multifarious duties of the police department is furnishing emergency aid to injured or wounded persons, and for this work the receiving hospital is specially designed. Unless the injured person refuses to go or another hospital is much nearer and the case is urgent all who are hurt on the streets or are wounded in brawls or quarrels are taken in the police ambulance to the hospital, which is now located at 110 Hill street, just around the corner from the Central Police station. There the surgeons in charge have every facility for giving emergency treatment. There is no better equipped receiving hospital in the country than we have now. Aside from the examination room and offices, there are wards for men and women, a surgical ward and operating room, a laboratory, a diet kitchen and a ward for insane persons. The latest improvements for giving scientifically correct care to the injured have been installed, including a dressing sterilizer, sanitary water heaters, instrument and utensil sterilizers, an X-ray outfit, with dark room for developing, and so on. Many a life is saved through the prompt and skillful action of these receiving hospital surgeons, and thousands of dollars are saved poor persons who meet with accidents and who are given the immediate attention necessary to obiate the necessity of going to a private hospital and paying for an operation. Besides the five police surgeons there are five nurses in attendance constantly. In no case is a patient kept more than a few hours at the receiving hospital, all persons unable to pay high hospital charges being taken to the county institution and others being removed to their homes or private hospitals when they can stand the strain of moving. Incidentally it may be remarked that the police surgeons give all necessary care to members of the police and fire departments of the city.

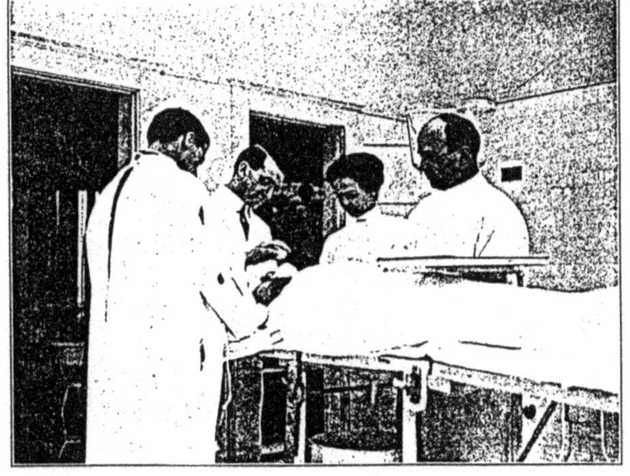

The police surgeons are C. E. Zerfing, Chief; C. A. Wright, W. E. Carter, F. W. Kidder and (Eastside) P. A. Off. The nurses are John Morgan, Gordon Johnson, Paul Engle, Ethel Beatty and Katherine Carson.

FIRST AID TO THE INJURED.

All the Los Angeles police officers are trained in giving first aid to injured persons, and each police alarm box contains a small kit of the essentials for dressing dangerous wounds. In an extreme case this ability has frequently saved a life that would otherwise have been lost before the hospital could be reached.

ARTICLE

Los Angeles Historical Landmark Slated for Demolition

by Jackie David, September 28, 2005

Back to Where and How It First Began

Los Angeles' famous and historical Central Receiving Hospital, located at 1401 W. Sixth Street, will be demolished in a few months. Along with the dust and rubble will be many, many memories - very personal for those who worked or were treated there - and a lot of history for such events as the Assassination of Bobby Kennedy who was initially treated at Central Receiving and quickly transported across the street to the Good Samaritan Hospital for brain surgery where he died. It was also the Central Receiving Hospital that provided emergency and paramedic services to Angelinos for some 120 years.

I had the honor of interviewing Dr. Alan Cowen recently - also known as Deputy Chief Alan Cowen of the Los Angeles Fire Department. Dr. Cowen is probably one of the few living historians left from an era that birthed the life-saving systems we have today: 911, Paramedics and Emergency Rooms. Dr. Cowen is retired and works full-time teaching Emergency Medical Services at Los Angeles Valley College - a staid existence when compared to the thrill of his 32 years of Paramedic work with the City of Los Angeles. He is currently chairman of the Department of Emergency Services for Los Angeles Valley College.

Dr. Cowen began working for the City of Los Angeles in 1967 at the age of 22. He promoted through the ranks to become the City's Chief Paramedic. He was the last Paramedic Chief in the Emergency Services Bureau of the Los Angeles Fire Department.

Here is Dr. Cowen's story... "his" story (and others) as well as history, as told via telephone interview.

Central Receiving Hospital, founded in 1868, was Los Angeles' first public hospital providing emergency care and paramedic services to the people of the city for more than a century.

It begins with a major smallpox epidemic that hits what is to become one of the largest and most progressive metropolitan areas in the world: the City of Los Angeles. The epidemic sweeps through Los Angeles in September 1868 and the City quickly builds a hospital in Chavez Ravine to aid smallpox victims. It is a small hospital. Dr. Henry F. Orme is the City's Health Officer.

Dr. Orme does an outstanding job handling the smallpox epidemic and, after a year, resigns from his post. The Los Angeles City Council presents him with a Resolution for his work with the Smallpox Epidemic of 1868. Chavez Ravine continues to care for smallpox victims even after Orme's departure. Thus, with this pain, is born Los Angeles' Emergency Medical Services.

It was a time of horse-drawn buggies. The Police Department was in charge of just about everything - including accidents and medical emergencies. Chavez Ravine Hospital was a long way to travel to bring accident victims for care. It was most certainly a much shorter ride to the only police station in town: the Central Police Station located at 326 West First Street. And so it was that the Central Police Station became an Emergency Hospital of sorts - although it was never officially called that until much, much later.

Just like Chavez Ravine, the Central Police Station was staffed with one doctor: Chief Police Surgeon Granville MacGowan. Later, in 1890, the City Council recognized the need to house emergency victims and so converted a room at the Central Police Station specifically for this purpose. Emergency power was provided along with a surgeon and staff to give emergency medical care to a quickly growing clientele. It was called the Emergency First Aid and Operating Room. A Police Ambulance, an open horse-drawn buggy, was also provided.

The Central Police Station served a total of 562 patients in 1889. It was also at this time that Chief Police Surgeon Granville MacGowan, like his Chavez Ravine predecessor, became the City Health Officer.

The reputation of the Central Police Station as a provider of emergency care continued to grow. Accident victims poured in. In a single year's time, between 1889 and 1890, the number of patients treated at the Central Station grew to 3,515. Dr. Ernest Bryant became the Chief Police Surgeon.

Los Angeles' population was at 65,000 and growing. The Central Police Station building moved to First & Hill Street to become the city's first Emergency Receiving Hospital, providing emergency medical services for 31 years, from 1896 to 1927.

In 1907, the Police Department continued to use Patrol Wagons as ambulances pulled by horses. There is a story of an ambulance driver named Bill Plischke who, it is said, through his interesting voice and tone, could communicate the severity of an emergency to his horses. Stories are that his voice alone, through commands, prompted his horses to move from a walk to a gallop - much to the delight of his needy passengers. Other well-known police officer ambulance drivers at the time were Jack Hills and Jack Mart.

Los Angeles forged ahead. It hired its first nurse in 1908 - a gentleman named Charles "Charlie" Whitehead. Services expanded. Where there was once only a single doctor, there was now a Surgeon, Charlie and two other police nurses running the one-room Central Police Emergency Receiving Hospital. Charlie was appointed Chief Police Nurse in 1916 and became the first nurse in the City to become a Chief.

On December 14, 1910, the City Council officially recognized the Receiving Hospital as a separate Department in the City and thus provided funding. The Department, in turn, also provided care for the City's Firemen (there were no women firefighters) and Police Officers while continuing to serve as an Emergency Receiving Hospital.

The official Central Receiving Hospital was finally established four years later and, in 1914, the one-room facility came to be called what it was for many years: The Central Receiving Hospital.

The City also purchased its first motor driven ambulance in 1914. It was called The Premier and had what no other ambulance had: an enclosed capsule for patients. For the first time in Los Angeles' history, patients who were transported for emergency care now had the comfort of much needed privacy.

continues on next page...

Central Receiving continued to work furiously to care for its patients. It was still a one-room Hospital. Between 1920 and 1921, it cared for a total of 29,957 patients. Five years later, in 1926, the number of patients ballooned to an astounding 67,210 - practically matching the population of the entire City of Los Angeles.

In 1927 it became increasingly apparent that change was in order. Chief Surgeon Edwin Goodrich, who now headed the Hospital, moved it to 1337 Georgia Street (near Central Street) where it became known as the famous Georgia Street Receiving Hospital. Another major change happened: nurses, for the first time, began to accompany police officers in the ambulances.

Georgia Street Receiving Hospital functioned for 30 years, from 1927 to 1957.

Also, between the late 1920s and early 1930s, three smaller branch hospitals were established to take care of Los Angeles' growing population: Lincoln Heights Receiving Hospital, Hollywood Heights Receiving Hospital, and Van Nuys Receiving Hospital.

There's a little piece of medical or seat-belt history that can be noted at this time. In 1952, Ambulance Attendant Jack Gilson was killed when he was thrown out of an ambulance in a collision. Gilson was the third Ambulance Attendant killed in this manner. After Gilson's death, Dr. Charles F. Sebastian from Georgia Street Receiving Hospital devised a series of straps to prevent ambulance occupants from being thrown out of the vehicle in a collision. He ordered they be installed in every ambulance. The City outfitted its 13 ambulances at a cost of $976.30. (Could this be how the seatbelt was born?)

Things really began to move along in 1957. The Georgia Street Receiving Hospital moved to its final location: 1401 West Sixth Street. The other address for this same facility, the other side of the hospital, was 500 S. Loma Drive.

The new Central Receiving Hospital opened its doors in 1957. Norris Paulson was Mayor. It cost $1.5 Million to build and retrofit the new 37,000 square foot facility. Its first floor had six emergency treatment rooms. It had six other rooms with 15 beds. Patient numbers were up to 107,000 a year. It was and continued to be the center where up to 20 physical exams were conducted per day for Police Officers and Firemen.

Dr. Charles F. Sebastian was Superintendent. His Chief Nurse was Vera Cooper. His Principal Nurse was RN John Stickles.

Police officers also continued to operate ambulances. The Chief Ambulance Attendant was Harold Patton. Jim Logan was the Assistant Chief Ambulance Attendant. He had two Senior Ambulance Attendants: D.V. Harris (who recently passed away in his late 90s) and Paul Clum.

In fact, it was Patton who hired Dr. Alan Cowen, in 1967, when Cowen was 21 years old. "I know it's ancient history but I remember Patton like it was yesterday," Cowen says fondly. "He was short and stocky and looked a lot like the actor Spencer Tracy. Patton was a hard-boiled egg, an old ambulance guy who ran a tight ship. He demanded and we gave," recalls Dr. Cowen.

A large commemorative event was held in 1968 at 1401 West 6th Street (Central Receiving Hospital's final location) to celebrate the Hospital's 100th birthday (remember the smallpox epidemic of 1868). "It was an event to remember", reminisces Cowen. We had everyone there. We had photos of folks when they were young and newer photos taken many years later. To many attending, it was their last official event."

"Central Receiving was amazing at rendering First

Ambulance Personnel, circa 1940

Aid considering we didn't have the tools or technology at the time," says Cowen. "CPR was unknown. Our tools, equipment and supplies would be considered ancient by today's standards. Our ambulances looked like "ambulasauruses. Yet, I watched our people stop hemorrhaging and do so many things to save countless lives. We absolutely saved lives, without a doubt, lots of lives. It was and continues to be an honor to have been a part of that."

On July 1, 1970, the Emergency Ambulance Service was transferred from the Central Receiving Hospital System to the Los Angeles Fire Department - after some 130 years. Medical emergency responders became known as Paramedics in 1970 and 911 came into being some 15 years after.

"It pangs my heart to know that the Central Receiving Hospital will soon be torn down. It is, to me, a real historical landmark," laments Dr. Cowen. In 1996, Deputy Chief Alan Cowen of the Los Angeles Fire Department organized and emceed a Central Receiving Hospital Reunion. Physicians, ambulance attendants, nurses, ambulance drivers, and other Receiving Hospital employees from yesteryear came from all parts of the country to attend the reunion. "It was like going back in a time machine," recalls Cowen. "These ambulance drivers, attendants and nurses were all the grandparents, the ancestors of emergency medical services in the City and they, we, were all joined by the common bond of helping people in emergencies."

Time moves on. Progress must be made. Amongst the rubble of what was once the Central Receiving Hospital will arise a brand new Police Station - back to where and how Central Receiving first began.

NEWS

City of Los Angeles • Personnel Department

700 East Temple Street, Los Angeles, California 90012 • www.LACITY.org

CONTACT: Jackie David (213) 847-9718
Bruce Whidden (213) 473-3935

FOR IMMEDIATE RELEASE:
September 28, 2005

A FINAL TRIBUTE TO A LOS ANGELES LANDMARK

A final salute and tribute to the life and history of the Central Receiving Hospital is scheduled for tomorrow, September 29, 2005, at 10:00 am – a few days before the landmark located at 1401 West 6th Street is literally demolished.

Along with the dust and rubble will be many memories – very personal for those who worked or were treated there – and a lot of history for such moments as the Assassination of U.S. Senator Robert F. (Bobby) Kennedy who, history tells, was initially treated at the Central Receiving Hospital. It was also the Central Receiving Hospital that provided emergency and paramedic services to Angelinos for some 120 years and birthed the life-saving systems we have today: *9-1-1, Paramedics and Emergency Rooms*.

As a final gesture, Los Angeles Fire Department engines, trucks and ambulances will flank the hospital. City dignitaries – the Mayor, Councilmembers, Police and Fire Representatives - are slated to attend. Photos and memorabilia will be on display. Dr. Al Cowen who retired as an LAFD Chief Paramedic and one of the Hospital's few remaining historians will take everyone for a walk back in time, via a slide show and video presentation, to a time of horse drawn ambulances to the city's first motor ambulance: *The Premier*. Glynn Martin, Executive Director of the Los Angeles Police Historical Society, will share with the public a scrapbook donated by the family of the City's first Chief Police Nurse, Charles Whitehead. Other historical pieces, including nurses' journals will be on display.

"We honor and celebrate the service provided by the Central Receiving Hospital and the many folks who have worked here," says First District Councilmember Ed Reyes. "This hospital has touched many lives and saved just as many. Although it is to be demolished, it will live on in our memories and in history as the City's grandparent of Emergency Services."

Los Angeles' emergency services began with a major smallpox epidemic in 1868 and with a single Police Station that provided ambulances and emergency care. Once the rubble has cleared, a new building will arise and Central Receiving will return to what it once was and how it all began: a police station.

The public is welcome to attend this final tribute.

The Gilson Strap

In 1951 two Central Receiving Hospital Ambulance Personnel were killed in traffic collisions in Los Angeles. One was Ambulance Attendant John H. Gilson, who was thrown out of the ambulance when the back doors of the vehicle came apart as a direct result of the collision. The collision that killed Ambulance Attendant Gilson was also responsible for injuries sustained by the patient on the gurney. Both the patient and the gurney he was strapped into flew out of the ambulance but thankfully the patient was not killed.

The Gilson Strap was installed in every ambulance in 1952. Could this be how the seatbelt was born?

Dr. Charles Sebastian, Central Receiving Hospital's Director, experimented with various devices to keep the Ambulance Attendant and patients safe during any kind of a mishap. It was determined that some sort of strap would be the most efficient and cost effective so a device was developed by William H. Harper, a Pasadena Physicist, and the Aircraft Belt and Trim Corporation. It became known as the Gilson Strap or Gilson Belt.

On March 24, 1952, Ambulance Driver Howard Smith and Ambulance Attendance Bob Roberts demonstrated the new safety belts in a City of Los Angeles Ambulance. A large nylon strap encloses the entire rear of the ambulance before the doors are closed and a seat belt is utilized by the ambulance attendant while the ambulance is transporting the patient to a hospital.

At the time there were 13 ambulances working in the City of Los Angeles as part of the Central Receiving Hospital System and the cost of the safety belts for all 13 vehicles was $976.00. The straps were compared to those used on an airliner. Each front seat in the ambulance had one and there was one to secure the patient to the gurney.

The new innovation was the large nylon webbing which buckled all the way across the rear of the ambulance, inside of the double doors. If the doors swung open in a collision, the webbing keeps those inside the patient compartment from flying out into the street. Dr. Sebastian is quoted as saying, "It's too bad we had to wait until two men were killed before we decided to do something. The safety straps have already proved their worth", said Dr. Sebastian, by preventing a driver from falling out of his seat when his ambulance went into a spin during recent rains.

The Gilson Belt was developed and incorporated in memory of John H. Gilson, who lost his life helping others.

Transfer of Ambulances and Personnel by City Council Action: 1970

Almost a year prior to the Los Angeles Fire Department taking over the Central Receiving Hospital Ambulances, discussions were being held between both administrations; meetings were underway as to whether a merger was possible and, if so, how would it take place.

It should be noted that in an **August 18, 1969 letter (see pages 42-47)** sent from then Chief Engineer and General Manager Raymond M. Hill to the Honorable Arthur K. Snyder, of the City of Los Angeles Governmental Efficiency Committee, that plans were underway to transfer the Ambulance Personnel from the Receiving Hospital to the Fire Department. Fire Department staff were grappling with the alternate method of organization that would happen if the transition occurred.

Central Receiving Hospital, founded in 1868, was Los Angeles' first public hospital providing emergency care and paramedic services to the people of the city for more than a century.

A study was conducted by Fire Department staff called "Central Receiving Hospital Services Study" and in the summary it was clearly indicated that the Los Angeles Fire Department did not seek extension of authority leading to control of emergency medical and ambulance services. Chief Hill stated that if the Fire Department was given the responsibility to direct and control these services, the ability and dedication of the officers and men of the department would result in services that would be a model for such operations it granted the essential support and means.

Total operations cost or comparison of costs with existing services would require detailed analysis and comprehensive evaluation of all phases of the operation to develop accurate comparable cost figures.

The report went on to state that public complaints on ambulance service can be corrected by Fire Department operation. However, facilities and quality of emergency care at hospitals must be upgraded to Hospital Council standards to do a complete job. This factor relates directly to the willingness of the City of Los Angeles to pay for superior care and the value placed on emergency care for our citizens.

Within the letter from Chief Hill was a section called General Discussion in which the following recommendations were made:

1. Discontinue operation of the Central Receiving Hospital and its branches for emergency medical care to the public.

2. Provide public emergency care entirely through private contract hospitals.

3. Transfer all present Receiving Hospital facilities to the Fire Department. Develop these facilities for operation of an occupational health program for firemen and policemen.

4. Provide firemen and policemen with full outpatient and inpatient care by private hospitals.

5. Unify ambulance service city-wide under administration of the Fire Department. Further stated was that any change in organization or operation of Central Receiving Hospital can be accomplished by Ordinance, inasmuch as the City Charter makes no provision for such Department.

Emergency medical care for the public and for fire-police personnel could best be provided by approved contract hospitals. Contracts should be negotiated with additional approved private hospitals to minimize travel time and provide more complete city-wide coverage. In certain depressed areas, City subsidy should be considered for providing emergency care facilities in private hospitals that presently will not provide this service.

Ambulance service, as presently constituted, is in need of change to bring stability to this operation and improve service to the public. Present morale of this service is at a low ebb and performance has suffered through lack of proper supervision and administrative support.

The City of Los Angeles is legally charged with providing medical care under certain circumstances for prisoners in custody of the Los Angeles Police Department. There has been a recognized need for an expanded occupational health program for firemen and policemen. The emphasis has been placed on routine examinations with little provided in the form of constructive (or preventable) health programming. There should be recognition of the physical and emotional environments to which fire and police personnel are subjected. In view of the above, definitive action should be taken to permit improving the performance of fire and police personnel.

(The copy above is transcribed from actual letter on pages 42-47)

continues on next page 48

BOARD OF
FIRE COMMISSIONERS
624-5211
STA. 3369

Russell L. Sorensen
President
Edward V. Hill
Vice President
Lee Hamer
Herbert Glaser
Johnny Grant

CITY OF LOS ANGELES

CALIFORNIA

SAM YORTY
MAYOR

DEPARTMENT OF FIRE
217 S. HILL ST
LOS ANGELES, CALIF 90012
628-6161

RAYMOND M. HILL
CHIEF ENGINEER
AND
GENERAL MANAGER

August 18, 1969

Honorable Arthur K. Snyder
Governmental Efficiency Committee
Los Angeles City Council
Room 242-B, City Hall

Dear Councilman Snyder:

As requested by your Honorable Committee on August 12, 1969, I submit the following Central Receiving Hospital Services Study compiled by my staff, dealing with an alternate method of organization for the Receiving Hospital Department:

CENTRAL RECEIVING HOSPITAL SERVICES STUDY

SUMMARY

The Fire Department does not seek extension of authority leading to control of emergency medical and ambulance services in the City of Los Angeles. However, if we are given the responsibility to direct and control these services the ability and dedication of the officers and men of the Department would result in services that would be a model for such operations if we were granted the essential support and means.

Total operational cost or comparison of costs with existing services would require detailed analysis and comprehensive evaluation of all phases of the operation to develop accurate comparative cost figures.

Public complaints on ambulance service can be corrected by Fire Department operation. However, facilities and quality of emergency care at hospitals must be upgraded to Hospital Council standards to do a complete job. This factor relates directly to the willingness of the City to pay for superior care and the value placed on emergency care for our citizens.

GENERAL DISCUSSION

Continuing criticism of Receiving Hospital operations has resulted in certain definite recommendations by diverse groups proposing changes in operation and procedure. The Fire Department, while not seeking to take over Receiving Hospital operations, must take a position regarding several proposals due to recommendations that certain facilities be placed under Fire Department control. These recommendations are as follows:

A. Discontinue operation of Central Receiving Hospital and its branches for emergency medical care to the public.

B. Provide public emergency care entirely through private contract hospitals.

C. Transfer all present Receiving Hospital facilities to the Fire Department. Develop these facilities for operation of an occupational health program for firemen and policemen.

D. Provide firemen and policemen with full out-patient and in-patient care by private hospitals.

E. Unify ambulance service city-wide under administration of the Fire Department.

Any proposed change in organization or operation of Central Receiving Hospital can be accomplished by Ordinance, inasmuch as the City Charter makes no provision for such Department.

Emergency medical care for the public and for fire-police personnel could best be provided by approved contract hospitals. Contracts should be negotiated with additional approved private hospitals to minimize travel time and provide more complete city-wide coverage. In certain depressed areas, City subsidy should be considered for providing emergency care facilities in private hospitals that presently will not provide this service.

Ambulance service, as presently constituted, is in need of change to bring stability to this operation and improve service to the public. Present morale of this service is at a low ebb and performance has suffered through lack of proper supervision and administrative support.

The City is legally charged with providing medical care under certain circumstances for prisoners in custody of the Los Angeles Police Department.

There has been a recognized need for an expanded occupational health program for firemen and policemen. The emphasis has been placed on routine examinations with little provided in the form of constructive (or preventable) health programming. There should be recognition of the physical or emotional environments to which fire and police personnel are subjected. In view of the above, definitive action should be taken to permit improving the performance of fire and police personnel.

SPECIFIC RECOMMENDATIONS

A. With transfer of all Central Receiving Hospital operations to the Fire Department.

1. Place Central Receiving under a Bureau of Medical Services. (See Exhibit A for organization.) This Bureau to be under command of a Deputy Chief with an Assistant Chief as Executive Officer.

2. As shown on the Organization Chart (Exhibit A) create a permanent Medical Advisory Commission to provide medical advisory expertise with respect to all phases of operations carried on within the Bureau of Medical Services. An additional and specific function of such a Commission will be to act as a final Appeals Board in medical rulings for pre-employment candidates and in-service members of the Fire and Police Departments.

3. Phase out public emergency care, with this service to be provided by approved contract hospitals. C.A.O. cost figures prove this would be a less expensive way to provide this service. There is better quality emergency care at contract hospitals, particularly those with complete facilities. There are approximately 100 hospitals in the Los Angeles area and many of these could provide emergency medical care.

   Deletion of public emergency medical care would apply to Central Receiving and all branches. The only facility retained would be for prisoner care.

4. Retire superannuated physicians presently on the Receiving Hospital staff. Reduction of emergency service to the public would permit major savings in salaries to physicians and nursing personnel. Employ fewer highly-qualified physicians at a salary conducive to attracting and retaining a quality medical staff.

5. Transfer Fire and Police Medical Liaison Units to Central Receiving Hospital Facility. This will provide more efficient service by using one file system; combining the three existing systems. Records and files would be updated and retrieval capability added to permit study and analysis of all health and care activities.

6. Develop an Occupational Health Program at Central Receiving and expand as needed to furnish the best possible medical care for firemen and policemen. The considerable investment by the City in fire and police personnel should be protected by adequate health programs. This could result in considerable sick time savings and retention of personnel that otherwise might be pensioned. Adequate record analysis could logically aid in improving quality of new appointees by introducing better quality control standards for appointment.

7. Expand bed capacity at Central Receiving to permit increased use for treatment and convalescence of firemen and policemen. Improve medical capability by updating diagnostic equipment. Improve x-ray equipment and establish procedures for 24-hour on-site staffing. Provide competent medical staff to furnish 24-hour emergency treatment and convalescence supervision. It may be possible to interest a medical school in staffing this operation. Improvement in staff and facilities would make treatment and care of firemen and policemen at the present location much more desirable. Better control of on-duty and off-duty provisions, plus bed care under competent supervision, could result in considerable reduction of off-duty illness or injury time.

B. With transfer of Central Receiving Hospital Ambulance Service to the Fire Department.

1. If this ambulance service is transferred to the Fire Department, total ambulance service city-wide should be placed under this Department. There could then be uniform standards of service for the entire City. This would mean elimination of all contract ambulances and result in improved emergency transportation service.

2. Ambulances would be placed at the best strategic locations, considering work load, distance, et cetera, in fire stations under direct fire officer supervision. This would replace existing locations. Service would be improved by quality supervision and substandard morale and performance would be upgraded. Cost would be approximately the same as the existing ambulance operation costs.

3. Failure to obtain satisfactory performance from civilian drivers and attendants would require replacement by uniformed firemen as present ambulance personnel left the service. Our ambulance experience in the Valley and more recently in the San Pedro-Wilmington and Watts areas proves our ability to render superior ambulance service using uniformed firemen. Use of trained firemen would make a large number of men available for ambulance work where necessary due to shortage of personnel in some unforseen circumstance. Use of civilians and uniformed personnel in combination on an ambulance should not be considered. If uniformed firemen were to replace civilians, the number of ambulances in service should be increased by 8 units to permit operation on Fire Department platoon schedules. The cost would be comparable to present operation of fewer units by civilians and result in much better service due to wider dispersion.

C. Emergency Ambulance Communications

1. Completion of the Fire Department dispatch control center would permit needed ambulances to be requested on a single telephone number. This would eliminate present confusion resulting from the public calling several numbers.

2. Dispatch of ambulances could be programmed into our new computors at no increase in cost to our existing contract. Location of available ambulances and contract hospital availability could be color coded on the master dispatch map and show on the console dispatch display. This would result in faster dispatch and treatment for a considerable improvement in service.

3. Present Central ambulances operate on radio frequency 155.28. This would be retained and extended to our present Fire Department ambulances. Two-way communication with hospitals could result

in medical decisions during transportation and improved treatment upon arrival at the hospital by having special staff or equipment ready for use. Existing use and proposed studies utilizing telemetric devices to monitor patients in transit by a doctor at a central point will save the lives of many patients in transit and by enlightened treatment at the hospital.

A spin-off of this program would be much higher qualified ambulance personnel due to the required advanced training. Such training could probably be obtained, at no cost to the City, under grant from the U. S. Department of Transportation, either direct, or in cooperation with, a medical facility.

As you are aware, time has been limited in the preparation of this plan. While additional findings have been compiled by my staff, I have not included them in this report, but will make them available to you upon your request.

Respectfully submitted,

Raymond M. Hill

RAYMOND M. HILL
Chief Engineer and General Manager

RMH:lm

cc Honorable James B. Potter

(The copy below is transcribed from actual letter on pages 42-47)

The Report

With the transfer of all Central Receiving Hospital Operations to the Fire Department, the specific recommendations are as follows:

1. Place Central Receiving under the Bureau of Medical Services (See Exhibit A for organization). This Bureau to be under the command of a Deputy Chief with an Assistant Chief as Executive Officer.
2. As shown on the **Organizational Chart (Exhibit A, see page 71)** create a permanent Medical Advisory Commission to provide medical advisory expertise with respect to all phases of operations carried on within the Bureau of Medical Services. An additional and specific function of such a Commission will be to act as a final Appeals Board in medical rulings for pre-employment candidates and in-service members of the Fire and Police Departments.
3. Phase out public emergency care, with this service to be provided by approved contract hospitals. City Administrative Officer cost figures prove this would be a less expensive way to provide this service. There is better quality emergency care at contract hospitals, particularly those with complete facilities. There are approximately 100 hospitals in the Los Angeles area and many of these could provide emergency medical care.
4. Retire superannuated physicians presently on the Receiving Hospital staff. Reduction of emergency service to the public would permit major savings in salaries to physicians and nursing personnel. Employ fewer highly qualified physicians at a salary conducive to attracting and retaining a quality medical staff.
5. Transfer Fire and Police Medical Liaison Units to Central Receiving Hospital Facility. This will provide more efficient service by using one file system; combining the three existing systems. Records and files would be updated and retrieval capability added to permit study and analysis of all health and care activities.
6. Develop an Occupational Health Program at Central Receiving and expand as needed to furnish the best possible medical care for firemen and policemen. The considerable investment by the City in fire and police personnel should be protected by adequate health programs. This could result in considerable sick time savings and retention of personnel that otherwise might be pensioned. Adequate record analysis could logically aid in improving quality of new appointees by introducing better quality control standards for appointment.
7. Expand bed capacity at Central Receiving to permit increased use of treatment and convalescence of firemen and policemen. Improve medical capability by updating diagnostic equipment. Improve X-Ray and establish procedures for 24-hour on-site staffing. Provide competent medical staff to furnish 24-hour emergency treatment and convalescent supervision. It may be possible to interest a medical school in staffing this operation. Improvement in staff and facilities would make treatment and care of firemen and policemen at the present location much more desirable. Better control of on-duty and off-duty provisions, plus bed care under competent supervision, could result in considerable reduction of off-duty illness or injury time.

With transfer of Central Receiving Hospital Ambulance Service to the Fire Department

1. If this ambulance service is transferred to the Fire Department, total ambulance service city-wide should be placed under this Department. There could then be uniform standards of service for the entire City of Los Angeles. This would mean elimination of all contract ambulances and result in improved emergency transportation service.

2. Ambulances would be placed at the best strategic locations, considering work load, distance, et cetera, in fire stations under direct control of fire officer supervision. This would replace existing locations. Service would be improved by quality supervision and substandard morale and performance would be upgraded. Cost would be approximately the same as the existing ambulance operation costs.
3. Failure to obtain satisfactory performance from civilian drivers and attendants would require replacement by uniformed firemen as present ambulance personnel left the service. Our ambulance experience in the Valley and more recently in the San Pedro-Wilmington and Watts areas proves our ability to render superior ambulance service using uniformed firemen. Use of trained firemen would make a large number of men available for ambulance work where necessary due to shortage of personnel in some unforseen circumstances. Use of civilians and uniformed personnel in combination on an ambulance should not be considered. If uniformed firemen were to replace civilians, the number of ambulances in service should be increased by 8 units to permit operation on Fire Department platoon schedules. The cost would be comparable to present operation of fewer units by civilians and result in much better service due to wider dispersion.

On July 1, 1970, the Los Angeles City Fire Department assumed total control of all Central Receiving ambulances and personnel.

Emergency Ambulance Communications

1. Completion of the Fire Department dispatch control center would permit needed ambulances to be requested on a single telephone number. This would eliminate present confusion resulting from the public calling several numbers.
2. Dispatch of ambulances could be programmed into our new computers at no increase in cost to our existing contract. Location of available ambulances and contract hospital availability could be color-coded on the master dispatch map and show on the console dispatch display. This would result in faster dispatch and treatment for a considerable improvement in service.
3. Present Central Ambulances operate on radio frequency 155.28. This would be retained and extended to our present Fire Department ambulances. Two-way communication with hospitals could result in medical decisions during transportation and improved treatment upon arrival at the hospital by having special staff or equipment ready for use. Existing use and proposed studies utilizing telemetric devices to monitor patients in transit by a doctor at a control point will save the lives of many patients in transit and by enlightened treatment at the hospital.
4. A spin-off of this program would be much higher qualified ambulance personnel due to the required advanced training. Such training could probably be obtained, at no cost to the City of Los Angeles, under grant from the United States Department of Transportation, either direct, or in cooperation with, a medical facility.

(*End of letter copy*)

At the end of this report, Chief Hill indicated that time had been limited in the preparation of this plan. While additional findings have been compiled by his staff, they were not included in this report. They will be made available upon request.

At midnight on July 1, 1970, the Los Angeles City Fire Department assumed total control of all Central Receiving Ambulances and personnel. All Ambulance Drivers and Ambulance Attendants reported to their respective fire stations on an 8-hour shift. Three shifts continued as was the practice at Central Receiving but instead reporting to the Police Stations and at two of the Emergency Hospitals in both Hollywood and Highland Park.

All of the Rescue Ambulance Personnel were civilians, including the Senior Ambulance Attendants and Chief Ambulance Attendant. Several of the very senior Attendants retired at the time of the transition since they had 30 or more years on the job but the vast majority, some happy and others not so happy, went to their new homes.

Because all of the members of Central Receiving Hospital Ambulance Corp. were not Los Angeles Fire Department members, they were paid far less and received very reduced benefits.

Not one single-function Ambulance member was consulted or played any role in the decision-making of this historic transfer of emergency medical ambulance personnel. None of the ambulance drivers or attendants were fully briefed on the impact of the transfer. Fire Department personnel were also not consulted as well. This led to numerous issues at the level of the fire station. There was no adjustment period and the impact was a negative morale on both sides.

What ended up was a two class system where firefighters and civilian ambulance members were doing the same job duties and responsibilities yet the firefighters were being paid far above the civilians. This led to additional negative morale and a total loss of professional identity for the rescue ambulance members.

The civilians worked three shifts: day shift from 0700 hours to 1500 hours, PM shift worked 1500 hours to 2300 hours, and a morning watch that began at 2300 hours until 0700 hours. The platoon system of the Fire Department was totally a 24-hour shift which meant that three different crews of the civilian ambulance personnel would work within the 24-hours platoon system. This complicated a multitude of problems with everything from time keeping to meals. It also meant that non-medical fire officers (Captains) would be supervising medical personnel from three entirely different crews. Those AM shifts from 2300 hours to 0700 hours rarely saw or even met with the Captains. This led to serious supervision issues and personality clashes.

Another colossal problem was that the civilian ambulance personnel were not aware of many of the Fire Department traditions, nor was any training given to them so as to inculcate the heritage and customs around a fire house. An example of difficult times for the civilian ambulance personnel was that some captains would not allow the civilian ambulance drivers and attendants to eat meals with the firefighters which caused tremendous animosity between the groups.

Brief History of Emergency Medical Services

In 1781 Los Angeles was a small pueblo under the authority of the King of Spain. An adobe and tile city. Volunteer Bucket Brigades.

It was February 1, 1886, not just any day, but LAFD's first day in service.
It consisted of:
4 stations
2 steam-powered engines (Pumpers) with hook and ladders
a hose wagon
and exactly 11 horses

There were 31 paid firefighters, 1 Chief Engineer, and 1 Asst. Chief for a service that had been done free for the last 15 years. By volunteers.

There had been 380 members of the LAFD volunteers. Most of the new paid members were from the old volunteer organization.

The City's alarm system was very crude; was an alerting procedure. Was long since disregarded.

200 years earlier, in Colonial Virginia, the townspeople used Musket fire to report a fire. It was called the "sounding of the alarm."

In Philadelphia, it was the Liberty Bell that alerted the city to fires. Fires at that time meant that blocks and blocks would be lost to fire.

Los Angeles had a telephone service in 1882, but few could afford it.

3 years prior to LAFD going into service, a fire alarm telegraph system went into effect. Located on 2nd Street between Spring and Fort (now Broadway).

An alarm turned in from a box sent electrical impulses, corresponding to the number of the box to the city hall system.

Thus, today's modern computerized system of the fire/ambulance dispatch system will be ice age archaic in a few short years. In 20 or so more years, today's system will be the "good old days".

The Council appointed George P. McLain, an engineer, to tend the engine for $100 per month.

LAFD's first Chief Engineer was volunteer Charles E. Miles. At the same time, Engine Co #2 was hard at work, not knowing that a firefighter would soon become the first paid Chief Engineer - Walter S. Moore.

City of Los Angeles has been in Emergency Medical Services for 130 years. Originally, it was within the Police Department. There was one hospital in LA and ambulances were horse and buggy. One of the first ambulance drivers was Jack Pliske. He was known as "cold-shouldered."

First African-Americans received the silent treatment. This was in the John F. Alderson regime.

Robert "Bob" Roberts began as an ambulance driver in 1928. After a long career he retired in 1957.

In 1952 Jack Gilson was killed after being thrown out of the back doors of a G-Unit following a collision. In 1951 two men were killed while on duty.

Dr. Charles Sebastian worked out of Georgia Street Receiving Hospital. Following the death of Jack Gilson he ordered that safety straps be installed in all G-Units to prevent ambulance personnel and patients from being thrown out during a collision. Total cost was $976.30.

In 1952, a total of 13 Ambulances were in service in the City of Los Angeles. They were known as "G-Units", since they operated out of Georgia Street Receiving Hospital.

EMS was defined as "a system of care for victims of sudden and serious illness and injury".

In 1992, heart attacks claimed 1.5 million lives. Deaths involving motor vehicles numbered 43,000, and of those 17, 800 were documented as involving ETOH (alcohol). Medical expenses due to unintentional injuries was $77.8 billion dollars. Total costs: $440.9 billion dollars

On June 7, 1957 it was known as a day of Thanksgiving; Rescue Ambulances were put into service in the San Fernando Valley by the LAFD.

Dr. Charles Sebastian, from Central Receiving Hospital, announced the cost of the new facility at $1.5 million dollars. It was located at 500 S. Loma Drive. It was 37,000 sq. ft, and replaced Georgia Street Receiving Hospital.

Mayor Norris Poulson and Councilman Ranson M. Callicot were present at the ceremony.

LAPD administered medical care to the sick and injured. Only one hospital existed in the city, located at 110 Hill Street, around the corner from the Central Police Station.

In 1996, nationally, there were:
750,000 providers
17,000 ambulance services
13,200 Board Certified ER physicians
23,000 Emergency Nurses
48,000 Emergency Rooms

The Receiving Hospital
110 Hill Street, and at the time considered very modern.

It had:
Exam Rooms
Separate rooms for male and female
Surgical ward
Laboratory
Ward for insane people
X-Ray and dark room

A police surgeon was on-duty.
Pre-1920s was staffed by:
C. E. Zerfing, Chief Police Surgeon
C. A. Wright
W. E. Carter
F. W. Kidden

Nurses included:
John Morgan
Gordon Johnson
Paul Engle
Ethyl Beatty
Katherine Carson

The Modern Era

Article appeared in *The Lancet* on Saturday, August 5, 1967. J. F. Pantridge wrote a paper ("The Pantridge Papers") that is likely the most significant piece of writing in modern EMS history.

In Belfast, Ireland, the risk of heart attack from M.I. (Myocardial Infarction) is increased and greatest within 12 hour period after onset of symptoms. Scheme was devised of "mobile units" enabling intensive care of heart patients that could go to the patient. Within the article, 10 examples were discussed; 5 were alive and well.

Most deaths from M.I. were within 12 hours. 60% are within 1 hour. Despite this knowledge huge numbers were receiving care well after a 12-hour period.

Mobile Intensive Care Units have been in operation since January 1966. Ambulances with a battery-operated DC Defibrillator with bipolar pacing catheters. This allowed monitoring for the first time.

338 occasions where unit summoned
312 patients admitted
155 had M.I.

The registrar or "houseman" was in charge of the MICU, and monitored patient in their own home. MICU's minimized risk of transport. In the study of 312 patients, none died en route.

No mention of the word paramedic anywhere in the article.

Problems

Problems have been inherent with EMS on the LAFD. In May, 1988, the union of the UPLA's (United Paramedics of Los Angeles) White Paper was published stating 94% of paramedics felt fire commission has not been effective in resolving EMS problems.

88% of paramedics felt the Fire Chief is doing poorly at managing the EMS system.

11% felt OK about the treatment of paramedics by department management.

40% of paramedics were seeking jobs elsewhere.

58% admit having made treatment errors caused by fatigue.

What was needed was increased effectiveness through improved management/supervision.

On May 5, 1983, the Board of Fire Commissioners approved the Department's proposal to improve the quality of patient care by establishing an improved EMS management system.

December 29, 1983 marked the date that the EMS Bureau was set up.

Problems:
Decreased quality of patient care
Need to increase level of out-of-station EMS supervision
Community CPR program

City Ambulance History

1850-mid-1860s Los Angeles initiated a paid police force. Sometimes a city doctor would stop by a house in a buggy or buck-board. LAPD officers went on patrol driving buck-boards.

1886 Fire Department Annual Budget was $11,500
1996 Annual Budget was $22,400,00
In comparison, the 2023 annual fiscal year budget: $782,870,860.

In 1887, Engine Co. #1 now serves as the location of S&M (Supply & Maintenance). It housed the first hanging horse harness, developed by Edward R. Smith, a uniformed member of the department, later to become an Asst. Chief.

Horses - early 1900s and particularly around 1880s. Overeager horses would injure/kill firefighters.

November, 1961 Bel Air Fire Over 500 structures were destroyed, desert-blown winds in excess of 50 mph caused a wind-driven fire with catastrophic results.

1974 Minority Recruitment Unit (Affirmative Action Program)
Equal Opportunity became the common denominator.

1976 Incident Command System

In 1990s, series of floods, civil unrest (1992), firestorms (1993), earthquakes (1994). CHALLENGES, CHALLENGES, CHALLENGES.

1970 Full City Rescue Ambulances
1971 Sylmar EQ (Earthquake) led to LA's EQ Plan / Paramedic training begins
1972 Recruitment begins
1973 First EMS Academy begins: 40 EMT I Ambulance Drivers
1974 ALS Ambulance Expansion
1975 CPR Training expands, until 1985
1976 Incident Command System developed, used at high-rise fires
1977 DC-10 crash at LAX / firefighter EMT training begins, 35,000 people trained
1978 Rapid response crash fire rescue developed at LAX
1979 Paramedic Engine Companies implemented
1980 Chief Paramedic position established, 10 administrative captains promoted and assigned to 3 divisions / 8 hours per day. MCI plan developed, high-rise drills, crane collapses
1981 Stress reduction introduced within Fire Department. Major Hazmat reduction ordinance
1982 50 Paramedics trained as EMT instructors. Dorothy Mae Fire. Olympic Flaming began.
1983 Bureau of Emergency Medical Services established. 1200 firefighters trained as EMT I's.
1984 Bureau of EMS was modified to six EMS Districts with 18 EMS District Commanders (EMS Supervisors). These were 24-hour shifts or known as platoon duty positions.
1992 A system of consolidation was introduced and single-function paramedics had the opportunity to become Firefighter/Paramedics. EMS Supervisors (Senior Paramedics) became Paramedic Captains.
1996 The Bureau of Emergency Medical Services and Bureau of Fire Suppression and Rescue merged together to become the Bureau of Emergency Services.

Promotion of First Senior Paramedics, 1980

On December 10, 1979, then John C. Gerard, Chief Engineer and General Manager (Fire Chief) of the Los Angeles Fire Department sent a letter to the Honorable Board of Fire Commissioners requesting additional Senior Paramedics and a Chief Paramedic.

After the first Senior Paramedics were promoted in 1980, they were sent to one of the three Los Angeles Fire Department Divisions on a platoon duty (24-hour tour of duty). Each of the Division Fire Stations were assigned a Division Chief (Assistant Chief Rank) and it was that person who supervised the Senior Paramedic.

Since each platoon worked 24 hours, it is easy to see how full coverage throughout the months would be covered. There was the "A" Platoon, "B" Platoon, and "C" Platoon, and on a Fire Department calendar the "A" Platoon was red, "B" Platoon was blue and the "C" Platoon was green - thus a member of the department who worked in the field setting on platoon duty could see exactly what days he/she would be working all year.

After Civil Service testing,
the first group of Senior Paramedics promoted were:

Alan Cowen
Merv Dunham
John Green
Fred Hurtado
Joe Martin
Larry Mayer
Allen Norman
Pete Segura
David Sirchuk

All of the Senior Paramedics were seasoned veterans as paramedics and each would be working in a Division with the exception of Arlyn "Shorty" Nine and Doug Brown, who was the Chief Paramedic's Assistant and was ultimately classified as a Senior Paramedic II; all others were classified as Senior Paramedic I.

In a letter addressed to all Division Commanders and Division Senior Paramedics on all three platoons from then Deputy Chief A. L. Schultz, Commander of the Bureau of Fire Suppression and Rescue, he outlined the approved equipment for Senior Paramedics.

Budget requests were placed for a tape recorder and camera to be carried in the emergency sedan.

The following were to be issued to each:
Turnout boots
White Rescue Ambulance Helmet
Brush Jacket
Work/Safety Gloves
Flashlight
Briefcase
Rain gear

Each platoon was to have an emergency sedan with Code 3 equipment:
Jumper Cables
Trauma Kit (Receiving Hospital type)
Clipboard
Resusci-bag (Laerdal)
1200 foot Hydrant Map
Earthquake Packet
Multi-Casualty Disaster Packet
(when available)

Front row (l-r):
Chief Jon Fasana, Larry Mayer, Alan Cowen, Arlyn "Shorty" Nine, Allen Norman, Danny Cypert, David Sirchuck
Second row (l-r):
Doug Brown, John Green, Don Lee, Tim Wilson, Harry Rich, Fred Hurtado, Joe Martin, Robert Linnell
Top row (l-r):
Captain Jim Jeffries, Captain Clarence Merriman, William Wells, Gary Inman, Steve Johnson, Wade Jones, James Denney, Michael Kleiner

Creating an EMS Bureau on the LAFD

Senior Paramedics worked within each of the three Divisions on the Fire Department. At that time each Senior Paramedic worked directly for the Assistant Chief who managed and supervised the Division. Although the rank was Assistant Chief, they were usually called Division Commanders.

I was assigned to Division II located at Fire Station 33 in South Los Angeles. It was a large station with numerous apparatus to include a engine company, truck company and Rescue Ambulance as well as the Division Chief and his driver's aide or later known as a "staff assistant".

We had functional supervision over EMS in the entire Division and only when the Rescue Ambulance was out on a call for service. When in the station house, the Station Commander with the rank of Captain was their immediate supervisor. Only when out in the field was the Senior Paramedic their supervisor.

Ambulance Driver Alan Cowen with Ambulance Attendant Fred Dumois, at Venice Beach Fair in June of 1967.

As part of the evaluation process, Senior Paramedics would schedule ride-alongs with each of their assigned Rescue Ambulances within their respective districts. Each district had more than 20 ambulances so we would set up a calendar for ride-alongs for the month and spend anywhere from 6 to sometimes 12 or more hours with a crew. Most of the Rescue Ambulances were very busy so we had ample opportunities to observe their performance and evaluate them.

We also had emergency duties:

- Respond as dispatched to any emergency incident to assist the Incident Commander with the management of the Medical Division, EMS planning or other related tasks.
- Respond to emergency incidents to provide on-scene supervision, coordination and evaluation of EMS activities.
- Respond to disasters and multiple casualty incidents to supervise EMS activities. This included functioning as the Medical Division Commander until relieved by an EMS superior officer, Triage Control or any other component officer in the Medical Division Command structure.
- During emergency operations involving participation of the Medical Alert Center, and/or County Health Services EOC (Emergency Operations Center) a Senior Paramedic could respond to one of these locations to serve as a Department Liaison Officer.

In addition to the above emergency duties, Senior Paramedics would investigate service complaints. Sometimes a Senior Paramedic would team up with a Battalion Chief to handle complaints involving paramedics and firefighters.

In 1972, the City Council of Los Angeles directed the LAFD to replace the firefighters assigned to rescue ambulances duty to single-function career EMS personnel.

Expansion of the EMS System on the LAFD

As the EMS system evolved and expanded, the need for additional Senior Paramedics became obvious as the system became more complicated. It was in July, 1970 when the fire service assumed the responsibility of providing City-wide Emergency Medical Services. The growth in size and sophistication caused a proposed Bureau of Emergency Medical Services to be born.

By 1983, the Los Angeles Fire Department was the largest Fire Department managed pre-hospital care delivery system in the United States. In fact, in fiscal year 1970-71 with the added ambulances from the Central Receiving Emergency Ambulance Service additional 12 units as of July, 1970, the Fire Department responded to over 106,000 EMS calls. The number of calls for EMS peaked at approximately 175,000 in 1979-80. It was estimated that EMS responses would approach 225,000 to 235,000 by 1990.

In 1972, the City Council of Los Angeles directed the LAFD to replace the firefighters assigned to rescue ambulances duty to single function career EMS personnel and in 1974 mandated the conversion of all rescue ambulances to Paramedic status.

It is noteworthy that in the 1970s the paramedic service seems appropriately assigned to the Bureau of Fire Suppression and Rescue. However, the dramatic growth dynamics of EMS have resulted in management and supervision problems that needed to be aggressively addressed.

These issues and problems included:

1. Lack of adequate supervision
2. Inadequate vertical lines of communication
3. Paramedics being isolated from an EMS Chain of Command
4. High attrition rate of trained and experienced paramedics
5. Paramedics feeling as "step children" in the Fire Department
6. Limited career ladder
7. Friction at the scene of emergencies
8. Level of service to the community

In a letter to the Fire Commission dated March 28,1983, Chief Engineer and General Manager, Fire Chief Donald O. Manning **(see pages 60-65)** wrote that Management of the EMS system by promoted paramedics and improved field supervision will result in an improved level of service and reduced liability to the City. He went on to say that the department has tried a number of solutions in the past but always in one organizational structure. He indicated that it was now time to be creative and use another approach. The

continues on page 66...

LOS ANGELES FIRE DEPARTMENT

DONALD O. MANNING
CHIEF ENGINEER AND GENERAL MANAGER

March 28, 1983

TO: The Honorable Board of Fire Commissioners
City of Los Angeles

FROM: Donald O. Manning
Chief Engineer and General Manager

SUBJECT: PROPOSED BUREAU OF EMERGENCY MEDICAL SERVICES

SUMMARY

Since the Department assumed the responsibility of providing City-wide Emergency Medical Services (EMS) in 1970, our Rescue Ambulance and EMS system has grown in size and sophistication to the point that today, it is the largest Fire Department managed pre-hospital care delivery system in the United States.

In fiscal year 1969-70, the Department operated 13 rescue ambulances staffed by "First-Aid" trained firefighters and responded to 33,500 calls for ambulance service. The service was supervised by fire suppression officers with the same level of first-aid training.

In fiscal year 1970-71, with the inclusion of the Receiving Hospital Department's Emergency Ambulance Service of 12 units on July 1, 1970, the Fire Department responded to 106,000 EMS calls. The calls for EMS peaked at approximately 175,000 in fiscal year 1979-80. It appears that EMS responses may approach 225,000 to 235,000 annually by 1990.

In 1972, the City Council directed the Department to replace the firefighters assigned to rescue ambulance duty with single function career EMS personnel; and in 1974, mandated the conversion of all rescue ambulances to Paramedic status.

During the decade of the 1970's, the paramedic service seemed appropriately assigned as an adjunct to the Bureau of Fire Suppression and Rescue. However, the aforementioned growth and dynamics of EMS have resulted in management and supervision problems that must now be aggressively addressed. Major problem areas include the following:

1) Lack of adequate supervision.

2) Inadequate vertical lines of communication.

3) Paramedics being isolated from an EMS oriented chain of command.

4) High attrition rate of trained and experienced paramedics.

5) Paramedics feeling as "step children" in the Fire Department.

6) Limited career ladder.

7) Friction at the scene of emergencies.

8) Level of service to the consumer.

Management of the EMS system by promoted paramedics and improved field supervision will result in an improved level of service and reduced liability to the City. We have tried a number of solutions in the past, but always within one organizational structure. In my view, it is now time to be creative and utilize another approach. The concept is to provide a total structure, the same as any of the other major functions of the Fire Department.

Submitted herein is the Department's proposal to establish a Bureau of Emergency Medical Services within the Los Angeles City Fire Department. The proposal was developed by a Steering Committee which included the following:

D. E. Thompson, Staff Assistant Chief
(Chairperson)
R. T. Rojo, Commander, Planning Section
J. A. Fasana, Chief Paramedic
D. E. Brown, Senior Paramedic II
A. M. Norman, Senior Paramedic I
W. N. Wells, Paramedic III
Representing the Fire Chief Officers Association:
R. L. Ewert, Assistant Chief
A. Vega, Battalion Chief
Representing United Firefighters of Los Angeles City:
L. E. Hall, Captain II
E. F. Lane, Captain II
Representing United Paramedics of Los Angeles:
R. A. Raya, Paramedic III

In addition to the above persons, input was received from all of the Senior Paramedics, the Department's Medical Advisor Dr. M.A. Rockwell, and members of the Department's Medical Advisory Committee.

RECOMMENDATION

1. That a Bureau of Emergency Medical Services be established and implemented as described in the attachments.

2. That the class title of Senior Paramedic be changed to Paramedic Commander.

3. That the Bureau of Emergency Medical Services be funded as proposed in Attachment #8, and #9.

FINDINGS

The City of Los Angeles has been providing a public sector emergency medical ambulance service since the early 1900's. The service originated as a program provided by the Los Angeles Police Department. In the mid 1930's, the service was transferred to the City's Receiving Hospital Department where it continued as the "Police" Ambulance Service serving the Metropolitan areas of Los Angeles until July 1, 1970. Private ambulance companies, under City contract, provided emergency service in the San Fernando Valley until 1957, when the Fire Department introduced its rescue ambulance service. On July 1, 1970, the Receiving Hospital Department was abolished and the emergency ambulance service was transferred to the Fire Department.

The decade of the 1970's was an extremely dynamic period in the history of Emergency Medical Services (EMS). In 1970, Cardio-Pulmonary Resuscitation (CPR) was being introduced as an adjunct to Advanced First-Aid; Emergency Medical Technician-1 training programs were being developed, and a pilot program to train firefighters as "Paramedics" was being tested in Los Angeles County. Since that time, EMT-1 training has become the nationally accepted minimum standard for all emergency ambulance personnel. EMT-1 and Paramedic programs are now being provided across the country by both paid and volunteer fire service agencies and law enforcement organizations. EMS has truly come of age in the American fire service.

The dynamic decade of the 1970's was not without its growing pains for the EMS system of the Los Angeles City Fire Department. The most significant problem was in the area of attrition of highly trained and experienced rescue ambulance and paramedic personnel. On July 1, 1970, the service consisted of 121 members. Since that date, the Department has hired and trained 447 rescue ambulance members, and lost 258 members, bringing us to our current total of 310 rescue ambulance members. This high attrition rate has taken its toll in training and replacement costs, loss of experienced personnel, and impacts directly upon the level of sevice provided and the members providing the service.

Today, the Los Angeles City Fire Department operates the largest fire service managed EMS, pre-hospital care, delivery system in the United States. The Department provides first-responder rescue ambulance EMS throughout the City of Los Angeles and, under contract, to the City of San Fernando. The service area encompasses approximately 470 square miles and a resident population of three million persons. The system includes 48 rescue ambulances, a paramedic engine company, and is supported by all fire suppression resources.

To improve the management and supervision of the Department's Rescue Ambulance and EMS System, the City Council authorized the hiring of a Chief Paramedic and 24-hour supervision by promoted Senior Paramedics in July of 1980. Our experience to date indicates that additional 24-hour supervisors are needed. The implementation of a Bureau of Emergency Medical Services should fully put in place the improved supervision intended by the City Council.

The primary objective of the proposed Bureau of Emergency Medical Services is to manage and administer the Department's EMS program. The Bureau has been organized in such a way as to address span-of-control and City geography and to maximize its effectiveness in improving management, supervision, training, evaluation and opening the lines of communications. The organization should be dynamic and flexible enough to meet the continuing growth in EMS.

It is intended that the following measurable objectives will be accomplished by the implementation of a Bureau of Emergency Medical Services:

1. Improved level of patient care
2. Reduced paramedic attrition
3. Improved cost effectiveness

The Bureau will be charged with the Department's goal to provide an effective EMS system.

The Steering Committee also addressed the appropriateness of the existing title of "Senior Paramedic". While the term "Senior" is a traditional civilian Civil Service class title, it is not a traditional rank designation used in the uniformed emergency services. Originally, the Committee considered a title change from "Senior Paramedic" to "Paramedic Captain", and a higher level officer with the title of "Assistant Chief Paramedic". After much consideration, it was the consensus to change the title from "Senior Paramedic" to "Paramedic Commander".

The issue of funding was explored in depth. If approved, the first year funding method explained in attachment #8, can fund the personnel costs of the proposed Bureau without additional costs to the Department by reallocating currently budgeted EMS resources. Additional funding is required for emergency sedans as shown in Attachment #9.

It is proposed that the Bureau office eventually occupy the space currently used by the Information Systems Section between the Bureau of Administrative Services and the Bureau of Support Services. The Bureau office should have adequate space for the following:

a. Bureau Commander's Office
b. Executive Officer
c. Medical Advisor
d. Conference Table
e. Office Staff

<u>CONCLUSION</u>

The concept of a Bureau of Emergency Medical Services is to provide a total structure, the same as any of the other major functions of the Department. Its implementation will fulfill that final element of the organization. It is my belief that the paramedics who will be in the position of recommending solutions to paramedic problems will come up with better solutions than people who have not had experience with these problems.

My goal is to improve the level of service to the citizens, reduce the attrition rate of paramedics and improve the paramedic's job environment. Through this vitally necessary change we will have a better organized fire and EMS system and thus a much stronger organization to serve the City.

Respectfully submitted,

Donald O. Manning

DONALD O. MANNING
Chief Engineer and General Manager

DOM:gd

concept is to provide a total structure and submitted a proposal to establish a new Bureau of Emergency Medical Services with the Los Angeles Fire Department. The proposal was developed by a steering committee which included an Assistant Chief, Commander of the Planning Section, Chief Paramedic, Senior Paramedic, a field paramedic, representatives of the Fire Chief Officer's Association, representatives of United Firefighters of Los Angeles City and representative of United Paramedics of Los Angeles.

JOB DUTIES OF THE BUREAU COMMANDER - CHIEF PARAMEDIC

GENERAL

The Chief Paramedic is assigned as the Bureau Commander of the Bureau of Emergency Medical Services and reports directly to the Chief Engineer. The primary responsibility of this assignment is to plan, organize and direct the activities of the Bureau.

EMERGENCY DUTIES

1. Respond to large scale emergencies to direct, coordinate and supervise the activities of the Medical Division.
2. Respond to emergencies to provide on-scene staff assistance to the Incident Commander with EMS planning, EMS liaison activities, evaluation of EMS operations, and/or management of personnel performing emergency medical services.
3. In the event of a County/City-wide Disaster or the activation of the EOC, respond to the Department Command, or as directed, to provide staff assistance to the Department Commander with the management of EMS Operations. This may include establishing liaison with the Los Angeles County Chief of Medical and Health Services.

ADMINISTRATIVE DUTIES

1. Plan, organize, direct and coordinate the Fire Department's emergency medical services program; formulate, recommend and oversee the implementation of policies, practices and procedures for providing emergency medical services.
2. Assist the Chief Engineer as a regular member of the General Staff, making recommendations on general policies, practices and procedures.
3. Participate in Department planning and EMS legislative matters and serve as the Department's Legislative Representative on EMS matters.
4. Provide liaison with other Departments of City Government, Civic and Community organizations and various State, County and local public and private agencies involved with pre-hospital emergency medical services as directed by the Chief Engineer.
5. Conduct field inspections.
6. Represent the Department at meetings and conferences as directed by the Chief Engineer.
7. Is responsible for the Bureau's budget formulation, preparation and submission to the Chief Engineer.
8. Is responsible for the assignment of Bureau personnel.
9. Manage and participate in long range EMS planning as directed by the Chief Engineer.
10. Take a leadership role in the Department's Affirmative Action Recruitment efforts.

11. Perform other duties as directed by the Chief Engineer.

JOB DUTIES OF THE EMS EXECUTIVE OFFICER (Paramedic Supervisor II)

GENERAL

A Paramedic Commander II assigned as the EMS Executive Officer is subordinate to the Chief Paramedic. The primary responsibility of this assignment is to assist the Chief Paramedic with the overall management of the Bureau of Emergency Medical Services and facilitate communications throughout the Bureau.

The Executive Officer maintains regular business hours, responds to large-scale emergencies to assist with the management of EMS activities, and acts as the Chief Paramedic in his absence.

EMERGENCY DUTIES

1. Respond to emergency incidents to function as the Medical Division Commander and/or to assist the Chief Paramedic with the management of the Medical Division.
2. Respond to emergency incidents to supervise and evaluate the performance of EMS District Commanders.
3. During large scale emergencies and/or disasters, respond as directed to assist the Chief Paramedic or other EMS Officers with EMS planning, coordination and other related tasks. The Executive Officer is subject to recall during a major medical emergency and/or disasters.
4. When assigned as the ranking EMS Commander at a large scale emergency, provide on-scene staff assistance to the Incident Commander with EMS planning, EMS liaison activities, evaluation of EMS operations, and/or management of personnel performing emergency medical services.
5. Serve as the On-Call EMS Officer.

ADMINISTRATIVE DUTIES

1. Assist the Chief Paramedic with the overall management and coordination of the Fire Department's EMS program.
2. Serve as the Chief Paramedic in his absence.
3. Research and prepare staff reports as directed by the Chief Paramedic.
4. Process, review, make recommendations, and take other appropriate action on reports forwarded to the Bureau Office.
5. Establish controls and monitor compliance of due dates on reports, action plans, and active projects being performed by members assigned to the Bureau.
6. Assist with EMS budget preparation and serve as the Bureau Budget Coordinator.
7. Coordinate equipment field evaluations and specification changes.
8. Facilitate the flow of communications throughout the Bureau.
9. Coordinate and supervise the activities of the Bureau office staff.
10. Coordinate and supervise paramedic field internships of both Department personnel and the personnel of other agencies interning on Department Paramedic Ambulances.
11. Coordinate and schedule the Ride-Along Program on Department Paramedic Ambulances, and

with EMS District Commanders.
12. Coordinate transfers and assignments of Rescue Ambulance personnel.
13. Serve as the overall coordinator of the EMS Reserve Program. (The EMS Reserve Program is currently being organized.)
14. Maintain liaison with various EMS Commissions and Committees as directed.
15. Assist with the investigation of complaints involving EMS personnel.
16. Provide consultation on EMS-related matters to Department management personnel as directed by the Chief Paramedic.
17. Maintain liaison with hospital administrators and other agencies regarding EMS matters as directed.
18. Maintain liaison with the Ambulance Billing and Arson Units regarding the control of confidential EMS records in response to requests for information as directed.
19. Handle inquiries from the news media, City Officials, and the general public in regards to Departmental EMS policies and procedures as directed.
20. Maintain status records relating to requirements for continuing education and certification of all Paramedics and EMT-1 Rescue Ambulance personnel.
21. Maintain liaison with the County Paramedic Training Institute, its standing and Ad Hoc Advisory Committees as assigned by the Chief Paramedic.
22. Take a leadership role in the Department's Affirmative Action recruitment efforts.
23. Assist other EMS Officers with special projects as approved by the Chief Paramedic.
24. May serve as a reviewer of grievances filed by subordinates.
25. Perform other tasks as directed by the Chief Paramedic.

JOB DUTIES OF THE EMS DISTRICT COMMANDER (Paramedic Captain)

OVERVIEW OF RESPONSIBILITIES

EMS District Commanders shall:
a. Be subordinate in rank to an EMS Area Commander.
b. Command EMS Districts in accordance with general rules of conduct.
c. Supervise the application of policy, Rules and Regulations, practices and procedures of the Department, and shall be responsible for the morale, efficiency, and distribution of personnel within their commands.
d. Respond to alarms and special calls when dispatched; command and deploy EMS personnel in the most advantageous manner for the preservation of life; and aprise the officers who relieve them of command concerning the situation as it exists at that time.
e. Keep such records as are necessary to insure efficient operation of their commands; keep journal records of their activities while on duty; and apprise the officers who relieve them concerning information essential to their commands.
f. Conduct Training Conferences of all their immediate subordinates at least once a month and at other times when necessary.

g. Visit each emergency ambulance over which they have supervision at frequent intervals to make inspections necessary to determine that proper care and attention is being given to Department property.
h. Have authority to prohibit the use of any EMS uniform, tool, medication, drug, solution or equipment which is unfit for service.
i. Be familiar with their assigned duties and response districts.
j. Permit members to go off-duty only in accordance with Department policy unless other arrangements have been authorized.
k. Within their discretion, impose penalties involving loss of privileges, or other penalties not unusual or excessive for the offenses committed, when subordinates under their commands commit infractions of the rules and regulations not considered flagrant; they shall thereupon report in writing through channels to their Bureau Commander all details involved, which reports shall be reviewed by intermediate Commanders who may impose additional penalties as warranted, attaching to the original reports their own written reports of any such additional penalties imposed.

Station Commanders also have responsibility for Items C, H, J and K as applicable to Rescue Ambulance Personnel while under the Station Commander's supervision.

GENERAL
A Paramedic Commander I assigned as an EMS District Commander is subordinate in rank and responsible to an EMS Area Commander. On a platoon duty schedule, the EMS District Commander's primary responsibility is to manage and administer the affairs of an EMS District. The EMS District Commander has direct supervision over single function paramedic and EMT-I rescue ambulance personnel.

EMERGENCY DUTIES
1. Respond as dispatched to any emergency incident to assist the Incident Commander with the management of the Medical Division, EMS planning or other related tasks. The Incident Commander shall be the highest ranking Fire Suppression Officer on scene.
2. Respond to emergency incidents to provide on-scene supervision, coordination and evaluation of EMS activities.
3. Respond to disasters and multiple casualty incidents to supervise EMS activities. This shall include functioning as the Medical Division Commander until relieved by an EMS superior officer, Triage Control or any other component officer in the Medical Division command structure.
4. During emergency operations involving participation of the Medical Alert Center, and/or County Health Services EOC, a Paramedic Commander may respond to one of these locations to serve as a Department Liaison Officer.

Bureau EMS 1983

On May 5, 1983, in a letter to the honorary board of fire commissioners from Donald O. Manning, Chief Engineer and General Manager of the Los Angeles Fire Department, it was recommended that the Los Angeles Fire Department's proposal to establish a Bureau of Emergency Medical Services within the Fire Department be approved. The department had just prior to that date proposed the conversion of existing "backup" non-paramedic ambulances to full-time single function paramedic status. The department was not prepared to implement the Bureau of EMS on an approximate 18-month trial basis.

It was determined that at least 18 months would be required for an adequate evaluation of the Bureau's operations. During the remainder of the fiscal year 1983/84, the Bureau of EMS will operate utilizing existing available resources. To facilitate the full implementation of the Bureau, additional funds will be requested for the fiscal year 1984/85.

The LAFD was well aware of issues and problems facing their EMS system and its ability to provide high quality patient care. It was recognized that there were management and supervision concerns that needed to be quickly addressed. The major concerns were: quality of patient care, inadequate level of EMS supervision, development of an EMS-oriented management structure, chain of command and communication, and retention of trained and experienced EMS personnel.

The lack of an adequate level of EMS supervision as part of an organized EMS-oriented management structure has a direct effect on the quality of patient care provided to the community. Existing Senior Paramedics are spending approximately 70% of their time performing non-medical related supervision functions. Currently, there is not a coordinated EMS management and supervision system, and no regular direct EMS input at the policy-decision level of the department.

The solution is the establishment of a policy-decision level organizational component, managed by EMS-oriented personnel whose primary focus will be the EMS system and improved field supervision; this will result in a more effective level of patient care.

The reorganization and improved EMS management and supervision will make our total EMS system more efficient, more effective and more productive. The resulting system will equate to more paramedic units being available to respond in a timely manner to the critical care/time dependent patient, and provide a higher level of care.

The non-medical related supervision functions, currently taking approximately 70% of the Senior Paramedics' working time will be reassigned to free the Senior Paramedics for EMS supervision, evaluation and training of our EMS personnel. This will be accomplished by centralizing the non-medical related supervision tasks within the administrative organization. This change will reallocate the field Senior Paramedics' time.

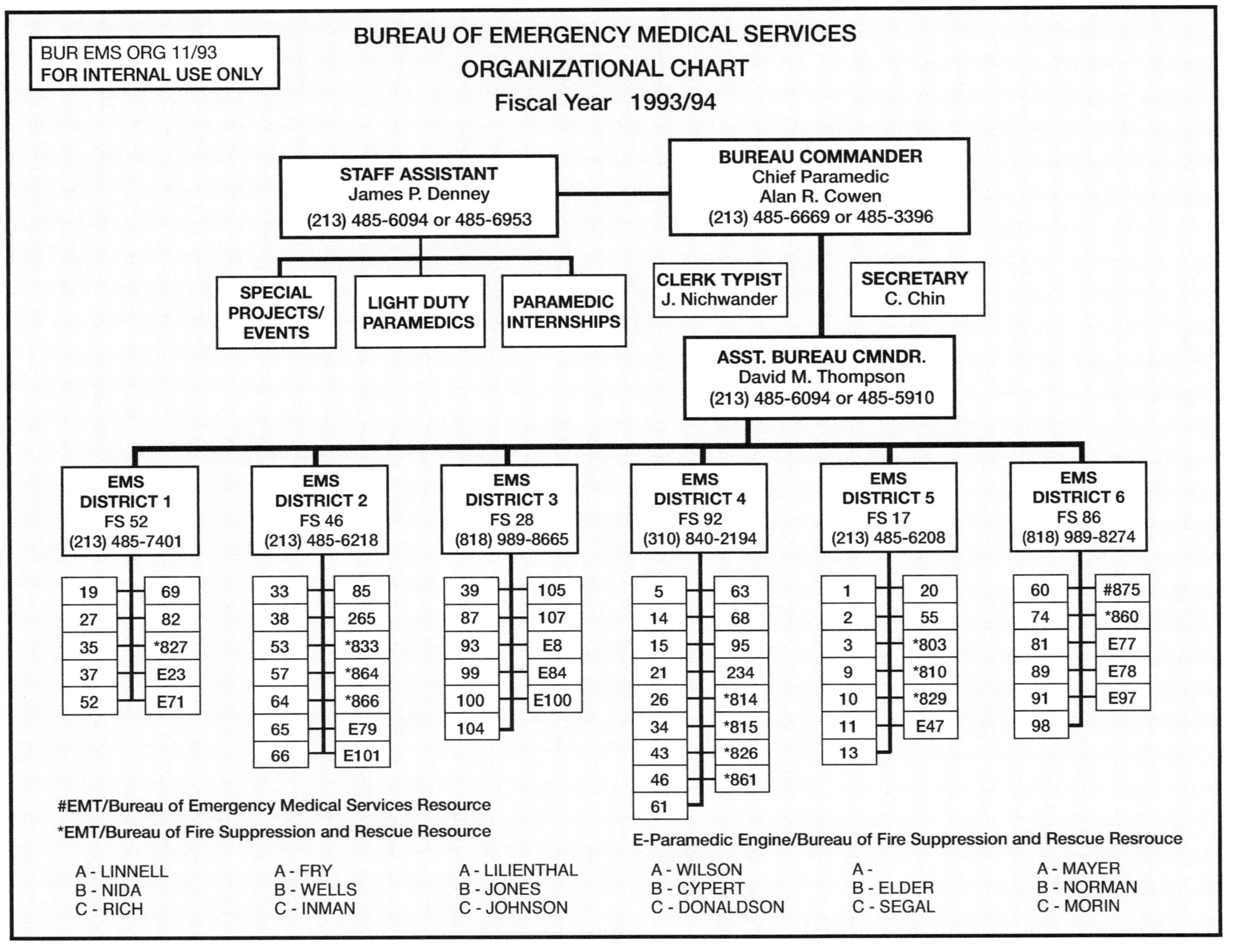

BUR EMS ORG 11/93
FOR INTERNAL USE ONLY
BUREAU OF EMERGENCY MEDICAL SERVICES
ORGANIZATIONAL CHART
Fiscal Year 1993/94
STAFF ASSISTANT
James P. Denney
(213) 485-6094 or 485-6953
BUREAU COMMANDER
Chief Paramedic
Alan R. Cowen
(213) 485-6669 or 485-3396
SPECIAL PROJECTS/ EVENTS
LIGHT DUTY PARAMEDICS
PARAMEDIC INTERNSHIPS
CLERK TYPIST
J. Nichwander
SECRETARY
C. Chin
ASST. BUREAU CMNDR.
David M. Thompson
(213) 485-6094 or 485-5910
EMS DISTRICT 1
FS 52
(213) 485-7401
19
27
35
37
52
69
82
*827
E23
E71
EMS DISTRICT 2
FS 46
(213) 485-6218
33
38
53
57
64
65
66
85
265
*833
*864
*866
E79
E101
EMS DISTRICT 3
FS 28
(818) 989-8665
39
87
93
99
100
104
105
107
E8
E84
E100
EMS DISTRICT 4
FS 92
(310) 840-2194
5
14
15
21
26
34
43
46
61
63
68
95
234
*814
*815
*826
*861
EMS DISTRICT 5
FS 17
(213) 485-6208
1
2
3
9
10
11
13
20
55
*803
*810
*829
E47
EMS DISTRICT 6
FS 86
(818) 989-8274
60
74
81
89
91
98
#875
*860
E77
E78
E97
#EMT/Bureau of Emergency Medical Services Resource
*EMT/Bureau of Fire Suppression and Rescue Resource
E-Paramedic Engine/Bureau of Fire Suppression and Rescue Resrouce
A - LINNELL
B - NIDA
C - RICH
A - FRY
B - WELLS
C - INMAN
A - LILIENTHAL
B - JONES
C - JOHNSON
A - WILSON
B - CYPERT
C - DONALDSON
A -
B - ELDER
C - SEGAL
A - MAYER
B - NORMAN
C - MORIN

The EMS Bureau will hold the field Senior Paramedics accountable for the EMS supervision, evaluation and training of our EMS personnel. The Senior Paramedics will provide an improved level of supervision by the following assessment methods:
1. On-scene unannounced audits of field EMS operations.
2. Structured skills evaluations.
3. Inspection of EMS units and personnel.
4. An improved interface with base hospital physicians and nurses to actually assess EMS personnel performance by case review of the quality of care.
5. Review of response times, out-of-service at hospital times, and other periods of being unavailable for response.

The department's ability to maintain, let alone improve, its current level of pre-hospital patient care will soon be challenged by the following:
1. The implementation of a limited number of trauma centers and other specialized care hospitals serving large geographical areas.
2. The implementation of the Automatic Call Distribution (ACD) System, emergency telephone number 911.
3. The utilization of both public and private medical helicopters for on-scene patient care.

These issues are in addition to the other demands placed on our EMS system by external regulatory agencies, diminishing fiscal resources, and the ever-changing complexities of emergency medical care.

We have tried a number of solutions in the past, but always within one organizational structure. It is now time to be creative and utilize another approach. The concept is to provide a total structure, the same as any other major functions of the Fire Department.

The target date for implementation of the EMS Bureau is 0800 hours on Monday, December 5, 1983.

Historical Perspective

The City of Los Angeles began providing a public sector emergency medical ambulance service as part of the Los Angeles Police Department in the early 1900s. In the mid-1930s, the service was transferred to the city's Receiving Hospital Department, where it continued as the "Police Ambulance Service," serving the metropolitan area of L.A. until July 1, 1970. Private ambulance companies, under city contract, provided emergency service in the San Fernando Valley until 1957, whereupon the Fire Department introduced its rescue ambulance service. On July 1, 1970, the Receiving Hospital Department was abolished and the emergency ambulance service was transferred to the L. A. Fire Department.

In the fiscal year 1969-70, the department operated 14 rescue ambulances staffed by first-aid-trained firefighters and responded to more than 33,500 calls for ambulance service. It was supervised by fire-suppression officers who had first-aid training.

In fiscal year 1970-71, having taken over the Receiving Hospital Department's 13 ambulance units, the Fire Department responded to 106,000 EMS calls. Calls for EMS peaked at approximately 175,000 between 1970 and 1980, and it looked as though it might approach close to 235,000 annually by 1990.

By 1972, the city council directed the department to replace the first firefighters assigned to rescue ambulance duty with single-function career EMS personnel and, in 1974, mandated conversion of all rescue ambulances to paramedic status. In 1979, the department established a Medical Advisory Committee consisting of volunteer experts from the medical community to provide input to the EMS service.

Growth of EMS

The decade of the 1970s was an extremely dynamic period in the history of emergency medical services. In 1970, cardiopulmonary resuscitation (CPR) was being introduced as an adjunct to Advanced First Aid. Emergency Medical Technician-1 (EMT-1) training programs were being developed, and a pilot program to train firefighters as Paramedics was being tested in Los Angeles County. Since that time, EMT-1 has become the nationally-accepted minimum standard for all emergency ambulance personnel. EMT-1 and Paramedic programs are now provided across the country as both paid and volunteer fire service agencies.

The dynamic 1970s were not without growing pains for the EMS system of Los Angeles City Fire Department. The most significant problem was in the area of attrition of highly-trained and experienced paramedic personnel. On July 1, 1970, the service consisted of 121 providers. Since that date, the department had hired and trained 447 rescue ambulance members and lost 265, bringing the total to 303. The high attrition rate had taken its toll in training and replacement costs, and impacted directly the level of service provided and the remaining members providing it.

On May 5, 1983, a letter sent to the honorary board of fire commissioners from Donald O. Manning, Chief Engineer and General Manager of the Los Angeles Fire Department, recommending that the LAFD's proposal to establish a Bureau of Emergency Medical Services within the Fire Department be approved. Just prior to that date, the department had proposed converting an existing "back-up" nonparamedic ambulance to full time, single-function paramedic status. It was determined that at least 18 months would be required to adequately evaluate the Bureau's operations, and, during the remainder of fiscal year 1983-84, the Bureau of EMS would operate with its existing available resources. To facilitate full implementation of the Bureau, additional funds would be requested for fiscal year 1984-85.

In 2016, the Los Angeles City Fire Department operated the second largest fire-service-managed EMS prehospital care delivery system in the United States, providing first-responder rescue ambulance EMS throughout the City of Los Angeles and under contract to the City of San Fernando. The service area encompassed approximately 470 square miles and a resident population of three million. The service included 48 rescue ambulances, all supported by Fire Department resources.

AMBULANCE LOCATIONS

Unit designation = "G" and a number that usually coincided with the Police Division number, but not always.

G-1 Was based at the City Health building on 1st. St.

G-2 Was based at Lincoln Heights Receiving Hospital located at Ave 26 and Pasadena Ave. Later to be moved to Rampart Police Station.

G-3 Was based at University Police Station located on Santa Barbara Ave, (now known as Martin Luther King Boulevard).

G-4 Was based at Hollenbeck Police Station located at 1st. and St. Louis streets.

G-6 Was based at Hollywood Receiving Hospital, next door to Hollywood Police Station on Wilcox.

G-7 Was based at Wilshire Police Station on Pico Boulevard just west of La Brea.

G-11 Was based at Highland Park Police Station located on York Boulevard just west of North Figueroa Street.

G-12 Was based at 77th. Street Police Station located on 77th. Street just east of Broadway.

G-13 Was based at Newton Street Police Station located just east of Central Avenue

G-14 Was based at Venice Police Station located on Washington Boulevard.

G-15 Was based at Georgia Street Police Station, which was also the home of Georgia Street Receiving Hospital prior to the equipment and personnel being moved to the new Central Receiving Hospital located at 6th. Street and Loma Drive.

G-16 Was only in service for a short time, it was used as a roving unit to help in busy areas, but it could go just about anywhere in the city.

G-17 Was based at Spalding's Mortuary located at Jefferson Boulevard and La Brea. This unit was put into service in the 1960's.

G-18 Was based at Central Receiving Hospital located at 6th. Street and Loma Drive.

Central Receiving Hospital Ambulance Personnel, circa 1940-50s Roster

Central Receiving Hospital Ambulance Personnel, circa 1950-60s Roster

Central Receiving Hospital Ambulance Personnel, circa 1967-68 Roster

Equipment through the years

Ambulance Drivers on scene, March 1937

First Ambulance, Receiving Hospital, circa 1914

Ambulance Driver
John Gaston, circa 1936

Ambulance Driver Nate Rubin, circa 1954

Administrators and Drivers of downtown Receiving Hospital, 1940s

Ambulance Driver
Ray Worthen, circa 1948

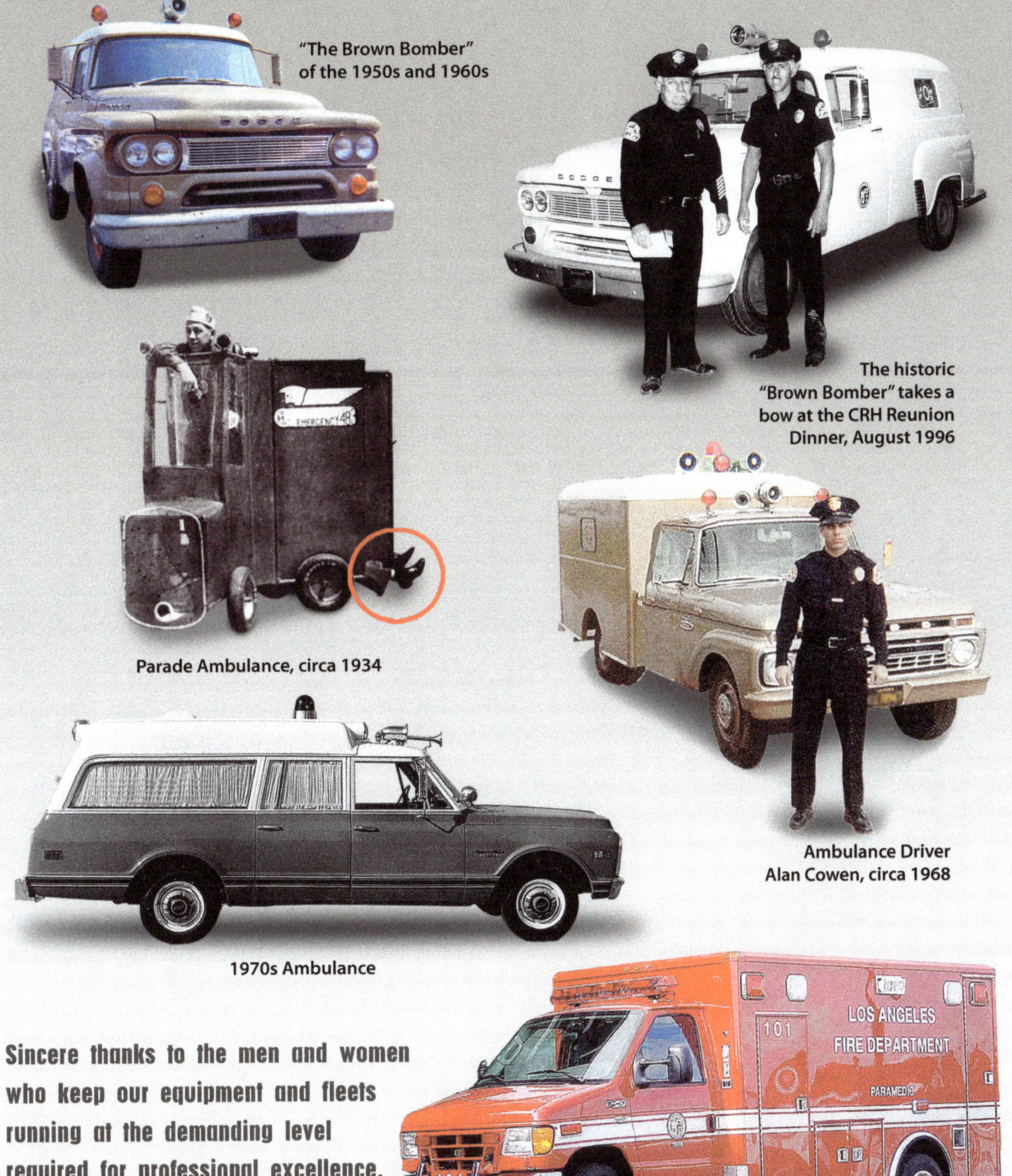

"The Brown Bomber" of the 1950s and 1960s

The historic "Brown Bomber" takes a bow at the CRH Reunion Dinner, August 1996

Parade Ambulance, circa 1934

Ambulance Driver Alan Cowen, circa 1968

1970s Ambulance

Today's modern LAFD Ambulance

Sincere thanks to the men and women who keep our equipment and fleets running at the demanding level required for professional excellence.

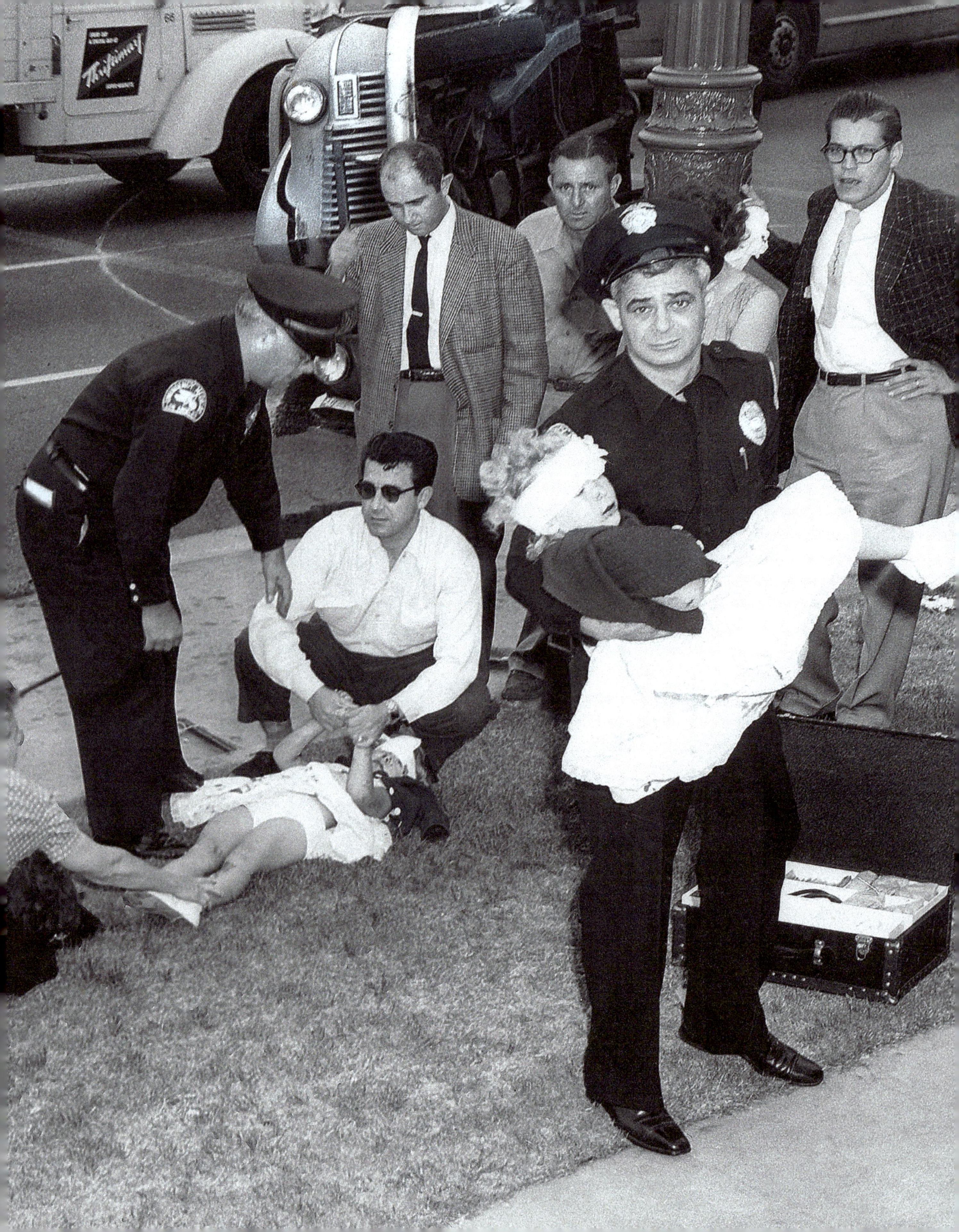

MEMORABLE CALLS
Central Receiving Hospital

Ambulance driver Nate Rubin and dispatchers

Central Receiving Hospital had a grand opening in 1957 after moving from the original Georgia Street Receiving Hospital. Many early police officers and firefighters owe their lives to both facilities as it was THE hospital for firefighters and police officers since 1927 when Georgia Street Receiving was located on the third floor of the Georgia Street Police Station. Georgia Street Receiving was the fourth hospital since the inception of the City Hospital system.

Central Receiving Hospital was located in a two-story structure at 1401 West 6th Street in Los Angeles. It was at 6th and Loma Drive, just west of downtown and was the hospital's fifth location. The cost was 1.5 million dollars. It closed to the public in 1970, but as late as August 2005 it was used for physical and psychological examinations for police and firefighter candidates. I personally had some physical exams done at Central Receiving during my career with both while working there and then while on the LAFD.

In October 2005 the old Central Receiving Hospital was to be demolished for the new Rampart Police Facility that was to be constructed. A large celebration was planned and a writer contacted me and asked for the real story behind the Receiving Hospital. I was interviewed by her extensively and she wrote the story as if it was my story. Naturally it is mine and hundreds of other people's story as well. I spoke at the event and had a slide show to go with the talk. It was a huge event where I arranged to have the only known Central Receiving Dodge Ambulance show up with two members who worked there with me. They put on their old Police-style uniforms and came in red lights and siren going, even stopping traffic as they made a grand entrance. The ambulance belonged to Joe Ortiz, one of my very early-on partners (1968-69).

Left:
Ambulance driver Nate Rubin responding to two young accident victims

First Day on the job

One of the earliest recollections of my career working for the City of Los Angeles was an Auto vs. Pedestrian that occurred in the early evening at the intersection of Venice Boulevard and Lincoln Boulevard. It was an emergency call that came in at the Venice Police Station on Shell Avenue in Venice. We had the ambulance parked in front of the station 24/7. It was my first assignment after being hired by the City. All ambulances worked out of Central Receiving Hospital located at 1401 West 6th Street in downtown. There were numerous substations around the City of Los Angeles, among them Venice Police Station. Other ambulance stations were out of Hollywood (G-6), Lincoln Heights (G-4), 77th Street Police Division (G-12) and the ambulance out of Central Police Division (G-1) to name a few.

Venice Police Division was known as Ambulance G-14, my first assignment. I arrived for the PM shift which was an 8-hour shift from 3:00PM until 11:00PM. The PM, or afternoon shift as it was called, was the busiest of all three shifts. The 11:00PM until 7:00AM the next morning was generally the least busy, at least most of the time.

On this first day at G-14, I arrived 45 minutes before my shift began and was delighted to be assigned in the west side of the city (Venice) since I had grown up there and knew the geographical region better than any other part of the city. One of the fears that plagued me early in my career was that I might find myself in an area unfamiliar and may not know the main streets within the district and had to depend on my attendant partner for help. That assistance might not be available given the personalities of some of the "old timers". I was soon to find out just how bad things could be.

I entered the Police Facility in full uniform, which was an identical LAPD uniform but with a different badge and no sidearm. In those days, City of Los Angeles Emergency Medical Ambulances were staffed by well-trained drivers, who just drove and assisted the Ambulance Attendant who was far more experienced and much older than most of the drivers. The Ambulance Attendants were a Civil Service Promotion position and were in charge of the ambulance and drivers.

I walked into the Ambulance Squad Room and noticed the older gentleman at a desk doing some paperwork. He was at least 50 years of age and was the Attendant, since his badge had the word Attendant on the top. The driver's badge had the designation of Driver. Attendants also had a silver band on their hat, whereas the driver had the traditional black band. This gentleman looked at me and I said "Hello, my name is Alan and I am assigned here on the PM shift." He said nothing in return and so I took the time to walk around the room and become familiar with the area and upstairs the bunk beds that the morning watch utilized.

At approximately 2:45PM, I heard someone coming down the stairs so I walked up and we met half way. I introduced myself and we exchanged names; his name was Pete Segura. Both he and I were hired the same day and were to become close friends in the years to come, particularly on the Los Angeles Fire Department where we were to end up together. In fact both of us were promoted to EMS Supervisors (Captains) in 1980, thirteen years in the future.

After a few minutes of discussion, I said goodbye and went outside to "check out" the ambulance, to ensure bandages, splints, oxygen and all of the other tools of the trade were indeed stocked up and in ready condition. While I was busy in the ambulance and first aid kit, I noticed an older gentleman exit a white Corvair and realized he was the attendant since he had on the same uniform as I except the silver band was reflecting the sun light. His name was Dan Cesarotti. He was to teach me many good things; some not so good.

I said hello to Mr. Cesarotti and he ignored me. As I watched him enter the police station there was a strange feeling in my stomach that this evening was not going to be fun. Mr. Cesarotti went into the Squad room and sat down. As I entered he did not give me eye contact. He wouldn't talk to me nor even acknowledge me. I attempted to engage him numerous times, and when he relieved his counterpart (the day watch) he was heard to say, "I have to work with the kid!" I could feel the growling in my stomach knowing this could well be a nightmare of an evening and I said a silent prayer that we would not have calls.

I was 21 years of age and just a month away from my 22nd birthday and my dream was coming true. I was working the Police Ambulance that I had chased on my bicycle when I was 10 years old. I rode my bike to this station dozens of times and watched this very ambulance respond red lights and siren around the area for years. Now I would be at the wheel.

I turned the red lights on and proceeded on the call feeling like a million dollars with about 20 dollars of change in my stomach gurgling.

It wasn't but 15 minutes later that the telephone rang in the office, on the same desk that Mr. Cesarotti was sitting at. He would not answer since that was the job of the ambulance driver. I lifted up the phone and stated, "G-14, Cowen". The operator was from downtown at Central Receiving Hospital and stated, "G-14, you have an Auto Ped. at Lincoln and Venice".

My first call at this assignment, and my partner had not even said hello to me. I told him what it was and where it was. He silently walked outside and got into the light brown Dodge, sitting in the attendants seat. I said "It is just down the street", since the police station was at Shell Avenue and Venice Boulevard. I turned the red lights on and proceeded on the call feeling like a million dollars with about 20 dollars of change in my stomach gurgling.

Within 45 seconds we arrived on scene, and in the street was an elderly gentleman very dead. By today's standards he was "obviously dead" with brain tissue everywhere and had sustained multiple fractures and severe multi-system trauma. His condition was deceased on scene, but since he was in public view, the attendant had the authority to transport to the local hospital. An LAPD traffic officer had arrived and was observing the scene and taking notes. It became obvious from bystanders and the police officer that this man was killed and that the vehicle had left the scene.

We loaded the patient onto the gurney and placed it in the ambulance. Mr. Cesarotti said, "Give me a slow 3 to the hospital". That meant red lights and siren but slow and safe.

We arrived at Santa Monica Hospital about 10 minutes later and placed the patient on a gurney adjacent to the emergency room. I removed the gurney outside next to the ambulance and thoroughly cleaned up the blood and brain tissue, having left the "Central Receiving" sheet in the ER. Mr. Cesarotti completed his paperwork and entered the ambulance where we returned to the Venice Police Station. He said nothing to me all the way back into the area from the City of Santa Monica.

I had my taste of what it was going to be like working with a person without a personality. It was March, 1967, an evening that is as clear to me now as it was 56 years ago.

The Jumper

The call came out as a "jumper" - unusual but not as uncommon as one in emergency work would anticipate. My partner was Fred McCuistion, an excellent ambulance driver and quite calm in a crisis. We were working out of Central Receiving (G-18) and headed out on 6th Street in the downtown area of the City of Los Angeles. On Figueroa we headed south and then east into the skid row region as it was called. Within two minutes we arrived on scene of a female who had taken her life by jumping off the 9th or 10th floor of a hotel. What I will never forget is the massive damage she caused to the vehicle she struck parked below. She was quite dead with massive injuries which were magnified by her eyes that were wide open and glazed over. In life she would have been considered quite good looking and even in death she maintained that.

Fred and I looked at each other and then mentally figured out that maybe she did not fall but rather was pushed: accident or homicide?

The top of the car was demolished which surprised me but then again it had been struck by perhaps a 120-pound body traveling at high velocity. Fred and I looked at each other and then mentally figured out that maybe she did not fall but rather was pushed; accident or homicide? We did not know but there were two police vehicles on scene and one officer told me to be careful with the remains so as not to disturb the scene. He was correct of course so I carefully determined that she was, in fact, dead and pronounced her such.

I could not help but think, what happened? She may have been a wife and mother and had parents and family. These thoughts ran through my mind over and over at the scene and much later, even years would go by and I would still think of her.

One of the hallmarks of emergency medical work is that we run calls for service and then we're done and move to the next call. We don't dwell on the first call (at least at the time I did not think so) and we then concentrate on the next call. All of the feelings and emotions don't vanish but rather are placed in that knapsack we carry on our backs for a lifetime and rarely if ever empty it. Thus, it fills up and overflows and then we act out and don't know why. Tears at the scene may have helped but that does not happen since we must keep "cool at all times" no matter what.

After pronouncing our "Jane Doe" dead we returned to Central Receiving and waited for our next call. In less than 10 minutes we were off again but both of us could not help but keeping thinking about "Jane Doe". After all, we had just met her 30 minutes earlier, left a clean white "Central Receiving Hospital" sheet over her since she was in public view and left.

After taking our next patient to Central Receiving Hospital, we returned to the scene of the "jumper", something we usually did not do. In reality I was searching for some type of closure even then. Perhaps I did not truly know why but we needed to know more about this woman and why she was dead. By then LAPD detectives were on the scene and quite closed-mouth about everything. They indicated that the case was under investigation but that they believed they had her name and would be able to solve the case. I was struck by the professionalism of the two detectives; they wore suits, not uniforms, and were well-groomed. In the LAPD the detective bureau is a rather elite group within the agency. We knew it and they knew it; they acted deliberate, as if everyone's eyes were upon them.

Since the Central Receiving Hospital had a small sub-station of LAPD within one of the offices, I had a good relationship with one of the officers. With one phone call, he ascertained that a suicide note had been found in one of the rooms and the case was solved. While this was several days later, the fact that we knew what occurred seemed to diminish the mystery somewhat and gave us a breather but we still thought and talked about her.

Soon thereafter, I was working out of a different station but with the same partner. Most of my partners did not speak much about each case we responded to but this one had been different. Fred and I continued to ruminate about "Jane Doe" for the next year, seemingly not being able to get her out of our systems. To this day, when in a pensive mood I will close my eyes and see her again, her big eyes wide open, seeing nothing ever again.

Special Deliveries

It was a cloudy day, threatening to rain when we received a call I would not forget. The radio cracked, "Obstetrics call in a car at Olympic and Western, northwest corner". While I had assisted in obstetrics calls prior, this one would be different as I would find out. With lights flashing and siren blaring, I was quickly heading eastbound on Olympic Boulevard toward downtown. Olympic is a major thoroughfare that goes from East Los Angeles all the way to the ocean; there was not much traffic as we rocketed eastbound. Within 4 minutes we approached Western and I could see the only vehicle stopped at the northwest corner. I pulled just passed the vehicle and stopped, leaving my emergency lights burning.

I was on the wrong side of the road and it was routine to leave the headlights on while traveling Code 3. I exited the ambulance and took the First Aid Box and OB Kit. Willie looked at me and said, "Why don't you handle this one" and I said OK. The driver was quite frantic and appeared nearly hysterical while his wife was lying across the back seat in distress. It was quite obvious that she was full-term and in labor. I quickly assessed her and she said the "baby is coming". As quick as I could, preparations were made to assist in the delivery of her baby. I had little time to do anything since crowning was starting to occur and I knew this would be a "field delivery". Willie and I placed our gloves on and I opened the OB Kit and laid it out so as to have everything I needed available.

By asking questions, we determined that they tried to make it to the hospital but could not. The husband stopped and dialed the operator and asked for help. There was no 911 system in place in 1968 so all calls for service were directed to the Receiving Hospital by the operator. I was just visualizing the perineum and preparing for the baby when suddenly and without warning the baby explosively exited the birth canal and was thrown into my lap. Amniotic fluid was splashed all over my face, eyes and mouth. There had been no time to do anything and the delivery was immediate and startling. I quickly took control of the newborn and ensured its safety by grasping his legs and neck, holding it carefully due to the slippery feeling.

I cleaned the baby off and was just about to place it on the mothers chest/abdominal area when the second baby suddenly emerged. I said to Willie "Open another OB Kit, we have a second baby". To say the least, we had our hands full of babies. After the second baby emerged, about a minute after the first, I managed to clean them and place umbilical clamps on each and cut the cords. Willie was observing everything and assisted me as requested. Both babies were crying, pink and healthy.

I completed the Birth Certificates and signed both. When I asked the names of the babies the mother asked us our names, and so somewhere out there are two boys that go by the name of Alan and Willie.

As required in those days, I completed the Birth Certificates and signed both. When I asked the names of the babies the mother asked us our names and so somewhere out there are two boys that go by the name of Alan and Willie. Both bundles of joy were transported to Central Receiving Hospital and did fine. Both Willie and I were the subject of discussion around the hospital for about a month given that this was an unusual event even then.

As we returned to the Wilshire Police Station Willie and I talked about the delivery and he said, "You did a great job, kid" and at the same time I actually noticed that the clouds had parted and sunshine was coming through; the entering of two new lives to live and the hope and promise of being promoted to Ambulance Attendant, a position I believed, after this call, that I could do - and do well.

Even in some emergencies, there is humor. I responded to a call one Friday night in the San Fernando Valley, where there was a party going on. When I arrived, I was told there was a woman in the back who needed help. I remember this was a rough neighborhood and these were unruly, beligerant people, and my partner and I got a little nervous when a guy closed the door. When we asked him what was wrong with the woman, he said, "There's something in her - check her out." She was complaining of intravaginal pain, and I said, "Well, I'm not a gynecologist - maybe we should take her to the hospital." But he insisted we check her and we were afraid not to. I put on a pair of gloves, reached in, and brought out a potato. When I asked her how it happened, she said, "Well, it was on the bed and I sat down on it."

Another time in Hollywood, as an Ambulance Attendant, I was training the Driver on delivery techniques. He had his gloves on while guiding the baby's head and he suspected that he inadvertently stuck his thumb into the baby's fontenells (soft spot on the baby's head). I quickly took over and realized that this was a Frank Breech (buttocks first) delivery. Luckily everything turned out alright. That was a long time ago, when I used to deliver two or three babies a week. I worked with guys who had gone back to deliver kids in the same families. Those people didn't have much money and we had a hell of a time getting them to go to the hospital. I had several kids named after me, and the parents would bring them to the station when they got older to show them the guy who delivered them.

I remember one baby I delivered at Adams and Western. I went into the house where a woman was getting ready to give birth and told me, "It's coming out!" So I put on the gloves, and while I'm delivering the baby, she's eating chicken.

Another time, I was examining a woman and, when I asked her what happened, she said, "I'm bleedin'." When I asked where from, she said, "You know, I'm bleedin' from my virginia."

Ogden/Hollywood

It was an evening call for service when G-6 (Central Receiving Hospital City Ambulance) was zig-zagging down Sunset Boulevard in Hollywood. I was in the driver's seat and the attendant was George Antonelli; the year was 1968, As we headed out of Hollywood Receiving Hospital, where we were based, I was somewhat concerned because I was not familiar with the geography of the Hollywood part of the City of Los Angeles. George had worked the area for many years but it was my second week at Hollywood. I had attempted to check the map before we began the response but George snapped at me for not knowing the streets in the area. In fact, George said little to me the first week, except to get upset and criticize me. It gave me a bad taste in my mouth when working with this individual because he was from the "old school". He believed that the driver should be seen and not heard and he was the attendant and in charge of the ambulance and driver. Instead of assisting me with the fastest route to the address he would rarely assist me, yet did not want to see me open a map book. I remember getting a pit in my stomach the first time he refused to help me. After all, we were a team in my view and he apparently did not know what the word team meant.

As I closed the map book because of his criticism, he said "It is one street past Ogden" and I said "I don't know where Ogden is." He said "Let's go." I turned on the lights and pushed the horn rim, where the siren was activated, and we were off. I watched every street but did not see Ogden, probably because I was most concerned with safety and being careful in an area I was not used to. It seemed like about 7 or 8 minutes had passed when he said, "Pull over." I immediately pulled over and stopped. He proceeded to tell me I'd passed Ogden 5 minutes earlier. I immediately apologized profusely and began to turn the ambulance around but he said stop so I did. It was then that he told me I needed to learn every street in Hollywood on my days off. I was embarrassed and also humiliated and simply stated, "What about the patient?" He said "Let's go" and guided me to the address.

It was a heart patient and the fire personnel on scene were rather irritated that we took so long, one even saying that they had heard us go right by the street without turning. I apologized to the firefighter. Ultimately we transported the patient to the hospital but I remained very bitter toward this ambulance attendant for a long time. This old-school mentality nearly cost someone their life and I vowed that if and when I learned the City of Los Angeles, I would not be an ambulance attendant like George Antonelli.

For many years the Central Receiving Ambulance system ruled the streets of Los Angeles. Drivers got years of experience and were promoted to ambulance attendants. This was a civil service promotion and paid more to be in charge of the driver and ambulance. I was perhaps the youngest ambulance attendant in the City's history, being promoted to ambulance attendant on January 1, 1969. From that point on, I thought it would simplify my life but that was not going to be the case.

I was perhaps the youngest Ambulance Attendant in the City's history being promoted to Ambulance Attendant on January 1, 1969.

All of my drivers that I supervised after my promotion had years of experience, yet their supervisor was promoted in two years. I immediately noticed an attitude by most that they did not like driving an attendant who was so young. I was about 23 years of age. The so called "grapevine" stated that they were not going to promote me due to being so young, but were afraid of some sort of grievance from me having scored number 6 in the entire city for the promotion. It took a year before I was "accepted" by my elders, which in reality was the whole organization, since I was the youngest of all personnel.

I had vowed to always help a driver if he did not know where a street was and that played many times. Unfortunately the old school personnel (attendants) did not help the drivers very much; it was an "I am in charge" attitude and it permeated the entire organization. I knew it would be impossible to change that mind-set so I did the next best thing - to treat my partners, whoever they were, with respect and got to know nearly all of them.

Years later, after joining the Los Angeles City Fire Department and going from ambulance attendant to Paramedic, then Senior Paramedic, then a name change to Paramedic Supervisor, then a major promotion to Paramedic Captain, I was on my journey. In 1985 I was promoted by Civil Service Examination to the Assistant Bureau Commander of the Emergency Services Bureau. I finally was promoted to the Paramedic Chief position on March 17, 1987. There I oversaw the entire EMS System for the Los Angeles City Fire Department. At that time I operated the largest Fire Department EMS system in the country. Now I was in a position to make, change, and articulate policy for the entire Fire Department as it related to emergency medical services.

While it took from 1968 until 1987 to work my way to the top, I never forgot that call while operating Ambulance G-6 out of Hollywood, California.

Venice Beach Surfer

My assignment at the Venice Police Station at Ambulance Designation G-14 continued for about one year whereupon the "transfer system" occurred. I desired to work in the Venice area because it was familiar, but working with a partner that caused me to feel like I was getting off a roller-coaster every time my shift started caused me to look forward to another assignment. After everyone put their bids in and recognizing I was a new employee it was quite a surprise to be assigned to what was known as the "Venice/Wilshire Relief". Three days at Venice and three days at the Wilshire Police Station allowed me to maintain the station but with a new partner. My nerves were rattled but it was short lived - my new partner was Willie Wilson.

Willie, it turned out, was talkative, informative and quite a bit younger than Dan Cesarotti. Since Willie was on vacation when the new transfer cycle began, I worked for a segment of three shifts with Fred Dumois, a silent but nice guy. We actually had some interesting conversations while working for a week together before Willie's return. Fred, who died about 30 years ago, liked the idea that I was attending San Fernando Valley State College, now known as California State University at Northridge. However, up until 1971, it had the former title. He always asked me about classes and how I was doing. Despite the fact that he never told me, I felt he was proud of me for going to college and working full-time. Few of the ambulance personnel were doing so.

A surfer had caught a wave and the worst thing happened: he had wiped out and injured his neck.

Our first call was at Venice Beach at the water's edge. A surfer had caught a wave and the worst thing happened: he had wiped out and injured his neck. It was the first time that a beach incident had occurred and the lifeguards had brought him to the shore. He was unconscious and obviously severely injured. We carefully took over his care and placed him on a board and then the gurney. It must be noted that this was a time where there were no paramedics, and no advanced life support of any kind. Naturally, we had oxygen and a Elder Valve, an old pressure-cycled resuscitator. After placing this young man (not much younger than me) into the ambulance, and as I was closing the doors, I became acutely aware of the huge crowd of onlookers around us - they seemed to be somewhat hypnotized and silent. A woman in the crowd yelled to me, "Thank you, bless you and take care of him." It was as though his life was in our hands, that what happened would be dependent on our actions.

I got into the driver's seat, looked back into the patient compartment and, for a moment, was caught up in the drama of what I was seeing. Fred was putting an airway (in those days it was metal) into the young man's mouth and then pressure-cycling oxygen into his lungs. It was what we do today with Bag-Valve-Mask devices but it was quite prehistoric, if you will. I could clearly see his chest rise as Fred blew air into his mouth. I pushed the button in the brown Dodge and pushed the horn ring which caused the siren to initiate. In a minute I was en route Code 3 with a critically injured patient and emotions were flooding through me. On one hand I was living what my dream was and on the other hand was completely concentrating on driving safely but quickly to Santa Monica Hospital. I zig-zagged through traffic, sometimes on the wrong side of the street, but cars would be pulling over to the right so I had the right-of-way. I was also fully cognizant that a smooth ride was essential so care was given on turning at intersections.

Shortly I arrived at the alley-way that led to Santa Monica's Emergency Department. I jumped out of the ambulance and opened the rear doors. I felt like a professional and noted that several private ambulance crews were standing by their ambulances observing our actions. After all, I was now a City Ambulance Driver, which was a position that every private ambulance in the county would have given their right arm for. As I opened the doors and released the safety bar, unhitched the "Gilson Strap" and then assisted in lifting the patient out of the ambulance, I felt like a million dollars - I had earned the right to be where I was. Finally I felt that when the shift was over, I had earned my pay.

On the way back to the Venice Station, Fred told me the ride was good and the patient received good care. Although Fred did not know, I was feeling elated and on top of the world. I could not wait for the next call.

Speeding Vehicle vs Bus

Thirteen years earlier I had been 10 years old and seen a horrific accident involving a train and vehicle. The scene was indelibly marked within my mind and had forged impressions of what I wanted to do in life and how to react in an emergency. These feelings were about to come awake in a call received in the late afternoon while working Venice Division. A speeding vehicle collided with a bus on Lincoln Boulevard at the intersection of Culver Boulevard in a somewhat remote area of what is now known as Marina Del Rey. The Fire Department was also responding due to trapped victims within the wreckage. Whenever the dispatch included the Fire Department, it drew out mixed feelings within the ranks of the ambulance personnel. It was not unusual for ambulance attendants to sometimes disagree with Fire Department personnel at the scene of various types of medical incidents. After all, we were the experts and provided the transportation of sick and injured people so when fire personnel arrived on scene sometimes there existed conflict.

One male nearly had a complete amputation of his leg were it not for a shred of tissue holding the leg to the body.

Years later when I was a member of the Los Angeles Fire Department beginning in July 1970, these conflicts did not evaporate; in fact they continued and increasingly worsened. Willie and I arrived to an unbelievable scene; overturned vehicles and what one now considers an MCI, or multi-casualty incident. More than a dozen patients were lying everywhere, some deceased, others screaming for help. Police and fire personnel were everywhere and continuing to arrive. I put out a call for additional ambulances and within 5 or 6 minutes several began to arrive, mostly privately-owned ambulances. While the City Ambulance system was the official and proper ambulances to handle emergency cases, there are times when it can be an overwhelming event and every ambulance is required, municipal or private. This was one of those cases.

I started to treat very serious patients, all adults with multiple injures; these included major lacerations with arterial bleeding, fractures, including obvious compound or open fractures, unconscious patients and numerous hysterical adults. It was totally chaotic initially but I watched Willie try and obtain some control over patient care despite the emotions that were running high especially in the hoards of people who pressed closer and closer for a better look at the scene. One male nearly had a complete amputation of his leg were it not for a shred of tissue holding the leg to the body. I had learned good bandaging techniques so I quickly dressed the gaping wounds with a tight pressure dressing. Then I put a rubber splint on the leg and ushered the man into a waiting ambulance. The young ambulance driver asked me where to go and what to do, so I told him to have the person in the back of the ambulance hold direct pressure over the bleeding area and transport Code 3 to Santa Monica Hospital. I could hear the siren wail as they took off heading north on Lincoln Boulevard.

Patient after patient was treated and transported. G-7 and G-3 assisted with this incident coming from other police divisions. There was blood everywhere and on everyone. I was covered with bodily fluids although I wore black gloves made of leather. No one routinely wore gloves for the protection of disease; in fact it was quite accepted to come back to the station covered with blood akin to a fighter after a bloody round or two. It meant you were in battle, the battle with death.

Well over an hour later, there were still patients to be transported. Major emergencies take time and energy. When the last patient was transported I was physically exhausted as was Willie. I had observed the Fire Department personnel extricate patients from under the bus and vehicles similar to, at the age of 10, the incident involving the train. This time I was part of the response and not a frightened child; this time I was a professional rescuer and still anxious.

Back at the station, Willie and I talked about all of the things that had happened. He was calm and helped to assuage my anxiety and trepidations. Had I done the right things? Could I have done better? Why was I anxious?

Only through time does one achieve expertise; guitar players must practice to become accomplished. I was getting quite an education in emergency care and I loved it more and more. I did not envision the EMS changes that were to overtake all of us in just a few short years.

The latter part of 1969 found me at 77th Division Police Station with a new driver by the name of Richard Houle. We did not know each other prior to working together but soon found that we shared the same interest in motorcycles. Richard owned a Triumph Bonneville and I had a Triumph Tiger. The difference was that he had dual carburetors and I had but one. He drove it everywhere on our days off, through the mountains of Malibu and Topanga to the desert areas. Riding was our way of cleansing our thoughts of the trauma and sickness we saw on a daily diet. We partnered the "day watch", 7:00AM until 3:00PM, and while not as busy as the PM shift we did have our share of high call load. Part of the 77th Police Division allowed for us to handle parts of Baldwin Hills and one specific area was quite rough. One call stands out in my memory due to the inherent dangers we faced on a typical day, one that I will always remember.

continues on page 98...

Chief Ambulance Attendant
Bob Roberts' badge

Chief Ambulance Attendant Harold Patton and Ambulance Driver Nate Rubin, circa 1955

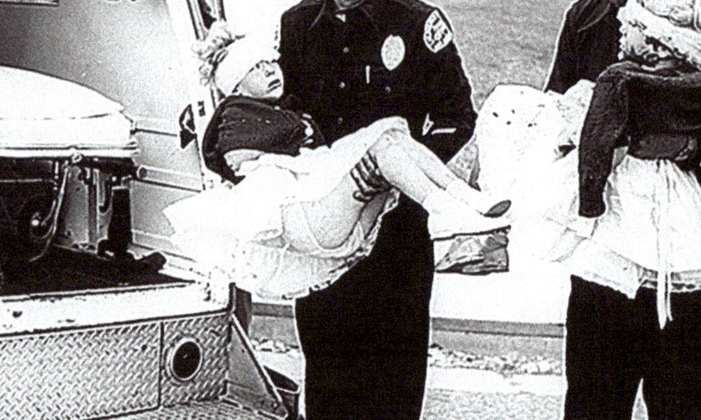
Two little girls in a traffic accident being put into ambulance, circa 1960

Drivers and Attendants uniform shoulder patch

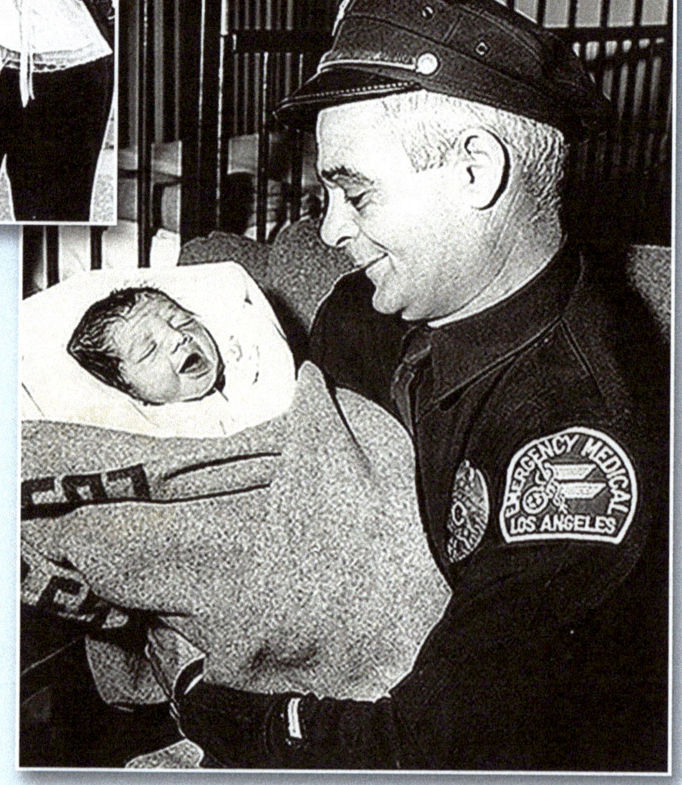

Ambulance Attendant Nate Rubin holding an abandoned infant left at a church

Deputy Chief Al Schultz presenting Captain Cowen with a 15 year pin, Fire Station 33

EMS Supervisor "on duty", 1981

October 1970 Fire Department News in Pictures

UNUSUAL REQUEST IN LINE OF DUTY

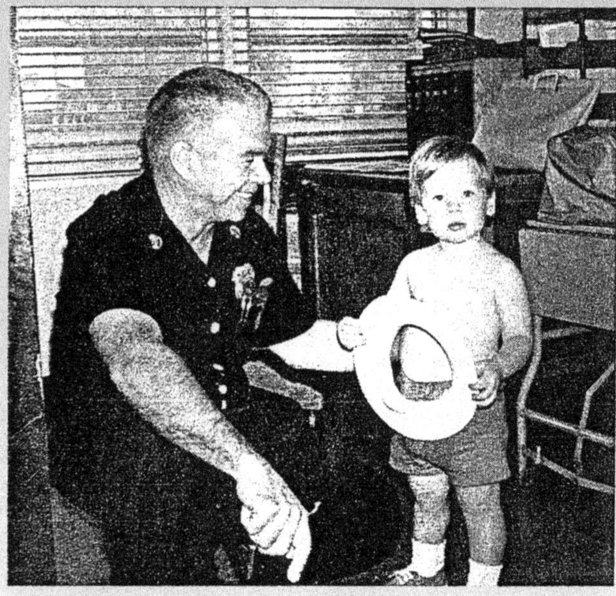

"And I will faithfully serve the City of Los Angeles in the discharge of my duties as fireman to the best of my knowledge and ability so help me God."

Little did Captain Harold Fowler realize that when he, as a rookie fireman, took this oath of office, it would include such things as—removing a toilet seat? This was the problem that two-year-old Kevin Tschekaloff brought to Engine 93. His mother tried to explain; but only Kevin knew for sure how it got there.

VISITING JAPANESE FIRE CHIEFS HONOR CHIEF HILL

by Len Lakin

Left to right, Chief Shigenao Murayama, Chief Raymond Hill and Chief Masao Kuromiya.

Chief Hill was recently honored by two Japanese Fire Chiefs. The two Chiefs presented Chief Hill with a picture painted by one of Japan's renowned artists, Mr. Shigekazu Ando.

Chief Shigenao Murayama is head of the Machine Division of the Tokyo Fire Board. Deputy Chief Masao Kuromiya is from our sister city, Nagoya.

Chief Hill presented the two visiting Chiefs with a Certificate of Commendation from the Mayor for their distinguished services to the City of Los Angeles.

YOUNG ATTENDANTS FIND NEW HOME WORKING WITH DEPARTMENT

Attendants, left to right, Dan Cypert, Allan Cowen, Robert Houle and John Stuckey have finished their first month with the Los Angeles City Fire Department at Engine 22. They responded to 606 emergency responses during the month of July.

All of the men shown right voiced that they enjoyed working with the Fire Department personnel and hoped that they had found a new home.

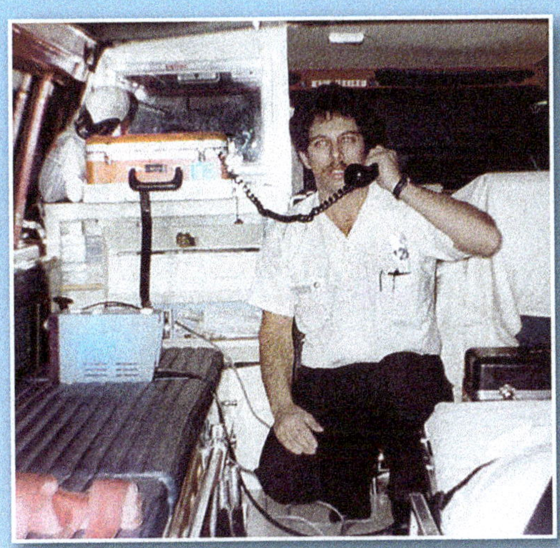

Talking to the hospital on the Bio-phone in 1974 while working Fire Station 105

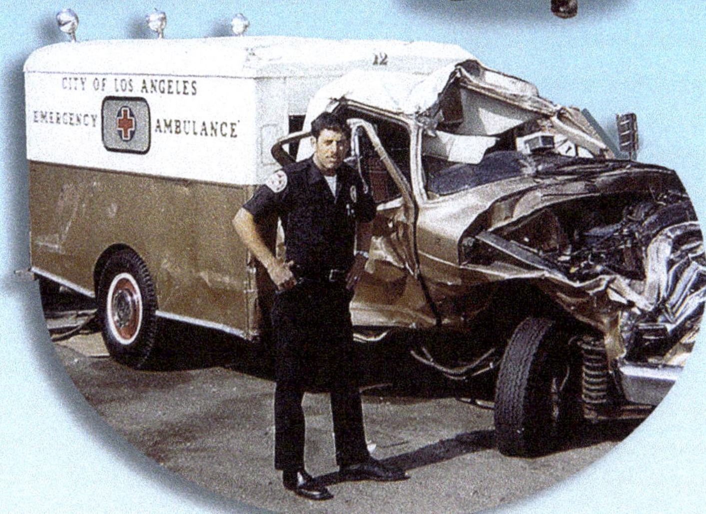

Among his many duties as Chief was working with the press.

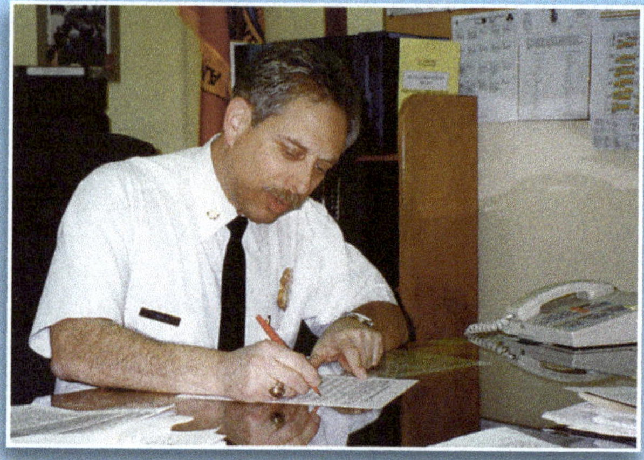

Chief Cowen in the administrative offices staying on top of things before the City's next big crisis.

Press Conference at LAX for the use of an AED (Automated External Defibrilator) that saved the life of an electrocuted utility worker, who died and then was revived.

Chief Cowen and EMS Supervisor (Captain) Kevin Nida "on scene" in the mid-90s.

Groundbreaking of Central Receiving Hospital, circa 1956

Groundbreaking for new Fire Station 41

Fire Department top staff at groundbreaking for a new fire station

Woman Thrown Out Window

On a Saturday morning we responded to an average-looking apartment house for an injury call. A woman was thrown out of her second floor apartment and sustained a serious fracture of her leg. As I was examining her with Richard assisting me, the woman had explained that her boyfriend tried to kill her by literally throwing her out of the window. She was crying and in severe pain. I had just place a rubber splint on her leg when a huge individual came out of the apartment and demanded to know what we were doing, at which time I replied, "Taking this lady to the hospital". I noticed he was very big and had no shirt on. His statement to me was, "You are not taking her anywhere".

I tried to explain that she was seriously injured and required immediate care. At the same time, I knew that our ambulance radio was also part of the police network and I could speak directly to anyone on the air, both police and ambulance crews. I considered this individual a direct threat to this patient and us. However, the ambulance was parked in front of the apartment beyond our ability to get instant police assistance via radio. I simply stated to this man, "We are taking her to the hospital".

Richard was a tall, lean and very physically fit ambulance driver who I felt could handle this guy. He had placed our patient on the gurney and tried to roll her toward the ambulance when he stopped us. A scuffle resulted and a physical altercation was inevitable. The unidentified man threatened us repeatedly and said he would kill her and us both if we did not do what he said.

The unidentifed man threatened us repeatedly and said he would kill her and us both if we did not do what he said.

As I tried to wheel the gurney toward the ambulance, he was in a pushing contest with my partner. My goal was to get the patient inside the ambulance and call for "officer needs help" which would have brought numerous police units Code 3 to our location. As they were pushing one another I was able to get the patient to the back of the ambulance but needed Richard to take one side of the gurney to place it in the ambulance. Richard broke away from the individual and assisted me and got her in the patient compartment. The man was again interfering with us and Richard said to me, "Can you drive on this call"? I said yes and got into the driver's seat. I realized that the man was not acting rational and was either on drugs or alcohol but his strength was beyond amazing. In attempting to remove the gurney from the ambulance, it became obvious he was beginning to get extremely violent and demanded to get into the ambulance. My concern was for the patient but we did not have the means to prevent this psychotic nut from hijacking the ambulance so he got into the patient compartment with Richard and our patient.

We had not gone one block when the fight began in the back of the ambulance. I started to pull over and was going to assist Richard but he yelled "get going". I turned on the siren but instead of going to Morningside Hospital, which was the closest emergency room, I elected to pick up my microphone and announce to all units and police listening that I was en route "University Police Station" Code-3 with a patient who was a violent male, mental, who was fighting in the back of the ambulance. My ETA (estimated time of arrival) was less than two minutes. I was speeding on Santa Barbara Avenue (now called Martin Luther King Boulevard) eastbound heading toward the station and could see Los Angeles Police Units converging to that area. As I got about two blocks from the station, I could see about a dozen police officers waiting in the street. At the same time, Richard hit the individual with an oxygen bottle as he was being choked by the crazed nut. I heard the 'clunk' of the bottle hitting him in the head without any results. He was feeling little if any pain.

I skidded to a halt and jumped out of the ambulance and opened the back doors. What then occurred was beyond anything I had ever seen: this giant of a man was throwing police officers off him like they were made of paper. His strength and power were absolutely scary and something that would give most people nightmares. Despite a dozen police officers, he was holding his own. Every time they would get him down, he would merely throw officers off of him like they were rag dolls. They had no luck in hand-cuffing this monster. It was as though he was a professional wrestler throwing fighters in every direction. At one point a motor officer parked his Harley Davidson motorcycle on the street and this brut tried to pick it up and throw it at other officers. lt ended up in the middle of the street.

LAPD Officers then called for more assistance and I gave aid to Richard who had done an excellent job in keeping this nut from killing our patient. He kept yelling in the back of the ambulance, "I am going to kill her and you too." When reinforcements arrived, a total of approximately 15 officers were able to get the man face down on the street and handcuffed him. They carried him into the station and placed him in one of the jail cells.

Richard had bruises and his uniform was torn, but, to his credit, wanted to take our patient to the hospital. We cleared the Police facility and drove her to the local emergency room for treatment. Afterwards we drove back to the police station for completion of reports. It was reported that the patient was high on PCP, which explained his superhuman and extraordinary strength. It was reported to me that officers transported him to a hospital for his injuries and in a rage at the hospital he pulled a sink off the wall in the emergency room.

This was not the first violent person we had encountered and certainly, as time went on, would not be the last.

Wrist Fracture

It was in 1968 when I responded to a call on Alvarado in the downtown area of Los Angeles. I had been working for the City of Los Angeles since March 17, 1967 and absolutely loved my job. As I recall it was on the day watch: 7:00AM to 3:00PM on G-18, the downtown ambulance that worked out of Central Receiving Hospital and handled the streets in the heart of LA. It was before noon that the call came in of a young man who fell out of a tree.

The address was on Alvarado near Third Street, where some tall trees were located. Within two minutes we were on-scene and at the foot of a large tree was our patient. He appeared to be approximately 17 or 18 years of age and had an obvious fracture of his wrist. He relayed the story that he had climbed the tree to rescue a small bird, a sparrow who he believed could not get back into the nest. So up he climbed to the nest to place the sparrow back into the shelter of its home. In doing his good deed for the day he managed to slip off the branch, bird and all, thus falling about 10 feet to the ground. Upon landing, the frightened baby sparrow flew out of his hand landing safely on the concrete.

Unfortunately, the young man threw his hand out to break the fall and instead broke his wrist. After splinting his arm and wrist, we transported him to Central Receiving Hospital for treatment - along with the baby sparrow, which I had placed in a small box that someone in the crowd supplied. In a 2005 article, the bird can be seen being fed by Central Receiving Hospital nurse Florence Mathews using an eye dropper. Someone, unidentified, took a photo of the feeding and sent it to me several years later. In attempting to do a good deed, one young man sustained a fracture to his wrist, while the bird received a nice lunch through an eye dropper. All in a day's work in the streets of LA.

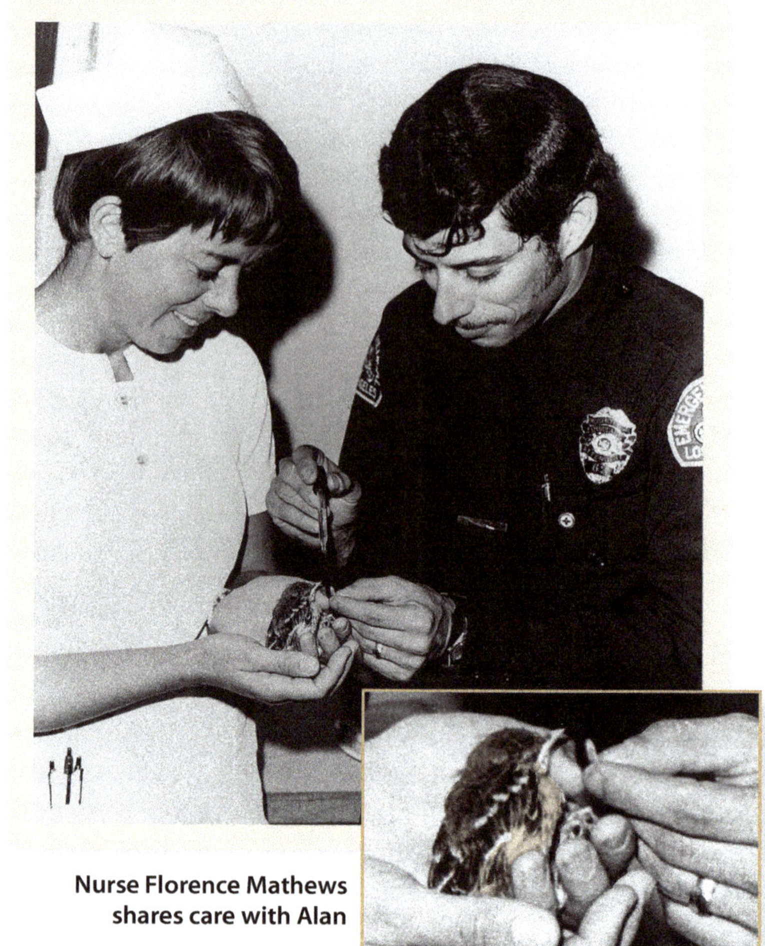

Nurse Florence Mathews shares care with Alan

Rape Case

With Willie Wilson back from vacation, I had a new partner who had a good sense of humor and a son slightly younger than myself. Willie lived in the Venice area so he got to work in his own backyard. He lived with his wife in a small house just west of Lincoln Boulevard; it was old but comfortable. My partner and I would work three days at Venice Police Station and three days at the Wilshire Police Station. G-7 was the ambulance in the mid-Wilshire region of the City of Los Angeles in the 4500 block of Pico Boulevard, our office was in the back of the station. We parked the ambulance outside in the yard that was shared with about 100 police vehicles, but we had a spot underneath the east side of the building which had a covering.

My first day at Wilshire (G-7) was concerning as I did not know the geographical layout of that portion of the city. Fortunately Willie was eager to show me around and he set the stage for what an ambulance attendant should do from my own perspective. He would sometimes check the wall map in the squad room if unsure of an address and taught me to do the same thing. It certainly would avoid both delays and embarrassment if you could not find an address or street. Willie was easy going, would answer all of my questions and also was part owner of a restaurant in our Venice division district. It was where we usually took our Code 7 (meals taken when on duty). It had many names over the years but while Willie operated it I recall it was The Snug Harbor.

The first thing an ambulance driver would do when beginning his tour of duty was to inform the off-going driver that he was present and in uniform, ready for a call. I would then check out the ambulance to be sure it was immediately available for emergencies; this included first aid kit, oxygen and various sized masks, extra bottles of oxygen, plenty of ZAT (a solution we used on open wounds) when we bandaged them, and an array of other checks. We also had an OB kit and some medicines. The Ambulance Attendant was always in charge of the ambulance and driver as that was how the system operated. It was understood that all calls would be handled Code 3 (red lights and siren) when responding to a location, but only the attendant could authorize a Code 3 to the hospital. It wasn't a matter of asking permission because in some cases it would be obvious, but usually the attendant would simply say, "Take it in", or "Give me a slow 3". In my case, Willie would just nod to me as I hitched the Gilson Strap and closed the back doors of the ambulance. I was cognizant of giving our patient and Willie the most comfortable ride as possible, since I was keenly aware that it was very uncomfortable in the patient compartment of the old Dodge Ambulances.

A man had entered the shop, motioned her into the back room holding a pistol in one hand. She had been the victim of a rape.

Our first call at G-7 was during a ride to familiarize myself with the area. Willie had told me to "suit up" and "let's get on the air" so I picked up the station phone and told "Eugie", one of the dispatchers downtown, that "G-7 is on the air". She said, "Okey Dokey" and we began to drive around. Next to the Wilshire Police Station was Sears Roebuck and Co., a very large store, and so there was lots of traffic in and around the area.

We had been on the air for approximately 30 minutes when our radio crackled, "G-7 come in". Willie answered with, "G-7, go ahead". Our first call was received about 4:00PM and it was a "woman down" at a flower shop on Pico Boulevard. We arrived in 2 or 3 minutes and everything looked calm from the outside of the building. It was the driver's responsibility to obtain the large black box with leather handles which contained all of our first aid supplies. I opened the back doors of the ambulance and picked it up and followed Willie. We entered a small flower shop and initially did not see anyone inside.

Willie called out and a young girl in the back room cried out, "Help". Upon entering the back room, it was obvious she was our patient. She had a look in her eyes that scared me; she stared at us and began hysterically crying. She relayed the story to Willie that a man had entered the shop, motioned her into the back room holding a pistol in one hand. She had been the victim of a rape.

It was no wonder that she had looked at both of us with rage. Willie told me to contact dispatch and have the LAPD respond to our location. I left the room and went out to the ambulance where I radioed to dispatch and requested the LAPD to send a unit. I returned to the back room where the patient, who was perhaps 19 or 20 years of age, was sitting in a chair, frozen, unable or not wanting to move. Within 5 minutes an LAPD unit arrived and they called for another unit with a female officer. At the time, I was relieved that the female officer finally arrived and began communicating with the victim who was now our patient. After an interview, it was determined that we would transport the patient to one of the local hospitals. She was crying and at times hysterical. The damage had been done and even though this was my first call at Wilshire Division, and certainly my first call involving a sexual assault, it would not be my last. Even when I recall this event it hit home that this young girl's life would be forever altered. I could not help but think about this case for weeks.

I thought about this young girl and often wondered whether the perpetrator had been caught and was in jail, where he belonged.

Within 5 minutes of clearing the hospital we were on our way to a traffic collision at Adams and La Brea, lights and siren operating.

Shooting on South Broadway

As time went on working with Willie and other ambulance attendants, I gained valuable experience. Like with anything, the more you practice, the better you become. So it is in Emergency Medical Services. Sometimes Willie and I did not need to talk on a response as if we knew what each other was thinking and what needed to be done. At times on quiet days we would drive the ambulance slowly along the Venice Boardwalk and enjoy the weekend crowds, many of whom had set up booths and sold creative fixtures; after all it was a time of "Flower Children", free love, and music that represented the times. Occasionally we would meet up with a police car while on patrol and stop to chat. I particularly enjoyed the summers working at the beach where there were concerts and "Flower Children" everywhere who called themselves "hippies". In a strange way I missed the 1960s and being part of it all because my job required me to play a different kind of role. At parties I attended, people would frequently offer me a "joint" but I always refused, not because I did not want to try it, but rather because of the responsibility I felt when on the job. Of course working with the police officers constantly and not wanting to be a hypocrite was part of it as well.

Before I accepted working overtime at other stations, I always asked who the attendant would be as I was reminded of how difficult some could react. Once, I worked in South Central Los Angeles out of 77th Police Division, where G-12 was located. Because of the high call volume, it was a sought after location to be assigned given the number of shootings, stabbings and violent types of calls. I accepted a Saturday night that I would normally have been off to work with Pete Manos, an ambulance attendant who was assigned there. He was unlike anyone I had met and treated me as an equal.

Our first call was a shooting on South Broadway at a market where we found an approximately 40-year old male dead on the sidewalk. What amazed me was not the drama of what had occurred but the fact that no one seemed to take notice that a dead body was directly in front of the doors to the business. Pete and I quickly determined that he was deceased with one in the 10 ring (shot through the chest), directly in the center left of the chest. I surmised that the projectile went through the heart and killed him instantly. Pete asked me to get a sheet from the ambulance to cover the man given that he was in public view. There were an abundance of police vehicles and then detectives swarming the scene. I requested the coroner and Pete completed the Medical Report. The police informed us that the victim was trying to stop a robbery in progress and was shot dead. It took months to stop thinking about the face of that man who did not know he was to die that day. He woke up living his life and died on a sidewalk trying to stop a crime from occurring. I still remember the man's eyes that were half open but seeing nothing.

On that particular day, Pete and I handled about a dozen emergencies, more than I had ever had in an 8-hour shift. I was both exhausted and exhilarated. The constant Code 3 calls and handling life-threatening types of injuries was new. I had gotten into the routine of traffic accidents, some serious, most not, and sick calls, but this non-stop action was very exciting and I wanted more. On one call, I was traveling on Slauson and going about 60 miles an hour, which to me was very fast on city streets. Despite red lights and siren, I knew the responsibility to be safe was mine. I was the driver and did not want to ever get into an accident. We were covering for a downtown unit so it was about 15 minutes away, when Pete said, "I'd like to get there sometime". Then he added, "Let's get going". I put the pedal to the metal and was doing above 70 miles per hour and Pete said something to the effect of "That's more like it". After the call, as we were leaving Central Receiving Hospital, I indicated that my speed was well over what was comfortable for me and he laughed. What worried me next was his statement, "I'll drive the next call".

It was the ride of my life. I have been scared before on the streets of Los Angeles but Pete Manos nearly scared me to death. At times he would be going over 80 miles per hour and I knew it was unsafe. I kept my oversized seat belts tight but feared the worst, that we would be statistics in the newspaper the next day. Thankfully, he gave me back the reins on the next call. He said that I should ride with Gil VanNess if you want a fast ride. Little did I know that in a couple of months, I had that opportunity and learned Gil's philosophy of driving an ambulance.

Laceration at Local Bar

As an Ambulance Attendant I was much more in the comfort zone when working overtime in other Police Divisions since most of the drivers were assigned to that area and familiar with its geography. Several times I worked G-1, the Police Headquarters area. My partner was Joe Ortiz, who was one of the most friendly and enjoyable partners. He had a brother by the name of Jessie who also worked for Central Receiving Ambulance Organization. Going to work on days with Joe was like being on vacation; easy going, relaxed atmosphere and his knowledge of the best restaurants where you could "eat on the run". Fluent in Spanish, Joe made his mark by being so professional with patients and handling any interpreting that was needed. In East Los Angeles it was extremely useful to have a Spanish-speaking partner and he was the perfect person to handle the sick and injured because of his pleasant personality.

Joe and I were "on the air" in the downtown area of Los Angeles and responded to a cutting, where an individual was in an altercation at a local bar and sustained a vicious laceration of the lower abdomen. He was initially holding his lower stomach and when he lifted his hands, a huge portion of intestines and tissue flopped out. Both of us were taken by surprise and after a few eye-popping moments, laid the man down and began treating him. I noted that an approximately 12-15 inch laceration, wide open, had neatly and almost surgically opened his entire belly. He had some pain, but the scene was quite horrific owing to what was coming out of this man.

I used what were known as lap pads, very large bandages similar to sponges, to cover the entire area, and moistened the entire 4 quadrants of his abdomen and kept everything in place with bandage tape. I remember bending his knees to take pressure off the abdominal musculature, which worked well. Joe went to get the gurney and oxygen and the patient said he was thirsty and wanted a drink from the bar. I told the patient that it would not be a good idea and he would need surgery to put everything back inside and sew him up. He was quite adamant about the drink, so I told him that when he gets out of the hospital he could drink all he wanted. For the moment it satisfied the patient, but my mind was on something else - who did the cutting and where was he?

As the police arrived on scene in large numbers, he was helpful to them in terms of who did the carving job and where he could be found. We were ready to transport and I felt that Los Angeles County General Hospital was the best facility for this patient. As we loaded up the patient, Joe said, "Shall I take it in"? and I replied in the affirmative. In the back of the ambulance, the gentleman explained that he was a veteran and it turned out that he fell on hard times, resulting in him living on Skid Row. From the looks of his wound, and the abdominal contents that had emerged, I was concerned that he could lose his life, but as fate would have it we would see him again several times over the next few months.

Joe went to get the gurney and oxygen and the patient said he was thirsty and wanted a drink from the bar. I told the patient that it would not be a good idea and he would need surgery to put everything back inside and sew him up

After clearing Los Angeles County General Hospital, Joe said, "Let's get some lunch" - a strange thing to think about after this type of trauma, yet we were hungry and there was some kind of humor to this scenario that only ambulance and emergency medical personnel get. We were so used to trauma that it did not seem to bother either of us and Joe added that we're headed to his favorite Mexican Restaurant not far from the hospital. It was called El Tepeyac and is still located at 812 Evergreen Avenue in the Boyle Heights area of the city. We requested a Code 7 (lunch break) and in we went. The dispatchers at the Receiving Hospital had the phone number of just about every restaurant that crews utilized and even private numbers to some. Joe knew everyone there and we had ourselves a feast which helped both of us put the visions and thoughts of our previous call out of our minds for the moment. For a change we were able to finish our meal and clear our Code 7. Immediately we received a most unusual call, one that is crystal clear in my mind and still talked about more than a half century later.

Amputated Penis

There are dozens of flea-bag hotels around downtown and particularly near Central Receiving Hospital. When the radio crackled, "G-1 report of an amputated penis" I wrote down the address and said to Joe out loud and over the sound of the siren, "Why would the operator put that out on the radio?" Everyone listened to police and ambulance calls in those days. It took less than 4 or 5 minutes to get to the 7th Street address, but in those few minutes we listened to other ambulances that were on the air make snide comments. These wisecracks were heard by everyone within 50 miles who were listening on a scanner or other device. When we arrived Joe grabbed the First Aid Box and we headed up the stairwell in what had to be the world's worst and dirty hotel. The elevator could only hold two people but he and I had a policy that he would always take the stairs for safety reasons. Besides, old elevators can get stuck.

We knocked on the door of the third floor room and heard someone moaning. I repeatedly called out "emergency ambulance" but no one answered the door so I opened it and pushed the door open. We could now hear loud moaning and crying from another room. We were very cautious as we walked to the bedroom and there in the middle of the bed, stark naked, was a gentlemen lying face up holding his amputated penis. Joe and I made eye contact with each other and approached the patient. He was about 50 years of age and covered with blood - lots of blood. In fact, this man was in shock. Both of us carried black leather gloves and put them on as we approached with Joe reaching into the First Aid Box and handing me a stack of 4x4 gauze pads and a lap pad.

Everyone in emergency services knows that direct pressure is the first treatment for bleeding. However, when an amputation occurs, if direct pressure does not stop the hemorrhage, then a tourniquet may be necessary. In a nano-second I ascertained that this man had a self-inflicted wound that resulted in an amputation of a body part. My immediate concern was where the knife was and would he use it on either of us, whether because he was a mental patient or in pain or a hundred other reasons. Before rendering treatment, I asked him what happened. He replied that his penis "did not work anymore so I cut it off". I said, "How did you do it?" He replied with a kitchen knife. My partner noticed a bloody knife in the sink. I proceeded to apply direct pressure to the wound. The penis was severed about 1 inch from the body so the majority of the organ was gone. I had studied the human body so I knew there were arteries and veins in the penis. Direct pressure seemed to have stopped most of the bleeding and I was aware that this patient needed immediate surgery. I told Joe to get the gurney and then heard lots of sirens outside. As I waited for Joe I asked the patient to give me the penis and he offered it to me. It appeared shredded and partially destroyed but I placed it in the lap pad and waited for Joe. Within a two minute period, I looked out the window and noticed at least three other G-units parked near our ambulance. The door opened and Joe had arrived with the gurney and at least 6 other Central Receiving Ambulance personnel, all of them offering their assistance to help in this particular case.

We were very cautious as we walked to the bedroom and there in the middle of the bed, stark naked, was a gentlemen lying face up holding his amputated penis. Joe and I made eye contact with each other and approached the patient.

We lifted the patient and placed him gently on the gurney. Everyone was willing to help and everyone also wanted to see the penis. I suspected that their eager assistance to help us was motivated by their genuine curiosity and morbid sense of humor. Instead of going to Los Angeles General Hospital, I chose to take the patient to Central Receiving Hospital simply because it was less than two blocks from our location. Because I elected to not show the ambulance crews the amputated penis, when G-1 arrived at the hospital, so did three other ambulances. I had not wanted to waste any time showing them the amputated body part. At the hospital, the physician determined that he had lost a huge amount of blood and began infusing him with IV solutions. The patient told everyone in the treatment room that after he sliced it off, he was going to eat it.

Later, we re-transported him to Los Angeles County General Hospital for surgery and then he was taken to the mental facility at the hospital for observation. This had to be one of the most interesting calls in my career.

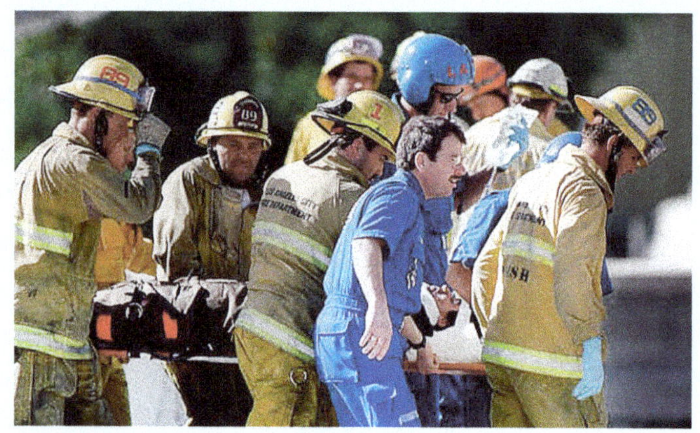

Partners in Rescue

Brotherhood in saving lives

A real honor in my career has been working side by side with talented and courageous men and women of our city.

Partners: Sid Kruger

One day, Willie didn't show up, but an attendant from the morning watch arrived in his place and introduced himself as Sid Kruger. He was much older than Willie, but youthful in many ways. We hit it off immediately. After his introduction, his first words to me were, "Let's get on the air." In five minutes we were on the air and he was showing me Nat King Cole's residence and those of other famous people. He was big on landmarks and I found I was listening closely to what he was saying. By remembering certain landmarks, he said, you can also remember the locations of hospitals, police facilities and good restaurants.

I was proud to be part of the team that day and will never forget Sid Kruger and his gentle way with patients.

Our conversation came to a halt when the radio dispatched us to Rossmore and Olympic to an auto vs. pedestrian. When we arrived a few minutes later, there was a large crowd waiting to see what we would do. I jumped out of the ambulance, grabbed the first aid box and followed Sid to the patient. Sid was cool, calm, and in charge as he asked everyone to give us room to examine the older woman who had been struck by a bus. After she was knocked down, the bus ran over her lower legs with its tandem rear wheels, and the damage was extensive.

The patient was in and out of consciousness and was critically injured. Her lower extremities were crushed and the bleeding was severe. She was in profound shock, her clothing had been ripped off, and she was dying. Sid wasted no time directing me to get the gurney, oxygen and splints. We treated, splinted, and administered high-flow oxygen, then rapidly transported her to the hospital. She received the best care any crew could render in the late 1960s. I was proud to be part of the team that day and will never forget Sid Kruger and his gentle way with patients.

Partners: Gil VanNess

I have worked with maybe a hundred different partners during my 50-plus years in Emergency Medical Services. One of the most unusual characters was a fellow by the name of Gil VanNess. The year was 1969 and I worked in downtown Los Angeles on G-18, a roving ambulance that, by nature and design, would float all over the city. It was called a roving ambulance because it covered areas while the regular ambulance crews took their Code 7 (meal). Gil was a short man, rather wiry in nature, with brown hair. He had a reputation of being one of the most experienced ambulance drivers in the Central Receiving Hospital system, having derived his recognition due to his many years in the downtown area of the city. I do not recall Gil ever looking at the Thomas Brothers map book no matter what the street address was. He had been there and done that in terms of the geography of this complicated city. The Hollywood area, particularly in the Hollywood Hills, can be very challenging in terms of streets and addresses. Some are even "walking streets" that are too steep or difficult to travel on by automobile, not to mention an ambulance. But Gil knew all the streets.

On one particular call I told him to slow down since he was traveling beyond what I thought to be safe. Keep in mind, back in the Central Receiving Hospital days, the Ambulance Attendant was in charge of the ambulance and the driver, and there was no mistake about that. It was a written and unwritten law that only the ambulance attendant could authorize a "Code-3" (red lights and siren) call to the hospital. While all calls were Code-3 to the location of the emergency, the attendant would notify the driver if he wanted the transportation to be emergency to the receiving hospital. The attendant would frequently use various terms to authorize a Code-3: some were, "take it in", give me a slow "3", and simply, "transport Code-3". This acknowledgement notified the ambulance driver to transport the patient or patients to the hospital with red lights and siren in operation. There was no discretion on this rule.

When I told him to slow down, Gil responded that he wanted to get there, and I said, yes so would I and in one piece. He obviously did not like being told to slow down. I noted the speedometer to be at 70 miles per hour in the downtown area. Of course, he did slow down but practically to a crawl to obviously show me he could take matters into his own hands. I told him we would address the issue later on when we delivered the patient to the hospital.

About one hour later, I could tell he was still bothered about the event so I told him to stop at a donut shop and I would buy him a donut and cup of coffee. We happened to be in the Wilshire District so he found his favorite location and we went in. After obtaining the drinks and donuts we sat down and he immediately told me he was the ambulance driver and although I was in charge, he knew how to operate the ambulance and was the assigned driver.

What makes this story unique is his reasoning as to why he liked to speed up rather than slow down, at intersections particularly. His rationale was this: the faster you go through the intersection, the less likely you will be struck by another vehicle. Naturally, I nearly spilled my coffee on the floor. He further tried to quote articles on ambulance driving to "prove his point". My recollection is that I started to laugh so hard that it took all I had to catch my breath. It was one of the first times I truly got serious with a partner and indicated to him that when working with me he needed to curtail the philosophy of his ideas and drive more safely.

Although Gil VanNess was perhaps an experienced ambulance driver, I sensed our little talk made some good common sense to him because anytime I worked with him he drove a bit fast but safely. In those days there were little, if any, rules on stopping at intersections. Finally one day, I said that we were going to switch roles and driving would be my responsibility. He agreed and it must have worked because he drove (at least with me) much more sensibly and carefully.

Giving direct orders to people can work, but sugar (with some coffee) can move mountains. That episode was 53 years ago and yet it seems like yesterday.

Partners: Pete Manos

I was working G-12 (77th Police Division) in 1968 with Ambulance Attendant Pete Manos and for the first time saw how a simple call can transform itself into a riot. It began like any other call with a dispatch to a home on 79th Street on the South Central area of the city. The police had followed an individual home and stopped him for a traffic violation. As the officers began to question the young man, he decided to not cooperate and did not comply with the officers direction to exit the car. This led to the two officers pulling the individual out of his car and then attempting to handcuff him.

Shortly thereafter Pete and I arrived on scene in the afternoon on a warm summer day. The suspect was being interrogated and apparently began to fight with the officers. As they tried to handcuff the suspect, he began screaming and his family exited the house. I observed his mother and father run over to where the altercation was occurring and yelling at the police officers. In a few minutes the crowd began assembling in the street while the officers were trying to control the suspect. The young man was shouting and badmouthing the police in no uncertain terms and more force was being applied to the young man in an attempt to take him into custody.

I began to hear his mother yell at the police officers that he was on medication and to let him go. The father also began to interfere with the officers and then the neighbors began to get restless and started to yell at the officers to let the young man go. All of a sudden I saw a coke bottle fly through the air and land next to one of the officers at which time the officer reached for his radio and put out an "officer needs help" call. Within 30 seconds I could hear sirens in the distance and getting closer quickly. I feared the worst; that the responding officers would converge in the area and get the melee under control. After all, at this point, the crowd had grown to about 50 or more persons, all yelling and surging toward the officers.

Pete and I crouched down behind the ambulance as rocks and bottles were being pelted at police officers.

G-12 was parked across the street and Pete and I were safe for the moment although I was physically in fear and wondered what was going to happen. This traffic stop had grown into what looked like a horde of people out to create a major disturbance. The initial traffic stop, albeit warranted, had become a potential near riot and I was worried.

Pete and I crouched down behind the ambulance as rocks and bottles were being pelted at the police officers.

They had finally been able to handcuff their suspect, but now the father and mother were in the faces of the officers who were threatening both of them with being arrested for interfering with the arrest. They were disregarding the officers request to back away as they tried to grab their son away from the officers.

Quite suddenly it seemed that this had turned very ugly as other neighbors began to attack the police officers. More reinforcements had arrived and about a dozen officers began using their night sticks to push people back. The incoming sirens had aroused many more neighbors who seemed to be attracted to the location like moths to a light. Within minutes battle was on; about 100 people facing the officers who meant business about keeping the peace. As more people joined in the attack on the officers, more officers arrived, red lights and siren, simply increasing the numbers of people jumping into the foray.

Thirty minutes later it was over. More than 50 police officers responded and took numerous people into custody. The young man who resisted arrest had been taken from the scene in a separate police vehicle and his parents were arrested along with more than two dozen others going to jail.

Pete and I evaluated about 10 persons but transported none. All of the screaming was over, all of the suspects taken away and some high ranking police administrators were on-scene trying to determine what had caused this disturbance. We were asked for our statements as well, and I was able to articulate what occurred and why. As it turned out, the driver was 17 years of age and had been drinking and struck several parked cars, then was followed by police when he refused to pull over.

The parents were concerned when the officers attempted to take their son into custody and began arguing and ultimately assaulting the officers. Neighbors jumped in to assist the family and all hell broke loose.

As we drove back to the station, Pete Manos said to me, "Think about it and whether it was worth all that the parents did to protect their son, when all of them are now being booked at the jail. All of this could have been avoided if everyone kept a cool head." I agreed. So much for the anatomy of a riot, although a small one in comparison to what was coming in 1992, 24 years in the future.

Partners: Willie Wilson

Another of my unforgettable partners in G-14 was Willie Wilson. We were quite the team. I looked forward to each and every day, both for the excitement but also because we were making a difference in the quality of life for others. Whether or not the quality of life issue was up front in my mind I cannot be certain but in later years, upon self-reflection, it is apparent that I thought a great deal about that. It is comforting to know what you do has a direct relationship in a positive way for others. Life was good in those early years on the City Ambulance system.

I learned much from Willie; the way in which he spoke to people, his bedside manner and the care shown others. He treated everyone the same, no matter what their station in life. We handled the homeless and less fortunate, the wealthy, the young and old alike and all backgrounds. One day, a Saturday in 1968, we received a call while working in Venice. This call had a profound effect upon me for years to come. Even today as I write about this particular call, I feel a tingling down my back.

At about 3:30PM we responded to National Boulevard in the Palms area of West Los Angeles. I remember parking on the opposite side of the road in front of a vehicle that was parked. I left my rear amber light flashing and both red lights in the front since I was parked on the wrong side of the street. Willie and I got out of the ambulance and walked over to the vehicle and looked in. There appeared to be a dead body, male lying across the front seat. In order to examine the patient, we opened the door and I reached in and immediately recognized the individual as one of my high school friends, Richard. We were not only friends but good friends in high school. I told Willie who he was and he asked me if I was sure. I said yes!

Further evaluation of Richard revealed a needle still in his arm, a spoon and tourniquet. He was, in fact, dead. He was my age and I was suddenly overwhelmed by the drama that had unfolded. Questions without answers flooded my mind and that was interrupted when the first of two LAPD officers arrived on scene. This was a coroner's case so we covered the deceased and filled out the Ambulance Run Book and left the copy for the police and coroner. We left the scene and headed back to the Venice Station but I felt stressed and strained. My high school buddy was dead of an overdose of heroin. It had been four years since we graduated and I had lost touch with him. Later I found out he "tuned in, turned on and dropped out" and became a user of heroin which cost him his life. I thought about him for weeks, another bit of stress I placed in that backpack of anxiety that holds all of the sights, sounds and smells of emergency medical care. It is my view that nearly all EMS providers suffer from some sort of what we know today as post traumatic stress. Some have learned to deal with it better than others, but it is always with you and will surely show itself later in life.

I still have remnants of post traumatic stress that occasionally take the form of nightmares, night sweats, and generalized anxiety. Death is dealt with in another chapter, from my perspective, but there exists a kinship with all EMS personnel regarding this subject.

Two hours after this response Willie said he was hungry so we headed for his restaurant, The Snug Harbor. One of his servers, an older lady said, "What will it be Willie?" He ordered and I decided not to have lunch. Willie insisted so I ate very light. Willie asked 'Sparkle Eyes' to take the order. I did not even know her name but for what everyone called her. She was a bit flirty and had at least 15 years on me. She must have used some flakes on her face that sparkled, hence the nickname. She could not have been nicer and I always enjoyed chatting with her during our visits when working G-14.

Dinner would be short however, as the telephone rang in the restaurant. I answered and the dispatcher said to respond to a "hanging in the garage" on Wade Street, 3600 block. We were out the door in a minute, rocketing north on Lincoln Boulevard, then a right turn on Venice Boulevard then a quick left turn and two blocks north. The wife met us out in front and she was screaming that she came home from work and found her husband in the garage. I quickly took ahold of the first aid box and followed Willie into the dark garage.

Despite the fact that I wanted to appear at ease in all situations, and in control at all times, the sight of her husband hanging from the beam with a rope around his neck stunned me for a few seconds. There was little doubt that this middle-aged man was deceased; in fact it appeared that he may well have been there all day. As neighbors began to arrive due to the ambulance with lights flashing in the street, it occurred to me how much this woman's life was going to change. Did he have children? parents? friends? My mind began its traditional swirling and I thought to myself, stay calm.

Willie pronounced the man dead and I called for the LAPD to respond. Given that he was not in public view, we were able to leave him for the coroner; we did not cut him down nor cut through the knot he had placed around his neck. We did not touch anything or move the step ladder he used to climb up. The look of death and smell of death permeated the garage. The LAPD Detectives arrived within 15 minutes and began their investigation which later turned out to be a suicide as expected. He had been despondent according to his wife.

We cleared the call and Willie told me to go back so he could finish his dinner. I wondered at that moment if my appetite would ever return.

Partners: John Flanagan

Days turned into weeks and weeks to months but I gained valuable experience working many different areas of the city. From South Central Los Angeles to Hollywood and Highland Park and from Venice to the East Los Angeles area including the Metropolitan and Hollywood areas I worked with as many ambulance drivers as possible. Some were excellent and I could depend on them to do a fine job; names like Fred McCuistion, Andrew Chapralis, John Flanagan, Norman Forsblad, Hal Fowler, Julio Gonzalez, Bob Holley, Robert Roddy, Ron Perkins and Richard Houle to name a few.

One call that I will never forget was with John Flanagan, who was assigned in the Highland Park area. We had responded to a female down in a market on York in Highland Park. After examining her and transporting to Huntington Memorial Hospital, John was replacing the sheets out in the ambulance area and I was finishing my paperwork in the emergency room. As I walked toward the ambulance I became aware of a verbal altercation between John and an unknown male about 40 years of age. I could also see the knife he was wielding from 50 feet away. I immediately ran and grabbed a full-sized hospital gurney in the ambulance area and quickly shoved it between John and the suspect. I saw a security officer walking and yelled to him for help. In seconds he was heading toward us and I realized he was quite old and suddenly had a bad feeling that he might be in a dangerous situation given his age. I yelled for him to call the LAPD, but he pulled out a canister of MACE and pointed it at the suspect squeezing the button. In the excitement, he shot himself in the face and went down for the count.

I yelled for some nurses to call the police and tell them that "an officer needs help" at the Emergency Room knowing they would respond Code-3. Every time the suspect lunged at John or me, he was yelling he would kill us. A couple of minutes later we still had him between the hospital gurney and the brick building, not letting him move. Finally sirens approaching, he lunged at us and we knocked the knife out of his hand and I was able to take him down whereupon the police officers handcuffed and arrested him on assault and battery. We were bruised up from the scuffle and my right thumb did not want to work very well. Both of us were placed off-duty for about two days. Afterwards we both realized how close of a call this was and what could have resulted.

Twenty-six years later in 1996 we would hug each other and reminisce this very incident at a Central

Receiving Hospital Reunion that I hosted at Petrelli's Steak House in Culver City, California. It had been a dream to have as many ambulance personnel, nurses and doctors, and others, attend what was called a "26-year Reunion". People came from across the United States to be part of it. It was an evening I will never forget and will cherish for my lifetime. People cried and laughed at the same time, hugging everyone, since most had not seen one another for 25-30 years. Lots of photos were taken and even a video was made.

After it was over I received dozens of letters, cards and phone calls, all thanking me for making a dream come true. Little did they know I had the same dream. Those who attended included Ambulance Attendant Daniel Cesarotti and Senior Ambulance Attendant and Supervisor D. V. Harris, both in their mid 90s. The event would not have occurred had it not been for the help of my Fire Department Secretary Cathy Chin, who is now gone from this world but deserves so much credit for helping to set everything up and meet and greet our guests. Thank you Cathy!

Author Alan Cowen with son Robby, who would later become a Fire Captain/Paramedic in Idaho.

A proud father passes the torch of life in rescue services

Robby Cowen

In the late 1980s and through the early 1990s, I would frequently receive dispatches day and night while off-duty. It was not unusual for me to be called at 1:00AM or 3:00AM to respond to major emergencies within the City of Los Angeles. I would wake up, put on my bright yellow brush jacket and head for the garage and respond. More than half a dozen times while on the freeway heading to some part of the City, I would look in my rear view mirror and a head would pop up and it became obvious that Robby would have heard the telephone ring and quickly gone to my department vehicle and hid. Once enroute, the rascal would pop up and make himself known. I would impress upon him to not get out of the car once we arrived at the site of the emergency. He followed my direction concisely. Robby would end up graduating from Paramedic Training at Daniel Freeman Paramedic School and be the youngest certified Paramedic at 18.

Robby is now a Fire Department Paramedic himself, and, at age 16, he attended the Central Receiving Reunion with me and had the opportunity to see and meet the forefathers of Emergency Medical Services in Los Angeles as well as the excellent nurses and doctors who came before us who helped make up today's system.

Central Receiving Reunion Dinner

In early 1996 the Los Angeles City Fire Department's Bureau of Emergency Medical Services sent out a nationwide search for any Ambulance Drivers and Ambulance Attendants, as well as Nurses, who worked at the Los Angeles Receiving Hospital System prior to July 1, 1970 for a 26-year reunion to be held on August 3, 1996.

These dedicated professionals who attended made this event a smashing success. It was quite an evening to see these people once again, after more than a quarter of a century, and know they served the City of Los Angeles for so long and so well.

Below is actual invitation to the Reunion Dinner event

ATTENTION
ATTENTION
ATTENTION

ALL "G-UNITS" COME IN

ALL CENTRAL RECEIVING AMBULANCE PERSONNEL, AMBULANCE ATTENDANTS AND DRIVERS

The Los Angeles City Fire Department's Bureau of Emergency Medical Services is pleased to announce a Central Receiving Hospital 26th Year Reunion. Join your fellow Ambulance Drivers and Attendants who once ruled the streets of Los Angeles in the infamous "Brown Bombers".

For an evening of fond memories and reminiscing of yesteryear, come and be honored for your part in the history making Emergency Medical Services System long before a Paramedic Program existed.

CENTRAL RECEIVING REUNION DINNER

Date and Time:	Saturday, August 3, 1996 Social Hour: 6:00 P.M. Dinner: 7:00 P.M.
Place:	George Petrelli's Famous Steak House 5615 South Sepulveda Boulevard Culver City
Food and Price:	Choice of: Filet Mignon, Grilled Salmon or Roast Chicken $30.00 per person, includes tax and tip.
Reservations:	Call Cathy Chin (Chief Cowen's Secretary), at (213) 485-6094 Emergency Medical Services Bureau Spouses are cordially invited. ALL RESERVATIONS MUST BE PREPAID July 20th is the deadline for reservations.

Some of L.A.'s finest Nurses were also in attendance:

1 Elizabeth Beaver   2 Virginia Eckvahl   3 Martha Morales Harl   4 Florence Mathews
5 Martha Beadles   6 Betty Eby Raines   7 Althea Sievertson   8 Rubye Smith   9 Reba Nelson

Dennis Bogard
?
James Just
Kenneth Clarke
Jerry Goens
Danny Cypert
Pete Manos
Richard Harris
Alan Cowen
Donald Rus
Donald Immerman
Richard Woods
Dorsett Harris (D.V. Harris)
Daniel Cesarotti
Kevin O'Connel

26th Anniversary Gala

Additional colleagues were in attendance this night but are not in the above picture:

John Flannagan • Forrest Painter • Marvin Randolph
Jesse Ortiz • Richard Houle • James Bailey
Hal Fowler • Pete Segura • Robert Holley

Retired Central Receiving Personnel, Ambulance Drivers and Attendants

Kevin O'Connell, Chief Cowen, Jessie Ortiz

Dan Lewis, Dan Cesarotti

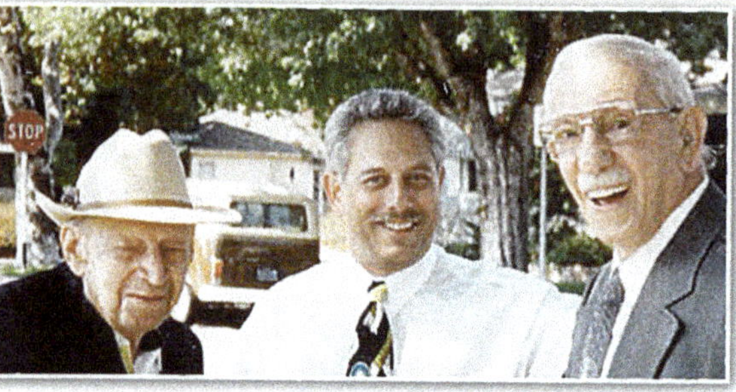

D.V. Harris, Chief Cowen, Dan Cesarotti

Jesse Ortiz displays Gilson Strap

Florence Mathews

Dave Thompson, Jim Denney

Richard Houle

D.V. Harris, Chief Cowen

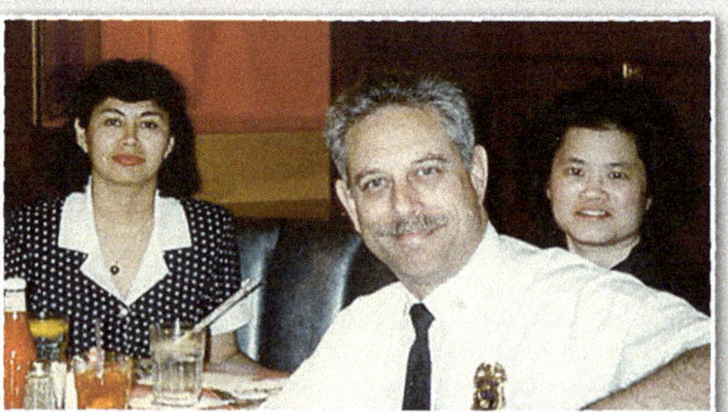

Racquel Borden, Chief Cowen, Cathy Chin

Dick Fowler, Don Rus, Richard Harris

Pete Segura

Ed McDaniels, Danny Cypert

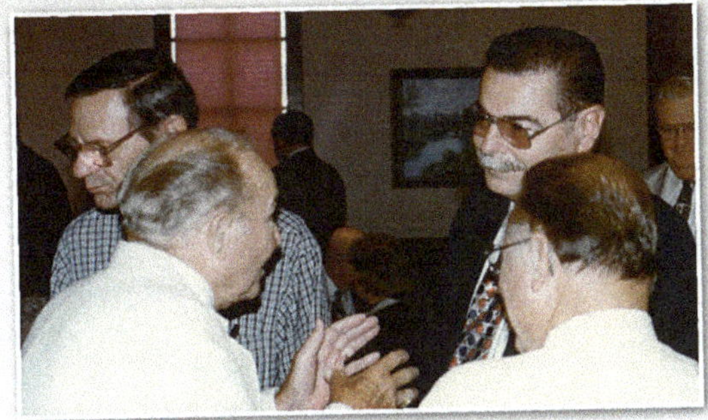

Dennis Bogard, Art Jenkins, Richard Harris

Dennis Bogard and spouse

Top row: Hal Fowler, unknown, Alan Cowen
Bottom row: Jim Bailey, Joe Ortiz

Cathy Chin

Chief Cowen's secretary

Dr. Douglas Arterberry

John Flannagan, Pete Segura

Central Receiving nurses reminiscing after 26 years

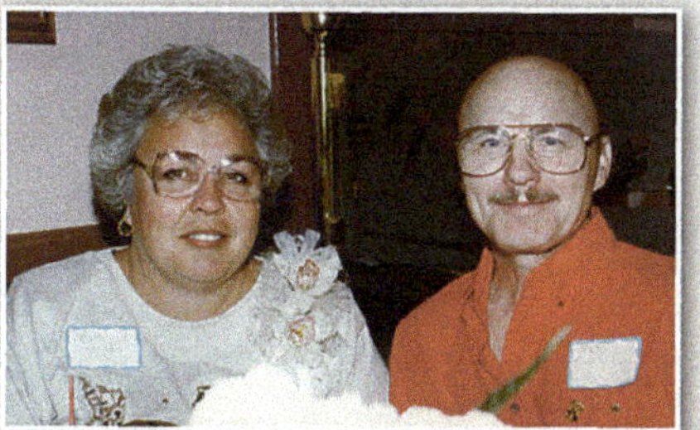

Ed Davidson with his spouse

Bob Holley, Jim Just, Alan Cowen, Rey Rojo

Bob Holley, Dan Lewis

Marvin Randolph

Ken Clark, Jerry Goens

Gordon Robb

Dave Miller, Arthur Jenkins

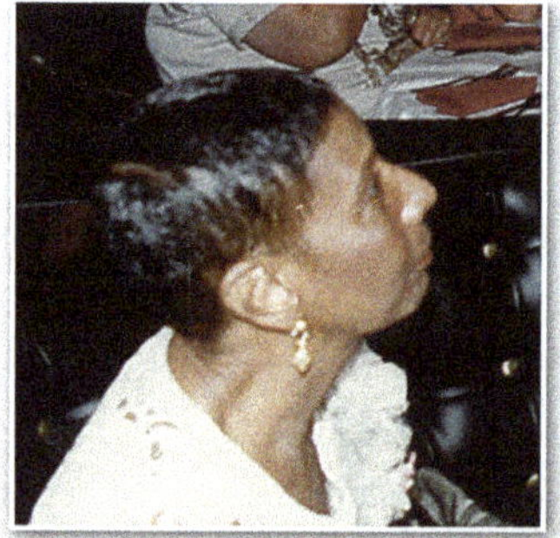
CRH Nurse

Art Jenkins

Ron Perkins

Mrs. Tom Fear, Forrest Painter, Tom Fear, Doug Brown

Doug Brown

Danny Jordan, Don Rus

Harry Rich

Gordon Robb, Richard Woods

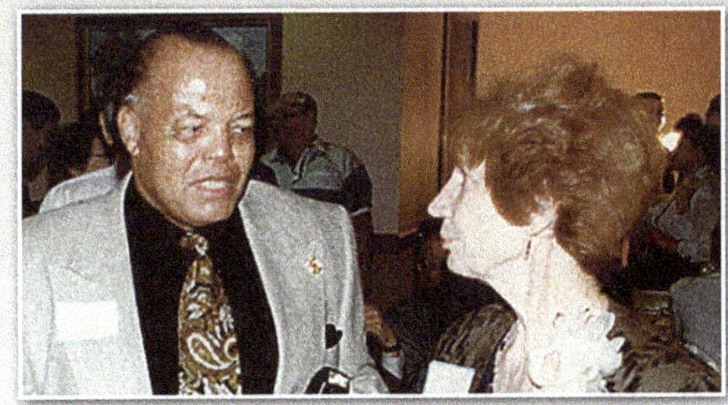
Ed McDaniels, Nurse Elizabeth Beaver

Tom Fear and spouse

Dan Cesarotti, Harvey Rhyne

Art Jenkins, Doug Brown

CRH Nurse

Ed McDaniels

D.V. Harris, Dan Cesarotti

Pete Manos

CRH Nurses

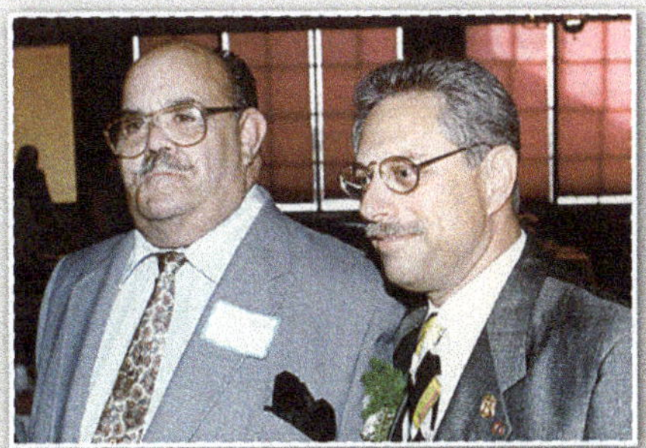
Max Shulman, Alan Cowen

Why We Serve

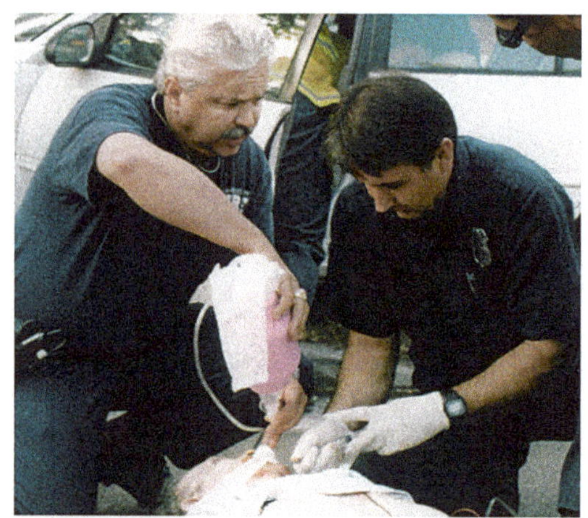

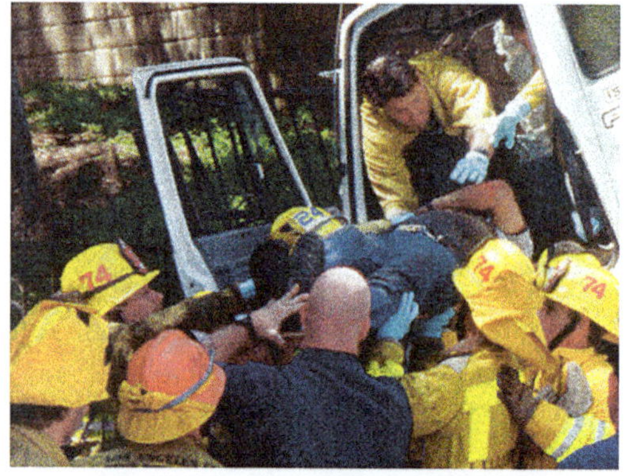

Photos by Joseph Ortiz

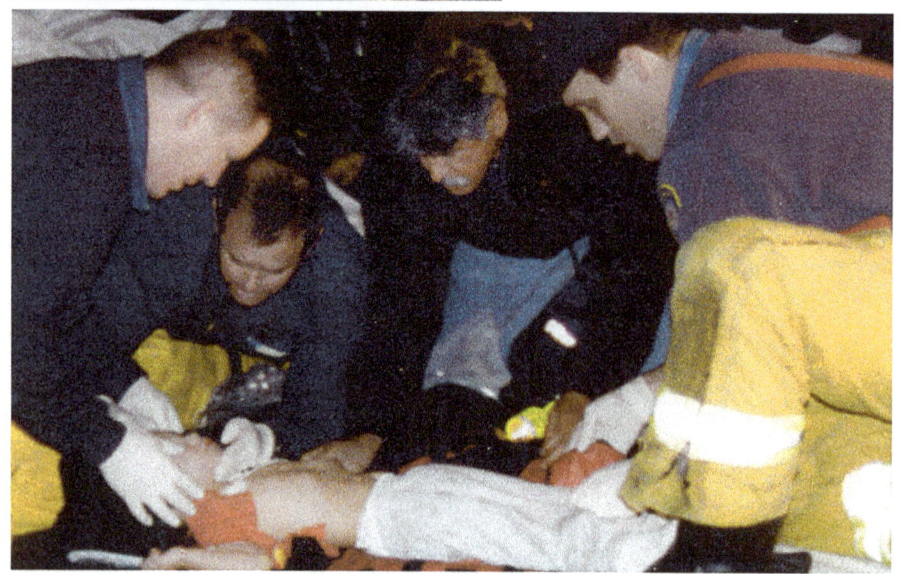

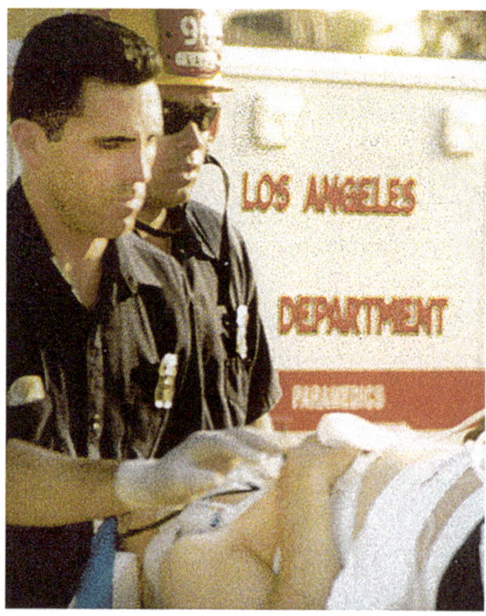

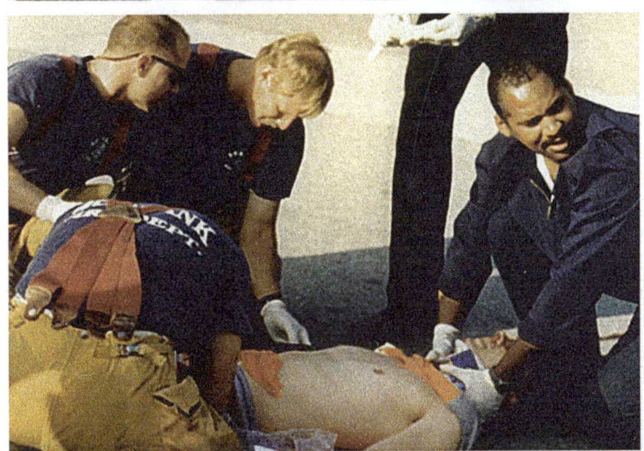

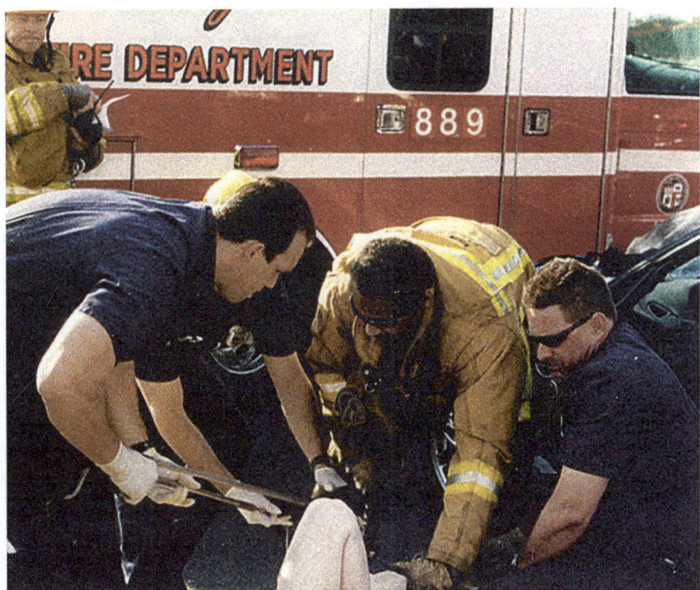

Fire Station 9 ranked #1 for the busiest station in the country with 33,380 total calls in 2017

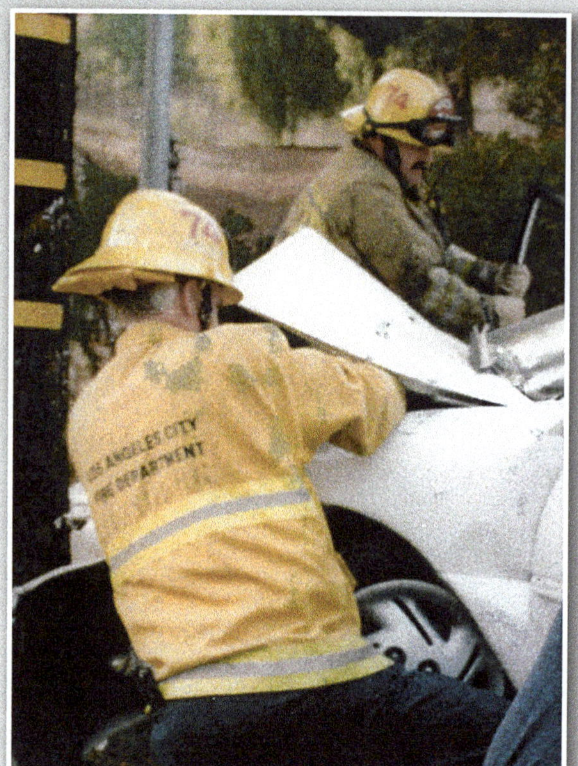

Where rubber meets the road

Photos by Joseph Ortiz

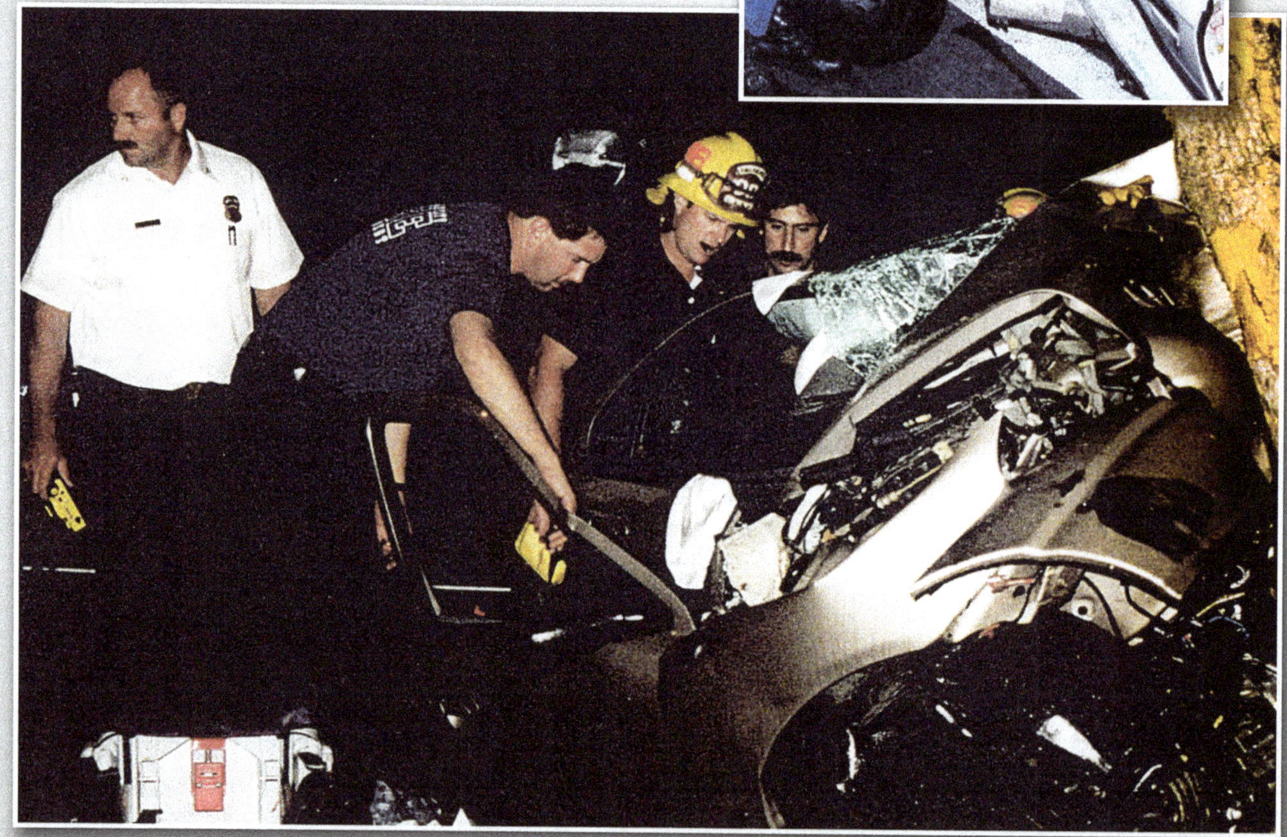

MEMORABLE CALLS

Los Angeles Fire Department

Of the literal thousands or tens of thousands of emergency medical calls I have responded to, there are some that cannot be forgotten and will always have a place in my memory - whether they touched my heart or brought tears to my eyes or were just plain unusual. These represent just a sample.

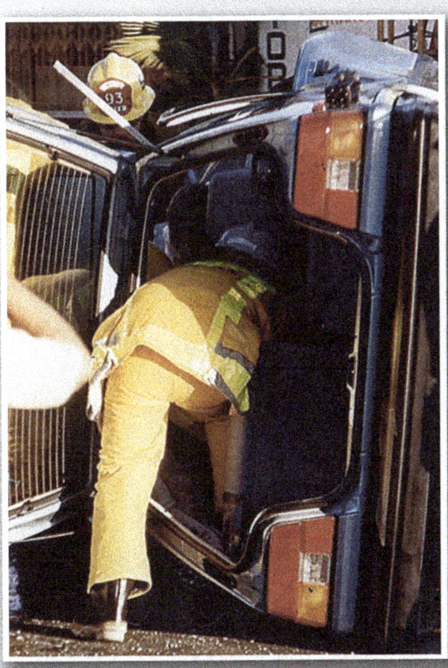

Bedridden Gentleman

The following is a true story and helps me (and my students) to be kind and compassionate.
Alan R. Cowen, Professor
Former Chair, Emergency Services Department, Los Angeles Valley College

As a Paramedic Captain for the Los Angeles Fire Department sometime in the early 1980s, I received a response to assist in handling a field problem in Central Los Angeles. Upon my arrival at the location, it became readily apparent that the field problem was indeed a big one: a male somewhere in the area of 600-700 pounds needed to be taken to the hospital. Unfortunately, the patient had been bedridden for several years and it was impossible to carry him out of the bedroom door. The engine company had indeed thought about it and requested a truck company for tools and additional manpower. Medically, the patient was stable and thankfully stayed that way during most of the planning and actual dismantling of the apartment. Several challenges faced the rescuers: first, not to injure the patient at any time; second, how to carefully and properly remove him from the bedroom; and third, how to transport him to the hospital. While I did not hear any adverse or untoward comments about the gentleman, I did sense some feelings from a few of the personnel on scene that this was so unnecessary and should have been avoided by the patient, family and doctors. Regardless, before we began the operation to expedite the patient I spoke with all members on scene in order to ensure that everyone was on the same page in terms of our tactics and strategies that were to be utilized in the mission. I recall even today, although it is more than forty years since this event, that obesity is not just the balance between calories and burning them off. In morbid obesity, it can be quite complicated and may be genetic.

I can only imagine how the patient must have felt with 8 to 10 fire personnel working to remove him from his confines in order to transport him to the hospital. Both on-scene paramedics were contemplating an IV "just in case" and the whole scene generated media as well. I could plainly see that the patient was terribly embarrassed by the ordeal, and began to cry. It took a couple hours to extract the patient from his apartment and was done so only by dismantling the entire door and wall. In fact, the crew literally took apart the walls and doors thus enabling the patient to be carried out. A large flat board was used to carry the man out and he was carefully strapped down to avoid injury. I oversaw the entire operation and it was flawless. It took 8 firefighters to carry this 600+ lb. patient to the ambulance and it was necessary to take out the gurney from the unit and merely lay the board down on the floor of the ambulance. I had the paramedics put two boxes under the head of the flat board to make it easier for the patient to breath. He was subsequently transported to a county facility for treatment and then to a different location for treatment of morbid obesity.

Five years later, I had the opportunity to meet up with this man and I did not and could not have identified him. He was a totally transformed individual, who perhaps weighed about 250 or so. He not only remembered me but everything that occurred on that summer day. He remembered the kindness showed to him by all present at that event, and he remembered being carried by careful hands. He told me how embarrassed he was and that was why he accepted treatment and subsequent surgeries to help stop his obesity and lengthen his years left.

It was a lesson for all who participated on that day - a lesson in tolerance, acceptance, and knowing that all present had done a fine job. Years later, when I had been promoted, firefighters and paramedics alike who were on-scene that day would come up to me and say, "Hey, remember that guy who weighed over a thousand pounds..." Interestingly, his weight has gotten heavier every year with the story, but isn't that how it always goes?

I tell my EMT college students that story as a lesson in tolerance and to treat each and every patient with respect. Whether overdose or any call, at 3:00PM or 3:00AM, we must do the best we can and stay compassionate.

5150

It was an early evening at Fire Station 61 in the mid-Wilshire district of the city when the radio crackled, "Rescue 61 from OCD" (Operations Control Dispatch center). I answered, "OCD from Rescue 61 go ahead".

The dispatcher calmly stated to respond to an apartment on a street just west of La Brea near 3rd Street for a "woman bitten by a bat". I picked up the microphone and indicated that Rescue 61 was responding and then reached over and turned on the red lights and beacon. At the same time, my partner initiated the siren and we were off. I tried to visualize what a bat bite might look like and what treatment I would be rendering to this lady. I was trying to formulate some sort of treatment plan and also be prepared in case the bat were to attack us. I also considered the possibility that the bat might have rabies, remembering from my training that rabies was a potentially fatal viral infection of the central nervous system. Although I knew rabies wasn't a common malady, I knew that wild animals, such as a bat, might well be infected, especially since it had attacked the woman.

Within three minutes we pulled up in front of the apartment and I picked up the microphone and notified OCD that Rescue 61 was on-scene. We then exited the ambulance with our equipment and headed for the door. I knocked loudly and said, "Fire Department". Almost instantly, the door flew open and a very worried woman, appearing somewhat anxious said, "There is a bat in here". I looked around and saw nothing and she then said that it was inside. I asked her where the bat was at this time and if she was OK. She replied that the bat had flown in through the door and bit her.

The woman then stated that a bat had flown in via the front door, bit her on the left ear and then entered her brain through the ear canal.

We put down our equipment, starter kit and medical kit and she pointed at her left ear. I asked her if the bat bit her face and she again indicated that yes the bat had gone for her ear. I did a thorough physical examination and assessment of the patient and found no evidence of any bite or injury and asked her what happened. It was at that time that I began wondering what really happened and where was the bat. The woman then stated that a bat had flown in via the front door, bit her on the left ear and then entered her brain through the ear canal.

My partner gave me a look that could only be interpreted as this woman was a "5150". It was a challenge to stay professional and not to smile or break out in a long belly laugh. I again looked into her ears and determined that no bite marks were present and that it was highly doubtful that a bat flew into her ear and then went directly into her brain, despite what she claimed. Just then, as I suspected, a Los Angeles Police Department radio car had pulled up and knocked on the door. My partner let them in and explained our situation. The officers had heard the call dispatched and wasted no time in responding to our location for assistance if we needed it. We both knew they just wanted to check out the "bat story" which we all knew was fabricated.

Upon further discussion, the woman admitted to being treated for psychiatric problems associated with her fear of bats and other flying critters. Once we thoroughly evaluated this lady, the police took over and said they would handle the followup. I recommended that they contact the lady's psychiatrist and follow-up could occur. I somehow knew that this particular call would be remembered for the rest of my career; to be told and re-told until I retired. I did not realize it would actually become part of the folklore of the LAFD. To the best of my knowledge, my partner and I never had another call involving a bat.

Burlington Fire 1993

As the EMS Bureau Commander of the Los Angeles Fire Department in 1987 it was common for me to respond to large scale emergencies anywhere in the City of Los Angeles. Anytime three or more ambulances responded to any incident I would be notified 24 hours per day. Most of the time the notifications did not require me to respond to the location as it was simply numerous patients at the scene that needed treatment and transportation. However, I responded to many multi-casualty events in which 5 or more ambulances and even 25 or more ambulances were needed to handle the event.

By nature, an EMS incident, unlike a fire, begins big and quickly and diminishes in size as more and more resources arrive at the location to resolve whatever has occurred. A fire usually begins small and slow then becomes larger and sometimes very large and again diminishes as resources arrive on scene and "surround and drown" whatever is burning. Either way, EMS or fire, it requires resources to handle and "knock-down" whatever is causing the emergency.

Sometimes both occur: a large fire such as an apartment building with many injuries and deaths. These events are particularly difficult due to both elements: life and property. One such event was the Burlington Street Fire that occurred on May 3, 1993 at 330 South Burlington Street about 4:30PM in downtown Los Angeles.

I was in my City Vehicle when contacted and was notified of this emergency. It came out as an apartment fire with "jumpers" and multiple casualties. I turned on my red lights and siren and began to respond to the location zig-zagging through traffic while hearing fire companies and ambulances arriving on scene and realized this was going to be a significant event. Upon arrival about 8 or 9 minutes later it became graphically obvious that additional resources would be required particularly in the EMS arena. It did not take long to realize that we were going to have critical patients and full cardiac arrests to deal with. What we did not initially expect is that we would be faced with multiple cardiac arrests which would be children and adults all at the same time.

To make matters worse, emotions were very high with hysterical family members running all over the scene, hundreds of bystanders and news media converging from all directions. Additionally, a shortage of law enforcement officers was evident as there was very little control over the surging of literally hundreds of people everywhere. Fire line yellow tape was useless as crowds moved through them.

Several EMS District Commanders were dispatched and each had a specific job; EMS District 5 was dispatched with Rescue Ambulance 11, 20 and set up a Medical Group near the intersection of Maryland and Burlington, about 75 yards just south of the fire. This was due to the numerous fire apparatus that were parked everywhere. It was a very crowded scene to say the least. Rescue 11 was assigned Medical Communications and started to obtain hospital status in that part of the city. This was done with the Medical Alert Center (MAC) wherein every hospital within the downtown and other areas let the Medical Communications Officer know how many beds are available at every hospital, whether it be emergency rooms, trauma centers or burn centers. This is vital information for field personnel so that one hospital is not saturated with too many patients and others receive none. The more critical patients are transported to the closest hospitals and the non-critical patients are taken to more distant hospitals based upon triage to sort determinations. Two additional ambulances were ordered and medical personnel had approximately 6 patients.

Rescue 20 and Engine 6 set up the Care Holding Areas that are utilized when an event has multiple casualties. Rescue 3 and 9 arrived as several more patients were being carried out. The initial patients were injured from jumping or evacuating the building. However, at this time an infant was carried out of the building in full cardiac arrest. The infant's pupils were fixed and dilated and showed asystole on the EKG. CPR was being administered and it was determined that immediate transport was necessary.

Rescue 13 and an engine company were assigned to handle triage directly in front of the building while Battalion 1 Commander was now Medical Group. EMS Commander of District 1 was reassigned as Treatment Control Officer. EMS 1 made the decision to have the care holding areas directly in front of the building.

Upon my arrival, I immediately ordered six additional rescue ambulances and announced on the radio that I was assuming the Medical Command. When I got out of my vehicle, I went to the command post and recall that it was so noisy and quite difficult to hear, both from hundreds of people everywhere and loud equipment operating. I walked over to the front of the building and EMS 1 reported that seven hospitals were being used for our patients. Despite someone on the air announcing that deceased patients were to be pronounced dead at the scene, I clearly articulated on the air that all full cardiac arrest patients were to be treated and transported immediately.

At this time, I noticed a gravid female, full-term, being given CPR and ordered her to be given top priority and immediately transported. Two such gravid patients, both in full arrest, were treated and transported. At one point in time, there appeared to be about 6 or 7 cardiac arrests being treated within the immediate care area. It was the most I had ever seen on a single incident within a 50 foot area. One particular sight still haunts me 30 years later. A young man, shirtless, perhaps in his early 20s, is screaming and crying while pounding his fists on a car as he looks at his wife and two children who perished in the fire. The look on his face and his grief and stark reality of what he saw has never left me and has sometimes caused me sleepless nights. I can still see him, and the pain and grief in his face, as he walks over to his deceased family and weeps.

All of the 9 deaths were caused by smoke inhalation and not burns. This major tragedy is one of the worst I have responded to and one I will never forget. In all, 17 Los Angeles Fire Department ambulances were utilized on this emergency and 12 hospitals received patients. A total of 20 patients were transported from the incident. Of the two pregnant women who were transported being given CPR, one newborn lived via C-Section and one did not. The injuries that patients received were from jumping from the second and third floors. A total of 44 people were treated for injuries, 20 of which were minor injuries and released on scene.

In all, 25 fire companies responded to the scene, two Battalion Chiefs, Assistant Chief, Deputy Chiefs and Acting Fire Chief. Dr. Russel Boxley, of the department's CISD (Critical Incident Stress Debriefing) Unit had eight teams who did debriefings to fire personnel after the incident.

Another sight that has stayed with me was the firefighters carrying out soot-covered victims, then laying them down next to dozens of fire hoses and performing CPR, using Bag-Valve-Mask devices on toddlers. All of this was done amid television helicopters who were broadcasting live on the air.

This was a major tragedy and one fire captain said it was "wall to wall bodies". 125 firefighters were involved in this 67-unit apartment incident.

Fire Chief Donald O. Manning reported that open fire doors contributed to the spread of the fire and smoke onto the third floor where most of the fatalities were found. At least 100 people/residents were left homeless and were bussed to Belmont High School gymnasium where they slept on cots and were helped by American Red Cross volunteers. Some residents said the smoke filled the hallways and forced them onto the balconies, where they handed down babies to people below, and jumped to safety.

After an investigation, it was found that at least 10 fire doors were either missing or did not operate properly at the 330 S. Burlington Street apartment. The City of Los Angeles has ordered the owner of the apartment to correct 19 separate conditions, including replacement or repair of fire-rated doors, automatic door closers, fire alarms, fire hoses and other devices. These violations led to what occurred on this incident.

Each semester I show raw footage of this incident to my Emergency Medical Technician classes at Los Angeles Valley College as part of their training. Each time I show this very graphic and horrific video, I see tears in some students' eyes and sometimes my own. Even my staff watches this footage despite having seen it time and time again, if for no other reason than to remember those lost and to learn how to do the job of an EMT better. It also serves to let our students know what they may encounter and offer ways to deal with it. The stress of an EMT cannot be understated.

NEWS FLASH FROM 30 YEARS AGO

"Man faces justice nearly 30 years after a tragic arson fire in 1993". It was known as the Burlington Street Arson Fire and one of the worst fires in the history of Los Angeles. It was deadly as seven children and three women, two of them pregnant, were killed in the fire.

The apartment was a 67-unit building that is located at 330 South Burlington and 10 people lost their lives that fateful day on May 3, 1993. Firefighters arrived at approximately 4:30PM and noted that several people were jumping out of windows to escape the dangerous smoke and fire. It was pitch black when firefighters entered the building with black smoke pouring out. I also listened to radio traffic while enroute to the incident.

Arson investigators determined the source of the fire as a mattress outside of the doorway of the property manager's apartment on the second floor. Patients that died did so due to the thick smoke and not from the fire.

The fire was the result of arson and witnesses implicated Ramiro Valerio and Juan Romero. In 1994 Valerio cooperated with Los Angeles Police as well as the FBI and Los Angeles County Sheriff's Department. The interview room was wired with hidden microphones and cameras.

As the years passed and witnesses had fading memories detectives continued to work on the case. In 2016 detectives received FBI files which included recordings that Valerio made as an informant; he bragged of organizing his gangs rackets. Prosecutors used his words to make the argument that Valerio, as a leader of the gang, ordered the horrific fire and with a motive to do so. The next year Valerio was taken into custody and arrested at his place of work and charged with murder.

LAPD Detectives never gave up on the case. Prosecutors said that Romero, the person who actually lit the fire, is currently a fugitive and believed to have fled the country. In the end, Ramiro Valerio was not testifying as a witness but was on trial for the deaths of seven children and three women who perished in 1993. He is now 49 years of age and bowed his head as the jury read the verdict. The jury found him guilty of first-degree murder with several special circumstances; he must be sentenced to life in prison without the possibility of parole.

Cat vs Dog

In the summer months of July or August, 1979, I had the good pleasure of working with a partner for just one 24-shift when my regular assigned person was off. The first and only time I worked with Paramedic Arthur Sorrentino was quite a shift. One call stands out from all the rest and may be one of the more interesting calls in my long career. We had numerous emergencies during the first 12 hours of our 24-hour platoon shift. However the second 12 hours was memorable.

It was about 2:00AM when the alarm came out of a woman screaming, police en route. We donned our jumpsuits and down the pole we went. I remember that ambulance-only calls were very quiet; we did not hear all of the sounds of boots and turnouts being put on or a bunch of firefighters hurrying down the pole, nor did we have the whole station wake up. It has always been strange to me how an audio alarm can go off and one can be absolutely wide awake in an instant only to realize it is a call for the engine or truck company and so one can close his or her eyes and be back asleep the next minute or two.

Goose bumps appeared on my arms and neck as I was quite sure someone was being murdered.

So it was on that early morning that we exited Fire Station 61 and headed just a few blocks away. As we pulled up to the side street address, I opened the Attendant's door and heard a horrible scream in the night that startled me. Goose bumps appeared on my arms and neck as I was quite sure someone was being murdered. A 6 or 7 foot fence that was brick blocked our view into the property, so I took a running leap and grabbed the top of the fence and in a second came face to face with the screaming that we had responded to.

No police had arrived on scene since we were within a few blocks of the residence. Art asked me what was going on and I had to collect my thoughts in order to articulate what I was observing. It was more dark on that street than I could imagine, perhaps pitch black is a better description. On the ground was a cat and attacking the cat was a large dog, that at the time I could have mistaken for a lion or tiger. However it was a Pit Bull. The screaming was the cat as it was trying to fight for its life.

The dog had somehow seen the cat in the yard and decided to defend its territory by moving in for the kill. The cat, what was left of its will to fight, was doing its best to stop the onslaught of the bigger and far more powerful Pit Bull. I told Art what was happening and just then a Los Angeles Police Department patrol vehicle arrived. Two officers jumped out and came over to the fence. I gave them an update of the misery I was observing and they decided to try and find an entrance into the yard. I remember saying, "You better be careful."

I also asked them to request Animal Regulations to respond to our location and backed that up with our own dispatcher. We stayed around the scene to ensure that the proper notifications were made and then determined if the cat could be helped - which it could not. The cat was deceased.

Neither of us were able to sleep the rest of the night and upon our return to Fire Station 61 we talked about the call. We still talk about that particular response and it has been more than 44 years ago. It is one of those experiences that stays with you and I often think of the cat, the dog, the police officers, how dark the night was and those horrific screams. I also think about each of us concerning that early morning call. It now takes its proper place in our hearts and enters the category of history and legend.

Dog vs Boy

Rescue 105 arrived at the apartment just after noon for a dog bite. What we saw practically turned my stomach; it was gruesome and scary. The boy, about 6 or 7 years of age, had climbed over a fence behind his apartment near Canoga and Saticoy in the San Fernando Valley. The dog, which we could not see nor hear, attacked him immediately and bit him repeatedly in the chest, neck, arms and legs. The boy was lying on the grass, barely conscious and asking for his mother. One look and I realized that his wounds were life-threatening and he was close to death. I asked my partner to call for the police to respond to the emergency because I was concerned that the canine might return. I then opened the starter kit and medical box, quickly reaching for 4x4 pads and lots of them. I proceeded to use my bandage skills to place pressure dressings on his avulsive wounds. I was also cognizant that at any time the dog might decide to pay us a visit. My partner called for the closest engine company for support and told them to bring an ax and load a hose for our own protection. All the while I was setting up oxygen via mask for this child and preparing two intravenous solution (Ringer's Lactate) for volume replacement. I pondered where to start the IV's as both extremities were massively avulsed and the tissue destruction was significant.

The engine company arrived within 3 minutes and was followed by the Los Angeles Police Department, each concerned with scene safety and security for our personnel. Blood was everywhere, and it resembled a meat packing facility; torn flesh is not easy to look at and I was busy doing several things at once. My partner had taken over finding a site for one intravenous infusion while I looked for another. My partner found one on an arm and I placed an IV into his jugular vein. It is hard enough to start a line on someone who is badly injured or very sick and, it seems, the most critical patients are much more difficult due to cardiovascular collapse. This was the case and we knew that large amounts of fluid were needed to ward off hypovolemic shock. Not once did the child complain about anything, but shock can sometimes do that. His color was poor and his pulse was very weak and rapid, his blood pressure was unable to be obtained. We were fighting against time and blood loss. I was convinced that if this child did not get into surgery quickly he would indeed lose his life.

It was one of those calls that we all think about but rarely respond to. An animal bite on the radio brings images to our mind of a simple dog bite with a few teeth marks and maybe broken skin. This was different; even his neck was torn open and chest ripped apart. I couldn't help but wonder why this occurred. Did the boy tease the dog? Had the dog been abused by his owners? Was the dog hungry? The "why questions" kept haunting me and I couldn't stop thinking about what happened.

Fifteen minutes later, our patient was bandaged, breathing oxygen, bleeding was controlled and IV's were running wide open. Blood can be difficult to measure in terms of loss, but in this case I suspected maybe a liter (1,000 cc) loss, as it covered everything and soaked his clothing. Even blood that was starting to coagulate was all over the area. There was little doubt of several factors: the child was critically injured, was in shock, and needed surgery.

A minute later, I was relieved by the fact that he started to talk to me on the way to the hospital. As we zig-zaged through traffic heading for Northridge Medical Center (many years later it would become a trauma center) I listened to the little boy, who asked if his mom was coming. I responded that she would meet us at the hospital and he was in good hands. And then I looked down and realized that I was the hands he was holding.

Six or seven minutes later, we arrived at the hospital and since we had called ahead on the H.E.A.R. system (Hospital Emergency Administrative Radio), the team was waiting for us. I was relieved that other hands would take over and deliver the kind of care this child needed.

The young boy nearly lost his life that day in 1975. Like many thousands of other responses I have gone on, I did not find all of the answers to my many questions about what happened. But to this day, 48 years later, I still think about it, and so many other calls.

Gentle Giant

I was working at Fire Station 105 in the west San Fernando Valley with my partner, Fred Courtney, who was physically big - truly his body was huge, perhaps 6 feet 5 inches. But he had a big heart, friendly, and was quite human, I would discover. We were partners for perhaps a year or slightly longer. I recall his soft approach to patients and his gentle touch and I thought of him as a "gentle giant". We took most of our patients in that geographical area of the city to Parkwood Hospital, a small ER close to the station.

I recall the years as being 1974 through about 1976 where we were paired together. Occasionally when other Rescue Ambulances were busy we would respond into their first-in district and then transport patients to Northridge Hospital or West Park Hospital or even Canoga Park Hospital. Westpark and Canoga were quite small in terms of what services could be performed there.

Those were the last days of psychiatrists and ENT physicians working extra days in the emergency department for extra money. It was quite obvious that they were not used to emergency work as I recall, even sometimes unable to do certain procedures. I recall once at Canoga Park Hospital, the ER physician could not intubate a patient and finally asked me if I would not mind doing it. I said OK and after the procedure was done, he repeatedly thanked me and could not stop congratulating me on a job well done. It was only then that he told me he had not intubated a patient in years. He informed me that his specialty was Psychiatry and he worked extra like many other physicians.

As I write these words it resonates within me that this period of time occurred more than 47 years ago. It seems just like yesterday and all of the visions return to me in black and white, crystal clear.

It was a late afternoon call to a home in Woodland Hills, a ranch-style house and lots of property. What I remember most was the wife and two children crying as they led my partner and me to the back bedroom. It was here that a man in his 30s was dying.

This was before DNR policies were in place and things were a lot less complicated. The father of two was in bed with two IV's running and his wife told me that he was going to die at home and that we did not have to transport him to the hospital. He was pale, thin, and fit the description of emaciated. I looked at my partner and both of us wondered why we were called and what, if anything, we could or should do. I personally wondered why we were even dispatched if the family did not want us to transport. From the looks of the patient, who was in and out of consciousness, his time was running out. I remember feeling terrible that we were unable to do much for him. He already had Morphine "on-board" and there was little left to do but wait for him to die.

I realized we were put into some strange position just staying there but the family did not desire us to take him to the local hospital. I did the appropriate action of calling our base station, which was Northridge Hospital. At the time, I knew that the likelihood of being told to transport to the closest hospital was imminent. I also knew that to sit with the family was to take us out of service for an extended time.

The patient was breathing in an irregular pattern and we recognized that there were periods of apnea associated, which was Cheyne-Stokes breathing, or lack of spontaneous breathing. The wife called her physician and he asked to talk to us. He was very nice on the phone and asked if we could support the family while he drove to the house. He explained that the patient and family wished to have him die at home and he would be there within the hour.

**This call caused considerable anxiety for both my partner and me.
In essence we were violating policy
yet something inside of each of us felt we were doing the right thing.**

The base station nurse asked me to speak directly with the ER Physician so I explained the dilemma we were experiencing. As an emergency ambulance service, we could not be out of service for an extended period of time and we should transport the patient to the closest ER. He understood our policies and indicated that he had spoken with the private physician who was on the staff at Northridge Hospital.

While I did not want to violate policy, we also did not want to abandon the patient and family who needed support then and there. As the Paramedic Attendant in charge of the ambulance, I decided to stay with the dying patient, but did call our dispatcher to try and explain why there was a delay in response and why we would not be transporting our patient.

This call caused considerable anxiety for both my partner and me. In essence we were violating policy yet something inside of each of us felt we were doing the right thing.

NOTE: As I am thinking about this call back in 1975, so long ago, I still feel the same feelings that just crept back into my consciousness. Sometimes in doing what is right, you end up violating some rules and regulations, which we were doing. Yet we were trying to do the right thing for the right reasons - and for this patient's family. These were real people - wife and children and grandparents, in front of us.

As it was, our patient slipped away from this life in front of all of us. He was already on oxygen so we did not administer any. He was medicated with Morphine so we did not administer any. We did not need to suction him nor breathe for him. Everything happened naturally, as was the family's wishes.

As he took his final breaths, I recall to this day that he opened his eyes for a few seconds and appeared to be looking around the room and at us. As strange as it sounds, there was a sense of calm in the room as his wife and children told him how much they loved him.

The private physician arrived after his death and was calming and reassuring to the family. He approached my partner and me and thanked us for not transporting him to a local ER where nothing could have been done.

We were emotionally drained after this particular call. We are trained to take action and treat patients - not sit and observe them die. But it seemed to both of us at the time that our patients were actually the family, who seems to need us more than the dying patient.

As we drove back to the station, we did not talk much. Perhaps retrospectively, we should have for it is times like these that great lessons of life (and death) are learned. I have thought about this call for four decades but never wrote about it until now.

It would be decades later that DNR policies and then most recently POLST and Hospice and Palliative Care Policies would become a reality. But back then we did not have such things and paid the price with our emotions which became fragile. I, for one, became a strong advocate for DNR, POLST and Palliative Care because of my experiences.

My partner and I became friends and enjoyed working together, and I will never forget his sensitivity and calm during this call. I was never the same after this response. It had a profound effect on me that I still mirror today.

Homeless Man

I happened to be monitoring EMS and Fire radio traffic from my office on the 10th floor of City Hall East in Fire Department Headquarters when a rescue ambulance called for a supervisor to respond to their location for a field problem. There was a delay in response by the EMS supervisor and as a result I contacted my Assistant Bureau Commander to follow up and asked for a full set of reports from all concerned. When a rescue ambulance anywhere in our system asks for a Field Supervisor I expect it will happen promptly. In this case it did not.

The ambulance had been dispatched to the 300 block of north La Brea Avenue to "an unknown problem" with a person down. This ambulance was configured as an "800 Series" ambulance which meant it was generally an EMT level ambulance operated by two firefighters. In this case it was staffed by a firefighter/paramedic and an EMT. Nevertheless, they had requested assistance and guidance from an EMS Supervisor and should have obtained it immediately.

When Rescue Ambulance 861 arrived on scene, they found a male adult transient, awake and verbally oriented and without complaints. However, further examination by the crew revealed that the patient was literally covered with several hundred larval insects, likely maggots. The infestation appeared to be covering most of his skin and clothing. No lesions or infections were identified on patient's body. In fact, the patient appeared completely unconcerned about this situation and EMS personnel also noted he was next to a shopping cart with his personal belongings; the cart was full of clothing, rotting food and a four-gallon bucket of what appeared to the crew to be fecal matter and urine. Additionally, two other shopping carts were in the possession of the patient, also filled with more four-gallon buckets of the same substances. The patient's personal hygiene was apparently part of what the shopping carts were used for.

It was obvious that the patient was unable to care for himself and thus the ambulance crew had called for direction.

The ambulance crew poorly documented their assessment and what they found on the appropriate F-902M report. The ambulance personnel did not perform a complete secondary assessment of the patient. The ambulance crew indicated on their reports that they called for the EMS Supervisor to assist them with a person with a health and sanitation problem. The supervisor, according to his written report and interview, was in the shower at the fire station and had answered his business phone. After speaking with the OCD dispatcher from the communications center, the EMS Supervisor acknowledged the dispatch then asked OCD to put him "en route" to the incident. At the same time the supervisor told the dispatcher that he would contact the ambulance on Channel 10 via radio to give advice to the crew. A moment later, the EMS Supervisor received an audio alarm at the fire station that included that they would place EMS 4 en route.

Instead of getting into his emergency sedan and contacting the crew on the radio, the EMS Supervisor used his office radio to contact the ambulance asking RA (Rescue Ambulance) 861 what they had. The crew at the scene of the event described in detail what they had encountered: the homeless person with three shopping carts, the rotting food, and the infestation of maggots. They were clear to explain they had encountered a serious public health problem, due to the proximity of the patient to lots of pedestrian traffic and a current placement problem. The EMS Supervisor inquired as to the status of the patient and transport destination. The ambulance indicated to the EMS Supervisor that the patient had no complaints and they could not leave him unattended and leave the scene.

Nearly three hours later, a captain and firefighter/lead paramedic from the QIS (Quality Improvement Section) arrived on scene.

The EMS Supervisor responded with a question, "If he has no complaints and you are not transporting, what is the problem?" The crew responded on the radio that they had a serious health problem at the location, since people were starting to gather in the area and that he had "maggots all over him". They added that the patient was constantly referring to his bucket contents as "gravy". The EMS Supervisor then asked, "Is there a problem with the patient?" The response by the crew was, "OK, there is no problem with the patient, but can you advise us who to contact, maybe the Department of Health Services or someone from Social Services". The crew repeated that they did not feel comfortable leaving the scene and leaving the person there alone. The EMS Supervisor then asked the crew for their address and told them he was still in quarters. He further stated he was ready to go to a meeting but could contact DHS and let them route it through to the appropriate agency and Los Angeles Police Department. Additional conversations continued between the ambulance crew and EMS Supervisor for well over two hours.

Thirty minutes later the ambulance crew asks EMS 4 if telephone numbers are available yet. The response by the EMS Supervisor is that he is on the line and to hold on. Approximately thirty-six minutes later, Rescue Ambulance, a Paramedic Unit, then requests the dispatcher to attach itself to the incident. Rescue had also requested LAPD respond to the incident. Nearly an hour had passed and EMS 1 (EMS Supervisor) offers to respond to the scene of the incident.

Finally, over two hours after the initial dispatch of Rescue 861, EMS 1 arrived on scene. Members of the LAPD SMART Team (Field Psychiatric Evaluation Team) took the patient into protective custody. Department of Street Maintenance personnel took possession of the patient's personal belongings, including three insect-infested shopping carts.

Nearly three hours later, a captain and firefighter/lead paramedic from the QIS (Quality Improvement Section) arrived on scene. Additional units from the LAPD provided security for the buckets of human bio-waste remaining on the sidewalk while Los Angeles County Health Haz-Mat arrived to take possession of the waste.

I directed that an investigation be initiated as the result of violations of the Department's Rules and Regulations. In this case the rescue ambulance tried to properly handle this call, but the EMS Supervisor failed in several ways to handle this response and did, in fact, violate the rules of the Los Angeles Fire Department.

Dump Truck Sand

Perhaps the worst EMS call I ever went on was in 1975, when I was working out of Fire Station 71 at Beverly Glen and Sunset in Bel Air. We got a call to Bottlebrush Drive, up one of the canyon roads in a nice neighborhood just off Beverly Glen. When my partner, Tom Gilmartin, and I arrived, people were screaming and yelling and directing us down the street to a house that was under construction. One of the workers had been operating the largest dump truck full of sand I had ever seen and had emptied out the wet sand, when something happened with the hydraulics. The driver got inside the framework to see what was wrong, when the bucket came down and completely flattened him. He screamed for a few seconds, until it came down the rest of the way and finished him. It's one of the worst things I've ever seen. Tom and I talked about it years later, and he told me it was the only call he ever puked on. I remember having to use three sheets to cover the guy because he was like liquid - the pneumatic press even crushed his bones.

Freddie Prinze

Another call I'll never forget was for actor Freddie Prinze. I was at the same station on Beverly and my partner and I responded to a little apartment building on Wilshire and Beverly Glen. When we walked into what looked like a hotel, I knew immediately it was either Freddie Prinze or Tony Orlando. The call came in as a shooting - Prinze had put the gun to his head and pulled the trigger. He was still alive, so we utilized a BVM (bag-valve-mask device) and covered his face to protect his identity from the photographer who had followed us. I remember how swollen and distorted his face was, and I kept wondering with all he had going for him why he would do such a thing. When we got to the hospital about 4AM, he was breathing on his own, although erratically, and the ER team continued oxygen and bored into his skull to evacuate a large hematoma. In spite of all they did, he died about 6AM.

Motorcycle vs Auto

It was a sunny day on a July afternoon when Rescue Ambulance 71 responded to Sunset Boulevard above the San Diego Freeway (405) where a motorcycle vs. an automobile collided. It is an overpass perched above the very busy freeway below. While it was like thousands of other calls I have handled, a few things made me never forget this particular response. First, high above the freeway below gave me a weird sensation as I could almost feel the movement of the "bridge". While it is solid and perfectly safe, nevertheless it gives me pause when I am on a bridge or over water or anywhere that poses a risk. As a field paramedic beginning in 1974, I tried hard to have what has become known as situational awareness. All it takes is a slip, a psychotic patient or a number of other things that can result in tragedy in a heartbeat. Scene safety and security has been a hallmark in my career and as a college professor teaching EMT.

It was apparent that he lost a huge amount of blood from the arterial injury and it was bright red, almost the brightest I had ever seen.

In this case, a male about 20 years of age, on a motorcycle, was weaving in and out of traffic when he misjudged a single car. It hit him head-on and as I arrived from the east it became apparent that this was a serious event with significant injuries. The patient, who was not wearing a helmet (in the 1970s there was no helmet law in effect nor had it even been considered) and suffered major head injures, to include an open skull fracture, with skull contents on the street. He also had an artery injury in the upper arm. It was apparent that he lost a huge amount of blood from the arterial injury and it was bright red, almost the brightest I had ever seen. My partner and I had our hands full with things to do and with the assistance of Engine Company 71 we went to work. Traffic was stopped and law enforcement were tending to traffic control and groups of people who were covering their eyes after taking a glimpse of our patient. He was, as they say, "hurtin' for certain" and his life was both coming out of his skull and his arm. I was surprised that no one had taken any steps to assist him and just were crowding around waiting for the Rescue Ambulance to arrive.

Those were the early days of the Paramedic program so even an intravenous infusion required base station contact. This was a 'scoop and run' type of call back then but a few things needed to be done: we carefully bandaged the massive head wound and used direct pressure to abate the blood loss. High-flow oxygen was administered since the patient was breathing on his own. I did hyperventilate this young man en route to the hospital. He also sustained bi-lateral femoral fractures and major chest and abdominal injuries. Two IV's were established: one in the good and viable arm and the other in the jugular vein. We poured in at least two liters of Ringers Lactate (Hartman's Solution) to replace the massive blood loss and used a backboard to lift him onto the gurney. Tom Gilmarton was my driver and he rocketed us to UCLA which was a couple of miles away. Tom was an excellent ambulance driver, one of the few who I truly enjoyed working with. I was so comfortable with his driving skills that I could read a newspaper and not even look up. I trusted his judgement.

In the patient compartment of the ambulance, l continued hyperventilating this young man and ensured his airway, while at the same time monitoring his EKG and was ready to do whatever was necessary for him. Within 5 minutes of driving time we arrived at the ER and quickly put our patient in a treatment room. A team of physicians and neurosurgeon were immediately called into the room and took over care. What makes me remember this call so vividly are several things: the bridge over the freeway, the nature of his injuries, seeing his brains on the street and elsewhere, the redness of the arterial bleed, the stark realization that this young man was losing his life - and that his life was in my hands albeit for a short time. I was acutely cognizant that my actions and those of my partner and engine company personnel would have a significant impact on his possible survival.

Sometimes, you just know things are not going to turn out well and this was one of those times. It was also one of those calls where you do things quickly and accurately and realize that time is running out. In this case the motorcyclist lost his life a few days later despite the care he received by the best specialists. I will not forget this young man!

Resurrection Case

On May 15, 1986 at 3:21PM, Rescue Ambulance 91 responded with Engine 91 to an address on Olden Street in Pacoima for a reported overdose. The patient, a 63 year old man, was in his workshed to tinker with his radios but did not come in when his wife called him for dinner. His wife indicated that he would lock himself in his shed and she was unable to get the door open.

Engine 91 made a forced entry into the workshed and discovered the patient bent over a table. According to the paramedics, the patient looked pale and was cold to the touch. One of the paramedics checked for a pulse but did not feel one. It was reported that the patient had rigor mortis (stiffness of death) and his pupils were dry, glassed over and unresponsive to light.

The junior paramedic went to the ambulance to obtain the EKG machine but when he returned, the other paramedic told him that he did not need the scope as the patient had rigor mortis. The lead paramedic determined this by moving the patient's arm and the upper torso moved because it was stiff. The patient was pronounced dead at 3:35PM.

The paramedics told the wife that her husband was dead. The Los Angeles Police Department arrived at the location and the paramedics informed the officer that they had a dead body. They led the officer into the workshed and viewed the deceased.

The Rescue Ambulance cleared the scene and returned to Fire Station 91 and at 5:21PM received an alarm to return to the same address for a reported seizure. Upon arrival, the officer met the ambulance outside the residence and told the paramedics that the patient was breathing. The paramedics put their EKG scope on the patient and found him to be in a bradycardia of 38 beats per minute. The patient was placed on the gurney and put into the ambulance. Contact was made with their Base Station and they were advised to start an intravenous infusion of Ringers Lactate and administer 50cc of Dextrose and 0.8mg of Naloxone (Narcan).

The first intravenous attempt was unsuccessful so they began transporting the patient and en route the intravenous was successful and the medications were administered. The patient was transported to Holy Cross Hospital and arrived at 5:42PM. The paramedics requested a Paramedic Supervisor respond to the hospital.

The patient's mouth was moving slowly and the deputy coroner pulled a wad of chewing tobacco from the patient's throat, whereupon he began breathing again.

After the paramedics left the residence the first time, a deputy coroner arrived at 5:10PM, and while examining him thumped his back. The patient's mouth was moving slowly and the deputy coroner pulled a wad of chewing tobacco from the patient's throat whereupon he began breathing again.

The wife of the patient spent approximately 2 hours thinking her husband was deceased only to be told by the police officer, after telling her to sit down, that he had something to tell her. "Your husband is alive."

The wife said she did not know how she felt and was unable to grasp the situation until later.

Ironically, in an article in the *Daily News Local* on Sunday, May 18, 1986, the wife praised the efforts of the two paramedics who pronounced her husband dead, saying she believed the two paramedics did everything they could have even though a deputy coroner later revived the man. The hospital later reported that the patient was in stable and improving condition after his brush with death.

The Los Angeles Fire Department suspended the two paramedics from field ambulance duty. Two separate investigations were conducted: one by the fire department and the other by Los Angeles County Department of Health Services.

Fire Chief Donald O. Manning stated he could not recall another case like this one ever happening.

This is one medical mistake that, while gravely serious, turned out for the better. As a result of this case, Los Angeles County EMS Agency now requires that an EKG be taken for at least one minute to confirm that the patient is indeed deceased.

Dr. Charles McElroy

I was at UCLA Medical Center after taking a patient there around 1978 and one of our other Rescue Ambulances, Rescue 5 brought in a gentleman from Los Angeles International Airport (LAX) who had been in Africa. He was very ill and one of his legs was three times the size of the other one. He had edema which was the worst I had ever seen in my career and I could not help but wonder if he had elephantiasis, which is chronic pitting lymphedema of the lower extremity. I had seen photos in medical books showing individuals with huge unilateral massive legs and also scrotums. Certain microorganisms are spread by mosquitoes and infected larvae migrate to the lymphatic system where they develop into threadlike adult worms within 6 to 12 months. Gravid adult females produce microfilariae that circulate in the blood. These filariasis are present in Africa, Asia, the Pacific and the Americas including Haiti and Southeast Asia. As of 1978 worldwide, more than 100 million people were infected.

This middle aged man looked as if he was going to die in the next 5 minutes; shocky, pale and diaphoretic and emaciated except for the huge leg. I recall hearing an intern yell out to have a tropical disease specialist get to the ER.

I had been to a continuing education lecture given by the Emergency Room Director, Dr. Charles McElroy, who I believed to be one of the most prominent physicians at UCLA. He was the doctor that doctors went to when they became ill. I had been talking to him when we both entered the main ER. He observed what was going on, with nurses and resident physicians running around trying to figure out what was wrong with this man. There appeared to be no one in charge and everyone was literally running around; an IV was being prepared, but no one seemed to be the leader of the team. That changed rather quickly.

Dr. McElroy suddenly got everyone's attention and asked who was in charge. One of the residents answered him and gave an update that the patient had just been picked up by Rescue Ambulance 5 at LAX - did not have additional information but he had called a tropical medicine specialist. I remember Chuck very loudly saying, 'People, let's get back to basics". He then started barking out orders such as blood work, vital signs, X-Ray of the chest. He also did not interfere with the medical personnel but rather guided them through this critical situation. He was Professor of Medicine at UCLA and the Director of the ER.

After the X-Ray was taken, he called me over to the view box and asked me what I saw unusual. I immediately noticed the size of his heart to be nearly double, so I answered cardiomegaly. He said, "Why?" I said, "I am not sure!"

He then ordered everyone to step back and ordered a 50cc syringe and very long needle. You could hear a pin drop in that ER area when he stepped over to the patient and talked with him very quietly and asked that a heart monitor be set up. The patient was in and out of consciousness and was having a considerably hard time breathing. It was obvious to me and everyone else in the room, physicians, nurses, paramedics and EMTs as well as the X-Ray operator and lab personnel that Chuck was about to do a procedure but as of yet no one knew what it was.

It was the first time I had watched a pericardiocentesis. This man was about to die and a true emergency existed. You hear about seconds counting and near-death but this was the real deal and it was happening in front of all of us. Chuck was about to treat a case of Cardiac Tamponade by taking the 16 guage needle and inserting it sub-xiphoid into the pericardial sac. Obviously, there is great danger and challenges when doing a procedure such as this but one needed to weigh those factors against not doing it and losing the patient.

I observed Chuck ever so carefully, push the needle into the pericardial sac and apply suction to the syringe by pulling back on it slightly. White and yellow pus suddenly filled the 50cc syringe and this occurred four times as it was repeated without moving the needle. It seemed surreal at the time - both exhilaration and fear filled the room as this patient's life hung in the balance. No one spoke, everyone watched. I observed the procedure but also the patient's face and reaction. After 200ccs were removed from this patient's pericardial sac, I observed him breathing easier and slower, and he made the comment, "I can breath now".

After the procedure and the patient was moved upstairs to the medical wing of the hospital, Chuck gathered everyone who was present and talked about the case. He did not dwell on what was done wrong as much as keeping an organized and methodical examination. He talked about how jumping to conclusions was not in keeping with a good assessment. Additionally, he said the chest X-Ray confirmed his diagnosis and he was certain that the only treatment to save this patient's life was an emergency pericardiocentesis. He had a very serious infection that had spread to his heart and caused this problem, but, most important, and a lesson to all those present that day, was to do a complete full-body assessment, vital signs, and chest X-Ray.

It was my impression that Dr. Charles McElroy, alone, saved this man's life. It is easy to get rattled on some difficult cases but this case-in-point is a lesson given so that we, as field providers, can learn to do the job better in the future. This was one of the most interesting cases I ever saw in my career and would tell this story to my EMT students each semester over and over again through the years as an example of staying focused on your assessment.

The patient was admitted to the hospital for three weeks receiving treatment before being released to go home. He completely recovered.

Long QT Syndrome

As the Commander of the Emergency Services Department I managed and supervised all aspects of the Paramedic Program within the Los Angeles Fire Department. It was not unusual, in fact common, for many different projects to be ongoing/concurrently happening.

The Prince family were forced to endure the death of their daughter, Cory, perhaps the saddest and most tragic event anyone can experience.

One day, a Captain from our Arson Section of the Department asked my secretary, Cathy Chin, if he could make an appointment with me. The Captain, Roy Prince, sat down in my office and told me a horrific story about his daughter, Cory, who at 24 years of age died suddenly in her kitchen while obtaining a bottle of milk for her daughter, Kaitlyn. It was later that afternoon that her husband would find her. What took her life was something known as the "Long QT Syndrome". The Prince family were forced to endure the death of their daughter, perhaps the saddest and most tragic event anyone can experience. The unexpected and sudden death of a loved one is shocking; when it is a child or young adult it is devastating.

Captain Prince asked me if I, as the Paramedic Chief, would write an article about this medical malady called the Long QT Syndrome in order to illuminate the subject so other parents would not have go through this pain and grief as the Prince family did. Having not been familiar with this syndrome I agreed to research it and write an article in memory of Cory. This was a project that I was not familiar with and started the next day to research it. Much of the reading and digging up information on this subject was done at home as I had a full schedule every day at Fire Department headquarters.

I titled the article, "The Long QT Syndrome, Remembering Cory Prince" and it was accepted for publication by *The California Fire Service News* in 2000. In order to find out additional information about this congenital disorder, I contacted an organization called the SADS, which stand for Sudden Arrhythmia Death Syndromes. They were extremely helpful as I progressed with the research and ultimate article.

Dr. G. Michael Vincent was President and Medical Director of the Foundation for the study of sudden arrhythmia death syndromes in children and young adults and believes that unfamiliarity of physicians contributes to the low number of Long QT Syndrome patient diagnoses. Long QT Syndrome, he stated, may be, in reality, as common among the nation's population as muscular dystrophy.

THE SAD FACTS:
The cause of Cory's untimely and tragic death is a congenital disorder associated with a high incidence of sudden death. It is an inherited disorder of the heart's electrical system that causes rapid and irregular heartbeat which leads to syncopal episodes.

continues on page 144...

Reprinted from the July, 2000 *California Fire Service News*

The Long QT syndrome

Remembering Cory Prince

BY ALAN R. COWEN, MA, EMT-P

"And then I think of one who in her youthful beauty died,
The fair, meek blossom that grew up and faded by my side:
In the cold moist earth we laid her, when the forest cast the leaf
And we wept that one so lovely should have a life so brief:
Yet not unmeet it was that one, like that young friend of ours,
So gentle and so beautiful, should perish with the flowers."

--*From The Death of the Flowers*
William Cullen Bryant

At 24, Cory Prince was a proud mother of her baby Kaitlyn. It was March 5, 1989 when Cory suddenly died in her kitchen while obtaining a bottle for Kaitlyn. It would be later that afternoon when her horrified husband would find her. Long QT Syndrome had taken away yet another of a long list.

The Prince family had to endure the death of their daughter – perhaps the saddest and most tragic event anyone can experience. The unexpected and sudden death of a loved one is shocking; when it is a child or young adult it is devastating.

The Sad Facts:

The cause of Cory's untimely and tragic death is a congenital disorder associated with a high incidence of sudden death called Long QT Syndrome (LQTS). Long QT Syndrome is an inherited disorder of the hearts electrical system that causes rapid and irregular heartbeat which leads to syncopal episodes with abnormal heart rhythm, and if the duration lasts for several minutes, death. It is recognized on ECG by an abnormally long interval called a prolonged QT interval. Frequently, the abnormality is not identified and a missed diagnosis results.

Dr. G. Michael Vincent, President and Medical Director of the Foundation for the study of sudden Arrhythmia Death Syndromes in Children and young adults believes that unfamiliarity by physicians contributes to the low number of Long QT Syndrome patient diagnoses. Long QT Syndrome, he says, may in reality, be as common among the nations populations as muscular dystrophy, which affects 30,000 Americans.

Long QT Syndrome once thought to be rare, is currently being recognized more frequently. This is due to the condition being publicized, and awareness by medical practitioners. People who have it appear to be healthy, normal individuals with no obvious abnormalities of the heart, neither structural nor mechanical. In fact, frequently only the presentation of a prolongation of the QT interval is observed on the electrocardiogram.

Paramedics who work in the field setting may be able to identify prolongation of the QT interval and the arrhythmias that do not infrequently accompany the syndrome.

The EKG is the single method currently available to diagnose Long QT Syndrome, specifically the accurate measurement of the QT interval. This, unfortunately, is not a simple matter, as each EKG is quite specific to an individual. It is quite difficult to determine just where the "T" wave ends. This is all the more difficult when "U" waves are present; as in some tachycardias where the "T" wave appears to coincide with the following "P" waves. Even with an adequate view of the QT interval, the exact measurement must be ascertained after taking into consideration the individuals heart rate and gender.

Practitioners who are experienced in diagnosing the Long QT Syndrome consider other factors for confirming a diagnosis. These include other EKG findings, family history, syncopal episodes, cardiac arrests and other family members with the syndrome.

Some other characteristics that can be looked for when suspecting Long QT Syndrome are bradyarrhythmias, large-notch "T" waves that enlarge with exercise, particularly in Leads V1 to V3, and QT intervals that do not shorten normally with exercise. "T" wave Alternans is an infrequently seen anomaly of the syndrome.

Paramedics can find themselves in the role of noticing EKG characteristics that can assist in increasing awareness to identify patients who are at risk.

First described in Europe in the late 1950's,

CONTINUED ON NEXT PAGE

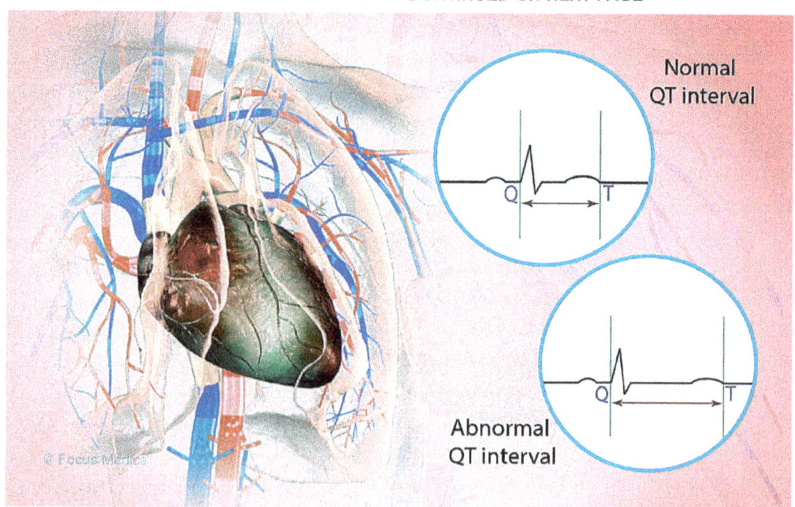

CONTINUED FROM PREVIOUS PAGE

Long QT Syndrome was little known; as such, few cardiologists could hope to recognize it. It was 1973 when Dr. G. Michael Vincent, a cardiologist and instructor at the University of Utah School of Medicine, began researching the death of a woman. Dr. Vincent began to recognize and understand something no one before him had. He began to unravel a medical mystery that had eluded many physicians. People had died suddenly, but nothing could be ascertained as to why. Post-mortem examinations revealed no abnormalities; nothing unusual with the heart.

It is extraordinary people, like Dr. Vincent, that add to that great body of medical knowledge that has been compiled since early medicine men began keeping records. The men and women physicians of today continue to learn from their medicinal ancestors of yesteryear.

Dr. Vincent tested family members of the women who had died making a dramatic discovery – there was a correlation, a familial link to the deaths. In fact, some members of the family had died very young. Descendents of the original family (named Christiansen) were spread all over – the family tree was broad.

Due to Dr. Vincent's work throughout the 1970's and 1980's, Long QT Syndrome groups/researchers were being organized in various countries. Long QT Syndrome was on the map, becoming known throughout the medical literature.

In one family reunion in 1986, Long QT researcher Katherine Timothy was present and administered 42 EKG's in one day. Over a dozen members of the family had Long QT Syndrome confirmed.

With the assistance of molecular geneticist Ray White and Mark Leppert, of the University of Utah School of Medicine, and project leader cardiologist Mark Keating, a study of the DNA images began. Dr. Keating was searching for evidence of a pattern on DNA bands that was specific to Long QT carriers, and thus proof positive that it was a hereditary syndrome.

More than a year passed after evaluating hundreds of DNA fragments without success. Then without warning, in November of 1990 Dr. Keating struck pay dirt. He had finally proved that Long QT Syndrome was hereditary in nature.

Today, it is known that four genetic defects exist that cause Long QT Syndrome. In future years it is likely that a blood test can be a screening point for Long QT Syndrome at infancy.

In Salt Lake City there exists the Sudden Arrhythmia Death Syndromes (SADS) Foundation. By 1992 a hotline was receiving thousands of calls yearly. Dr. Michael Vincent, a pioneer, has added to that host of medical knowledge to help future doctors who will take the place of those who practice today – tomorrow.

For additional information on Long QT Syndrome call the SADS Hotline at 1-800-STOP SAD or on the Internet at http://www.sads.org

This story has been told for Cory ... May she rest in peace.

Be careful out there ... ARC

References

"Inherited Long QT Syndrome," G. Michael Vincent, Cardiac Arrhythmias, J.B. Lippincott Co., 1995

"The Long QT Syndrome, Prospective Longitudinal Study of 328 Families," G. Michael Vincent, Circulation, 1991

"Looking For Long QT," Elizabeth Charuvastra, R.N., RN Times

"Sudden Arrhythmia Death Syndrome," (SADS) 1997

Deputy Fire Chief Alan R. Cowen, Los Angeles City Fire Department, served as the Commander of the department's Bureau of Human Resources. He is the former Paramedic Chief and Commander of the Bureau of Emergency Medical Services. Chief Cowen is a 31-year veteran of the fire service and has been a Licensed Paramedic for 26 years. He has earned a B.A., M.A., and Doctorate Degree. He is a member of the EMS Committee, and retied in 1998.

The author wishes to thank Roy and Joan Prince and especially Kaitlyn for permission for the privilege of writing this article.

The California Fire Service News, published six times a year by CSFA since 1927, is the state's only statewide Fire Service trade journal.

CSFA members receive the digital magazine as part of their membership, and a controlled print mailing is also sent to over 2700 fire stations throughout California. Readership exceeds 15,000.

Long QT Syndrome, once thought to be rare, is currently being recognized as being much more frequent. This is due to the publicity surrounding the condition and new awareness by medical practitioners. Persons who have it appear to be healthy, normal individuals with no obvious abnormalities of the heart, neither structural nor mechanical. In fact, frequently only the presentation of a prolongation of the QT interval is observed on electrocardiogram. Paramedics who work in the field setting may be able to identify prolongation of the QT interval and the arrhythmias that do not infrequently accompany the syndrome.

The EKG is the single method currently available to diagnose Long QT Syndrome, specifically the accurate measurement of the QT interval. This, unfortunately, is not a simple matter, as each EKG is quite specific to an individual. It is quite difficult to determine just where the "T" wave ends. This is all the more difficult when "U" waves are present; as in some tachycardias where the "T" wave appears to coincide with the following "P" waves. Even with an adequate view of the QT interval, the exact measurement must be ascertained after taking into consideration the individual's heart rate and gender.

Practitioners who are experienced in diagnosing the Long QT Syndrome consider other factors for confirming a diagnosis. These include other EKG findings, family history, syncopal episodes, cardiac arrests and other family members with the syndrome.

Paramedics can find themselves in the role of noticing EKG characteristics that can assist in increasing awareness to identify patients who are at risk.

First described in Europe in the late 1950s, Long QT Syndrome was little known and, as such, few cardiologists could hope to recognize it. It was 1973 when Dr. G. Michael Vincent, a cardiologist and instructor at the University of Utah School of Medicine, began researching the death of a woman. Dr.

Cory Prince: Long QT Syndrome

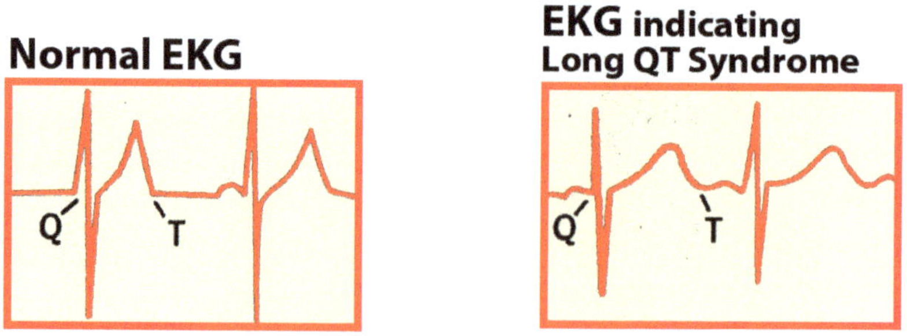

Normal EKG

Q T

EKG indicating Long QT Syndrome

Q T

This story has been re-told in the memory of Cory Prince.
May her family continue to find peace knowing that this painful loss contributed greatly to diagnosis and treatment for so many individuals and families nationwide.

Vincent began to recognize and understand something no one before him had. Thus he began to unravel a medical mystery that had eluded many physicians. People had died suddenly, but nothing could be ascertained as to why. Post-mortem examinations revealed no abnormalities; nothing unusual with the heart.

It is extraordinary people, like Dr. Vincent, that add to the great body of medical knowledge that has been compiled since keeping records began. The physicians of today continue to learn from the medical ancestors of yesteryear.

Due to Dr. Vincent's work throughout the 1970s and 1980s, Long QT Syndrome groups/researchers were being organized in various countries. Long QT Syndrome was on the map and becoming known throughout the medical literature.

In Salt Lake City, there exists the Sudden Arrhythmia Death Syndromes (SADS) Foundation. By 1992 a hotline was receiving thousands of calls yearly. Dr. Vincent, a pioneer, added greatly to the host of medical knowledge to help future medical personnel take the place of those who practice today.

Laurel & Hardy

Ever since I was 4 or 5 years of age I enjoyed the famous comedians, Laurel and Hardy. You know, the tall, skinny guy named Stan Laurel and the portly guy named Oliver Hardy. It has been said that we ought to truly analyze humor, perhaps the anatomy of humor, but in the case of Laurel and Hardy we should look at the humor of Anatomy: the poor skinny guy who played the bumbling yet innocent victim and the harsher Oliver Norvel Hardy, the "smarter one", who was the brains of the two. They were so innocent and lovable that l was absolutely fixated upon both of them. To me there will never be another Laurel and Hardy and l have loved them deeply for more than 70 years. I have seen every film they ever made and continue to "belly laugh" at the same skits and gags over and over again. They were the greatest comedy team that ever lived. They now belong to the ages.

Oliver Hardy and Stan Laurel

The following is a true story that occurred shortly before I retired in 1998.

This involves Joe and Jessie Ortiz, two lively figures on the Los Angeles Fire Department, who devoted their careers to Emergency Medical Services. These two funny brothers (though not nearly as funny as Laurel and Hardy) had a reputation that stills exists on our great LAFD. For whatever reason, these two guys loved Laurel and Hardy probably as much as I did and perhaps it goes way back into the 1960s when Joe worked for an ambulance company that was called Professional Ambulance Co. It was owned by a gentleman and actor by the name of Rand Brooks, who, among other programs, acted on "Rin Tin Tin". "Rin Tin Tin" was a German Shepard and it dealt with his adventures. Rand Brooks at one time was married to Lois Laurel, who happened to be the daughter of Stan Laurel. I knew her as Lois Laurel and Lois Brooks.

Joe Ortiz worked as an ambulance driver for Professional Ambulance and got to know Lois quite well. The reason there is a story behind this relationship is because around 1969, Joe took the Civil Service Test given by the City of Los Angeles and joined the Central Receiving Hospital Ambulance Corp. These ambulances became known as the "Brown Bombers" and ruled the streets of Los Angeles for many years. They got their name because they were stationed out of Georgia Street Receiving Hospital. Crews worked out of LAPD stations until July 1, 1970 whereupon they were all transferred to the Los Angeles Fire Department by the action of the City Council.

Joe and Jessie were affectionately known as the "Burrito Brothers" and became legendary due to some of the pranks they played on other members in their respective fire stations. At some point in time, of which I cannot be certain, they actually became partners, if not on a regular schedule, then occasionally. On one occasion, I became a witness to one of their stunts.

I was the Paramedic Chief for the LAFD from 1987 until about 1995 when I became a Deputy Fire Chief. I am unable to tell exactly when the incident happened but I suspect in the early 1990s. I was leaving Fire Department headquarters and was walking down Main Street southbound heading to meet someone for lunch. As it happened, I heard a siren in the distance that grew in intensity and so it was an opportunity for me to observe one of our ambulances while on an emergency response. I very frequently managed by being in the field setting and personally observing our personnel engaged in EMT and Paramedic skills. My eyes spotted some red lights far in the distance on Main Street approaching my location. It has been my habit that if I saw defensive driving techniques and the ambulance stopped at the intersections as per policy, I would drop a note to my Assistant Bureau Commander and have him send an "atta-boy" signed by me to the crew's EMS Captain for inclusion into their personnel file. It was another way to help evaluate performance. On the other hand, if I saw an ambulance driving too fast or doing something outside of our polices and procedures, then the letter might well be a Notice to Correct Deficiencies (F-1104). No one wanted an F-1104.

As the ambulance got closer, I noted that the crew stopped as is required at the red light and then carefully entered the intersection as they were looking first to the right, then left and then right again as they cleared the area. As they approached me mid-block, I was startled by what I saw: both the driver and attendant were wearing Laurel and Hardy masks. They were absolutely perfect and colorful masks of the great Laurel and Hardy. It seemed as though time stopped for a moment as I did a double take on what occurred. I could not stop laughing and at the same time recognizing that a complaint might be lodged by someone who saw what happened. After all, an ambulance traveling Code-3 should be a serious thing one would think. I pondered the question over lunch and had a good belly laugh.

I knew in a heartbeat it was the Ortiz brothers. Only they would perpetrate such an event as this and target me. I also knew that they did not know I would be walking along Main Street and that was mere happenstance. They obviously recognized me in uniform and probably thought about what they were going to do and then did it. I also knew that those masks were probably used frequently but had never received a complaint. I saw them both at a Laurel and Hardy meeting of the Sons of the Desert (the official fan club with "tents" all over the world) that still to this day I attend. In fact, I saw Joe Ortiz at the Sons of the Desert Meeting some time ago and we sat together. To this day we still attend meetings and enjoy and laugh at the gags I am sure will continue as long as possible.

What is ironic was that Joe told me that he and Jessie utilized their masks several times on calls they responded to, with positive results. In the case he mentioned specifically, the ambulance was sent to a "fight call" with the police, and the ambulance arrived prior to the LAPD. Both he and Jessie saw the fight in progress and by exiting the ambulance with their Laurel and Hardy masks on, noted that the fighters immediately ceased their fighting and began laughing hysterically. The crew, by their actions, averted what could have resulted in serious injures.

Comedy to the Rescue

Crowd Control as related by Joe and Jessie Ortiz

On an October afternoon in 1983, my partner Jessie, and I were working on Reserve Rescue 14, out of Fire Station 11, which is located just west of downtown Los Angeles. It was about 3:30PM. The fire company were all out and I was in the office completing some incident reports. My partner was restocking the ambulance unit.

Suddenly there was a banging on the apparatus doors and the doorbell began ringing over and over. Jessie and I rush to the front doors and find a 20-year-old Hispanic woman yelling and pointing down the street. After calming her down we learned that there was a big fight around the corner on Bonnie Brae Street. She told us there were several people injured.

Jessie and I jumped into the rescue unit and proceeded to the location. As we approached the scene, we observed approximately 25 individuals fighting each other with tire irons, sticks and knives. Some of the people were bloody and the scene was out of control. It looked like a war zone. LAPD was immediately requested: "A Back Up Call!" The fighting continued. Jessie attempted to stop the fighting by shouting "Alto! Alto!" (Stop! Stop!) in Spanish over the rescue unit's PA system. It seemed like forever waiting for the police back up.

It then came to me that we had in the rescue unit a pair of Laurel and Hardy masks, not department-issue, which we had purchased earlier in the day, for an upcoming Halloween Party. My partner, Jessie, who is my brother, and I put them on.

A few moments later, a bloody-faced man began yelling "El Gordo y el Flaco, el Gordo y el Flaco" which means "Look, Laurel and Hardy". Jessie and I were going through the Laurel and Hardy motions. People started laughing, we kept up the routine for a few minutes, more people started laughing, and the fighting stopped.

A few minutes later police units began arriving with red lights and sirens. Police officers approached with guns drawn only to find people sitting on the ground laughing.

It wasn't long before all the police officers were laughing too. One veteran LAPD sergeant, shaking his head and smiling, said, "Just when you think you've seen it all."

A few weeks after the incident, a Rampart Division officer sent me this photo.

Joe and Jessie Ortiz use quick thinking in a potentially volatile situation.

Echoes of  Service

Paramedic Chief, Alan Cowen, at Press Conference

Fire Chief William R. Bamattre

20 year Pin for Captain Paramedic

Chief Cowen with Paramedic Michelle Banks

Beverly Simms, my secretary from 1986-1990

Cathy Chin, my secretary from 1990-1998

The City of Los Angeles honors and respects the standards set by the LAFD. In my years of service I was honored to be a small part of the City's acknowledgement of these fine men and women.

Recognition for Paramedic Crew

Presentation of Service Pin at Fire Station

Service Pin presentation at Fire Station 100

Ambulance Billing Unit, Headquarters

20 year Pin for Captain Paramedic

15 year Service Pin presentation at Fire Station 91

I wanted to live my calling and to give the very best of myself, to be there for every neighbor and to save their lives and homes.

Fire Commission meeting at Fire Station

LAFD Top Staff with Fire Commissioner Harold Kwalwasser

Commendations to Paramedics

Paramedic commendations

Commendations to a Paramedic team

Presentations to Paramedics

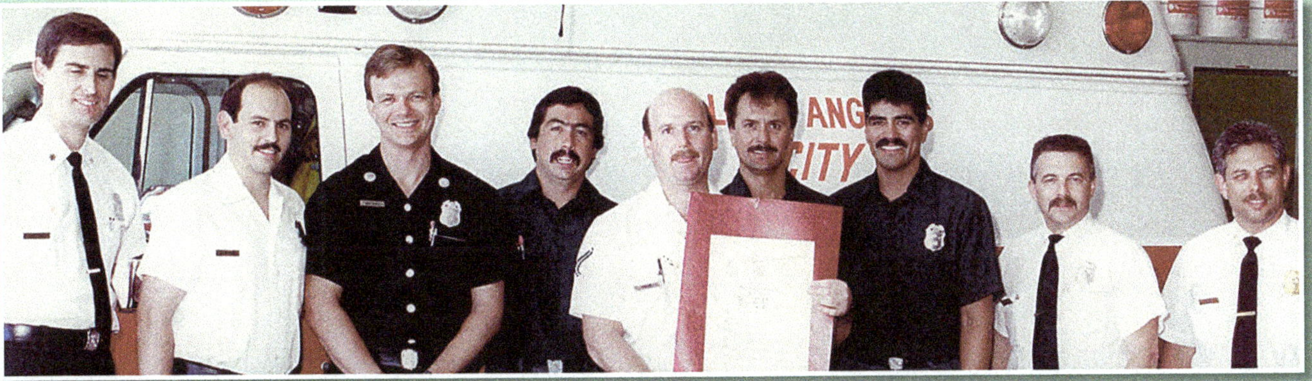

Recognition to Paramedics

15 year Pin presentation at Fire Station 105

Today's LAFD personnel stands firmly upon the shoulders of the servicemen and women who have served the Department for well over a century of duty to the City of Los Angeles.

Graduates of Paramedic School, LAFD, 1974

First Paramedics promoted to Senior Paramedics (Paramedic Supervisors), 1980

Paramedic Graduation, 1985-86

Fire Personnel at Fire Station 33, 1980-1981

Executive Officers, Top Staff, LAFD, 1988

Executive Officers, Top Staff, LAFD, 1990

Fire Commission President Terzian and Top Staff, LAFD

LAFD: 137 years of dedication and commitment to the citizens of Los Angeles. When life and property are on the line, the City has been depending on these devoted, brave men and women I've been profoundly honored to serve with.

James Denney, Steve Lilienthal, Don Lee, Charles Ryan, John Green, Danny Cypert, Alan Cowen, Robert Linnel, Larry Mayer, Harry Rich, Kevin Nida, Allen Norman

Timothy Wilson, David Thompson, Gary Inman, Joe Martin, Wade Jones, Beverly Simms, Steve Johnson, Marc Segal, William Wells

EMS Bureau Paramedic Supervisors, 1987

My promotion to Chief Paramedic, 1987 (with my wife, daughter and parents)

Northridge Hospital presentation to Pre-hospital Coordinator, 1996

Capt. Dave Thompson, Art Morin and Alan

Graduation from Paramedic School

EMS Bureau Staff and friends

Headquarters Staff

20 year Pin for service at Fire Station 63

Bureau Commanders with Chief Donald O. Manning

EMS District Captains with Bureau Secretary Cathy Chin

Fire Service Day at Fire Station 88; Tommy LaSorda, Honorary Fire Chief

Just a few of the many selfless servants of the Los Angeles Fire Department

Posing with just one of many cast of characters of the annual Hollywood Blvd. Parade

Community outreach programs of the LAFD have been a valuable opportunity for the general public and department personnel to come together as neigbors and simply have a fun and rewarding time.

Robby Cowen, Chief Cowen, and LAFD Medical Director Marc Eckstein at Fire Service day

My associates, Jose Ortiz and Kevin Nida

Dalmatians and classic cars are a strong draw for children and adults alike at these well-attended annual community events

Abby, the Fire Dog dalmation, with my daughter and her friend

Fire Service Day - Edward James Olmos, Honorary Fire Chief

Fire Service Day - Charlton Heston, Honorary Fire Chief

Fire Service Day - Tommy Lasdora, Honorary Fire Chief

Boxing referee, legend Mills Lane, at LAFD event

Fire Service Day has been a unique privilege over my many years with the LAFD

My longtime friend, Bobby Sherman

HOSPITAL CLOSURES

The Many Impacts

When I was the Paramedic Chief in the late 1980's and through the 90s, hospital closures was and still is a major problem even today. There were (and are) many impacts - in particular, a helicopter crash that killed two of our paramedics, one firefighter, and a 12-year-old girl they were transporting to Children's Hospital, and other significant calls that I responded to as well as Bee emergencies and how my plan was implemented for safety purposes when confronted with the Africanized Bees.

After Councilman Richard Alatorre requested that the Fire Department prepare a report on hospital closures, the Emergency Medical Services Bureau went to work on studying the issues that led to this flummox. The medical gridlock that resulted from the collapse of the Los Angeles County Trauma Center System that had began in 1983, and continued with the mostly private hospitals in the entire Los Angeles area compounded the problem and caused compromised patient care - with deaths reported from these closures. Additionally, there were many reports of inappropriate closures by individual emergency rooms throughout the City of Los Angeles and Los Angeles County.

Closures had been reported throughout the entire County of Los Angeles and the problem was escalating.

The closure of emergency rooms to 911 Paramedic traffic causes longer transport times to more distant hospitals. The longer transport times reduce paramedic availability for incoming 911 calls and increased paramedic response times to those calls. The temporary or permanent closure of emergency rooms affects all city residents. Closures have been reported throughout the entire County of Los Angeles and the problem was escalating. Centinela Hospital, for example, had announced the closure of its emergency department to 911 patients beginning April 26, 1988, and other hospitals did the same.

Although the emergency room closures have been primarily have been attributed to reductions in funding, it has also been reported that Los Angeles County Department of Health Services base station contact, Trauma Triage, and emergency department closure and patient diversion polices have contributed significantly to the problem. The City of Los Angeles' Police and Fire Public Safety Committee directed the Fire Department to investigate and report with recommendations the needed policy changes that could be developed and submitted to the Los Angeles County Board of Supervisors. This motion was presented by Councilman Alatorre, 14th District, and seconded by Councilman Woo.

In 1983 the Trauma Center Program in Los Angeles County began with a total of 23 hospitals that participated and met the requirements to function as a Trauma Center. By 1992 there were only 13 hospitals that remained in the program. Trauma patients are transported directly to trauma centers and bypass non trauma center emergency rooms. The Fire Department at the time believed that this was a problem because trauma centers were frequently too busy to quickly treat the patient and the nearest hospital may be able to adequately and more quickly threat the patient. There was a 20-minute transport criteria with operational considerations in mind, so that LAFD rescue ambulances would not be traveling great distances from their fire stations, which created a lack of coverage that other ambulances would need to cover but would take longer to get to their destination.

In November of 1988, the Department of Health Services issued Reference 808 "Base Hospital Contact". This reference mandated those specific times when paramedics must make base station contact from the field setting. The Los Angeles County EMS Agency which is part of the Department of Health Services has the legal authority to modify base station contact guidelines. At that time, paramedics were required to make base station contact when they encountered the following: signs of shock, cardiopulmonary arrest, primary complaint of chest pain or discomfort, trauma, hallucinations and childbirth or active labor. The policy intended to ensure that patients received the optimum level of care by paramedics. The Fire Department contended that the contents of Reference 808 were restrictive and removed the clinical judgement from the paramedics.

It was the opinion of the City Fire Department that Los Angeles City Fire Department Paramedics utilize standardized field protocols which are used by numerous other jurisdictions. These protocols would be standard operating procedures that dictate the modalities of treatment to be rendered for specific injuries and illnesses encountered in the field setting. The Fire Department believes that the use of field protocols would allow paramedics to exercise their clinical expertise and to proceed with appropriate treatment without spending an inordinate amount of time conversing with a base station, and receiving orders that would be covered under field protocols.

Interestingly, the Department of Health Services agreed with the Fire Department's contention that the obligation to make base station contact is restrictive to the paramedics, and that it probably extends the time that a paramedic spends with a patient in the field by a few minutes. However, this requirement has no impact on the transport time or the amount of time the paramedics must spend at the hospital with the patient when the emergency room is backed up. The Department of Health Services has a committee in place that reviews these polices. According to DHS, there is a move to modify, not eliminate the base station contact criteria. However, it was noted that review process would take a long time.

The Department of Health Services has maintained that the purpose of trauma triage is "to establish criteria and standards which ensure that patients requiring the care of a trauma center are appropriately triaged and transported". The goal of trauma triage is for patients to be transported to and from the scene as quickly as possible, transported to the most accessible medical facility appropriate to the patient's needs, with base hospital physician's determination in this regard being controlling, and when making base station contact, that this contact be accomplished in such a way as not to delay transport. The maximum transport time for trauma patients is not to exceed 20 minutes. The Fire Department maintains that the list of criteria that establish which patients must go to a trauma center is too broad, and thus more patients that are necessary must be transported to a possibly over-crowded trauma center as opposed to the nearest available facility. Earlier efforts by the Fire Department to have these standards relaxed have not been successful.

The problems of emergency department closures has two major effects on city Fire Department rescue ambulances. First, rescue ambulances are required to travel greater distances to deliver patients to a hospital, and secondly, those hospitals that are open will likely be more crowded and it will take longer for a patient to be turned over to the hospital's care, thus freeing up the rescue ambulances. It was not unusual for multiple hospitals to be closed particularly on weekends. There were extreme cases where rescue ambulances were tied up for two to three hours. The Fire Department maintains that rescue ambulances should not be at the hospital for longer than 15 minutes. It should be remembered that 911 calls keep coming in 24/7 and when ambulances are not immediately available, people suffer longer due to waiting for an ambulance that must come from an area further away from the caller. This back-up occurs more frequently than it should.

County USC, a familiar landmark for over 100 years.

The City of Los Angeles has a computerized dispatch system that automatically makes the ambulance "available" after 15 minutes at a hospital (unless advised otherwise). Records revealed that many times rescue ambulances remained at a hospital far beyond the 15 minutes. Examples include: at Martin Luther King-Drew Medical Center, rescue ambulances are leaving the hospital under 20 minutes 36% of the time, Los Angeles County USC Medical Center 39% of the time, and Harbor General Hospital 40% of the time. Amazingly, on average the paramedics are at Martin Luther King-Drew Medical Center for 28 minutes, Harbor General for 26 minutes and County USC Medical Center for 25 minutes. This time includes cleaning and restocking the rescue ambulance after patient delivery.

Martin Luther King Jr. Community Hospital opened in 1972 as a full-service medical center.

At that time in 1992, the City of Los Angeles could deploy additional rescue ambulances at an estimated annual cost of $700,000 each. However, this would only mean that more ambulances would be waiting at still crowded hospitals to deliver patients. It is acknowledged that the problem is insufficient hospital facilities for the number of people who are using them. There are 50 private hospitals that the city generally transports to (non trauma center facilities). These hospitals can close their doors at any time, thus further restricting the number of available hospitals. There are five county hospitals.

At that time, there were seven patient diversion categories recognized by the Los Angeles County EMS Agency which dictate under what circumstances hospitals can refuse ambulance patients. They are: 1. closed because of emergency department saturation, 2. closed because of neurosurgeon unavailability, 3. closed due to lack of CT scanner, 4. closed due to trauma center saturation, 5. closed due to pediatric center saturation, 6. closed due to intensive care unit saturation, and 7. closed due to internal disaster. These determinations are made by the hospital. The Los Angeles Fire Department would recommend the recognition of only two diversion categories; closed due to saturation or internal disaster. Although the EMS Agency desires to eliminate intensive care unit (ICU) saturation, the Hospital Council has adamantly argued against this action.

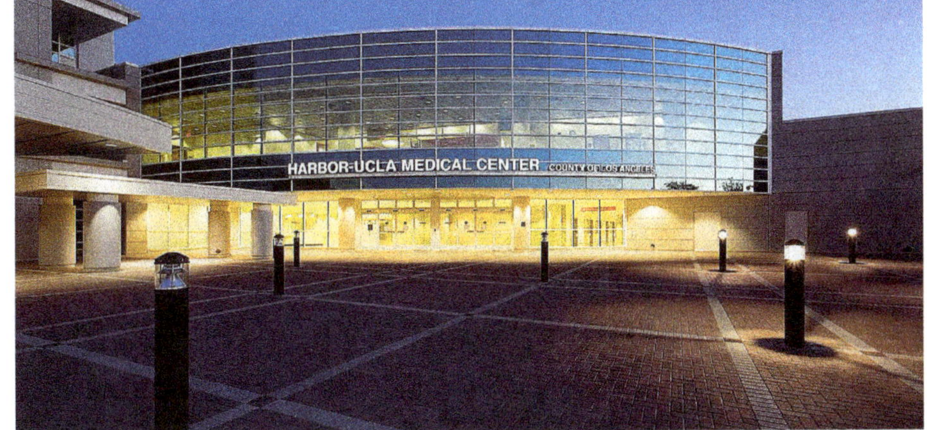

Harbor General Hospital was purchased by the County of Los Angeles from the United States Army in 1946.

NOTE: Due to an excellent relationship with the EMS Agency, I had the opportunity to invite the Chief of Prehospital Care and Trauma Hospital Programs, Virginia Hastings, to do several observational ride-alongs with me on weekends to monitor EMS activity in the City of Los Angeles. We would respond to numerous emergencies and also stop off at various hospitals - both trauma centers as well as non-trauma centers - but 24 emergency hospitals. There were some eye-opening events such as some hospitals that were closed to saturation that should not have been. To her credit, Virginia put a rapid stop to those hospitals that were violating the rules and regulations. In one case, as I recall, the staff was having a pizza party while the emergency room was "closed due to saturation".

In conclusion, the week-end emergency "back-up" still continues to this day and ambulance waits are as long now as they were 33 years ago. It is the belief of the Department of Health Services and the Los Angeles Fire Department that the majority of problems associated with pre-hospital emergency care are related to a funding crisis at the State and County level brought on in large part by the growing indigent population and the demand on the 911 system. Both entities are cautious in dealing with the problem because of the fear that the private hospitals will close their emergency rooms or trauma centers and further exacerbate the existing problem.

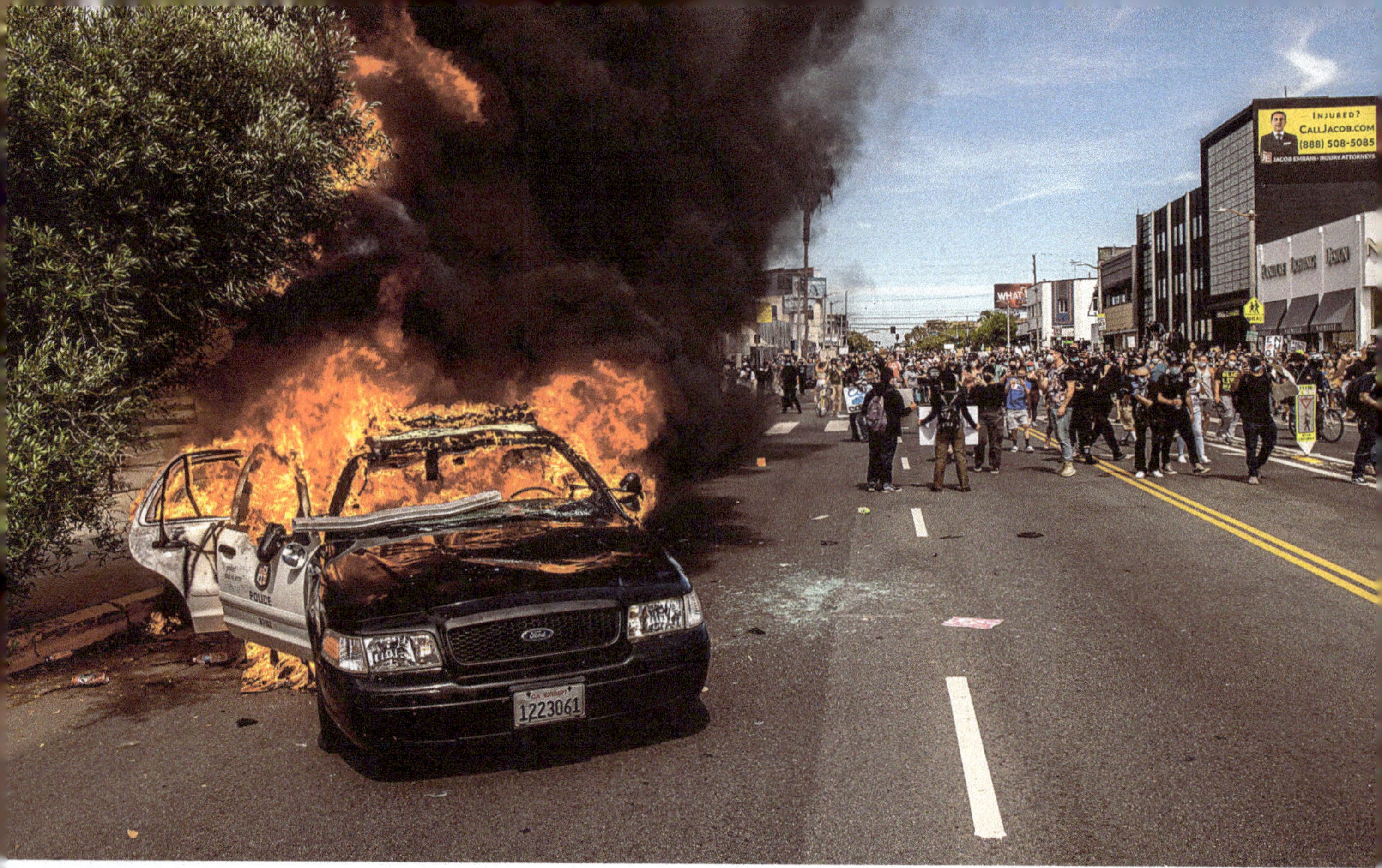
INJURED?
CallJacob.com
(888) 508-5085
1223061

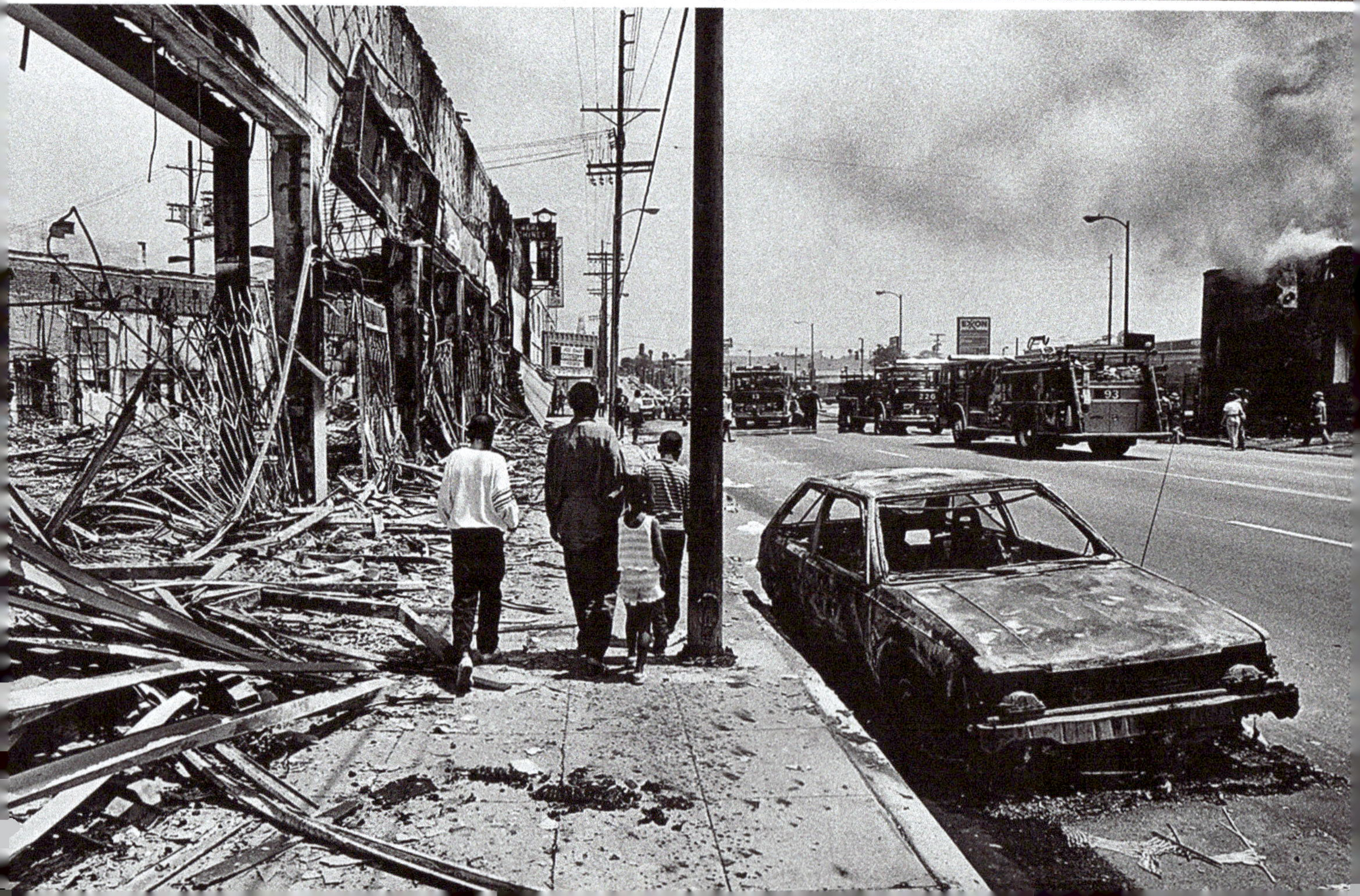
93

L.A. UPRISING

1992 RIOTS

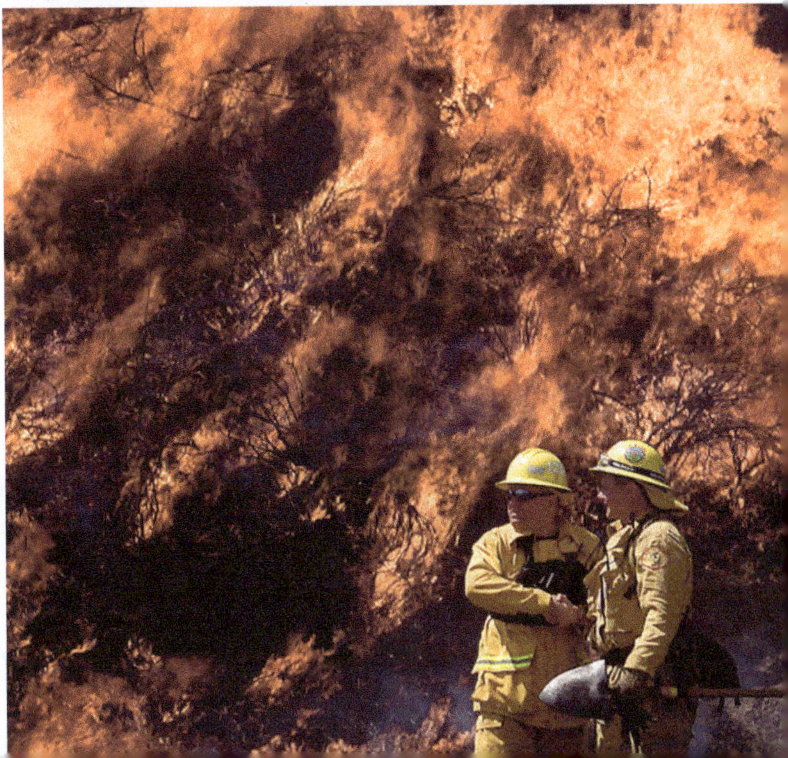

L.A. UPRISING

The 1992 Los Angeles Riots

DAY ONE - April 29, 1992
21:48 hours

"WE HAVE A FIREMAN SHOT . . .
WE HAVE A FIREMAN SHOT . . .
WE NEED HELP IMMEDIATELY!"

Light Force 35 broadcast this desperate message to our dispatch center, taking priority over every other call. Within minutes we learned that a dark-colored vehicle with its lights off had tried to pass the hook and ladder fire truck en route to a fire. The tillerman, who controls the back portion of the truck from the top rear, moved the hook and ladder to the right in an attempt to move the vehicle away. Instead of being repelled, the driver pulled up to the side of the fire truck. At the intersection of 34th and Western in South Central Los Angeles, the unthinkable occurred. The car's occupant fired into the cab, striking Apparatus Operator Scott Miller, the driver.

Miller slumped over the wheel. Other firefighters on the rig moved Miller from the driver's seat to the jump seat and took over the driver's position. The bullet had entered Miller's cheek, struck his jawbone and was deflected, lodging in his neck and severing his carotid artery. A resulting massive hemorrhage left him barely conscious. Fortunately, a firefighter paramedic assigned to the truck was able to reach Miller within seconds, stopping the flow of blood from the artery. Determining that it would be quicker to transport their injured crew member themselves, Truck 35's crew sped away from the area of the attack to Cedars Sinai Medical Center, a Level 1 Trauma Center.

Miller was in shock, unable to talk, and in critical condition. No one expected him to live. We had sent our firefighters and paramedics to assist those in need and now we were forced to save ourselves.

This image taken March 3, 1991 from video by George Holliday in Lake View Terrace shows the Rodney King beating.

The fire that Light Force 35 was responding to burned on out of control until additional fire units arrived.

Approximately 6 1/2 hours had passed since the announcement of the verdict in the Rodney King trial. Now the violence had brought down a firefighter whose only purpose was to help. Although the police were likely targets for anger in this situation, firefighters and paramedics usually enjoyed a sense of neutrality. But

Miller's injuries proved that there were no boundaries to this madness. No one was safe - not the community, not the injured, not the care givers.

Earlier that morning

The day had started well enough. A lovely spring morning was beginning when I left for work for the first time that day. I didn't know I would return to headquarters again that evening under critical circumstances.

I arrived at Fire Department headquarters about 6AM, as I do every morning. No one else is in my office at that time and I checked for messages on my secretary, Cathy's, desk. Finding no messages, I headed for the coffee room where I filled up my tall engraved glass which reads "Emergency Medical Services", a gift from Captain Dan Cypert. Back in my office, I sipped my coffee and scanned the newspaper. For the next few hours, I reviewed the usual amount of correspondence from field captains and paramedics and wondered what the day would bring. For weeks, the Fire Department had been preparing for the possibility of trouble when the Rodney King trial verdict finally came in.

Before noon

The Los Angeles Police Department notified the Fire Department that a verdict was expected in the afternoon. In response, the Fire Department held yet another planning meeting to finalize our course of action in the event of a civil disturbance. We sat through many similar meetings and thought we were prepared. By the day's end we would learn that no one was!

15:10 hours

The Rodney King verdict was announced in Simi Valley, a suburb of Los Angeles at 3:10PM. All officers were acquitted in that case and **I knew, instinctively, there would be trouble.**

Fire rages on both sides of Western Avenue along Santa Monica Boulevard in Hollywood on April 30, 1992.

15:55 hours

Chief of Police Daryl F. Gates partially activated the Emergency Operations Center (EOC) at City Hall East as a precaution. Fully activated, the EOG provides a central location for communications and resource control during an emergency.

The EOC and the Los Angeles Police Department's Communication Division were located adjacent to the Fire Department command center beneath city hall. Although these agencies were all located on the same floor, they were separated by security doors. Ironically, our communications systems would serve to keep us separated.

17:45 hours

The first report of violence came in. Pedestrians threw bottles and debris at passing motorists at Florence and Normandie in South Central Los.Angeles. In retrospect, there were sparks of violence around the city and this was one of them, but nobody had put it together yet.

Rescue Ambulance 66 reported to the dispatch center that rocks and bottles were being thrown at civilians, striking three people at Florence and La Salle.

The Fire Department had been meeting routinely with the police department as the trial approached. We had previously set up a program in which the LAPD provided the Fire Department a police escort to certain kinds of calls under normal operating procedures. These included shootings, stabbings, assaults with a deadly weapon, or any call in which there was the likelihood of a suspect remaining on scene upon prior to the arrival of the Fire Department. At the onset of the civil disturbance, that policy was supposed to remain in force. After the rioting started, however, there were few police escorts to be found. The escort plan would fail to work properly.

That evening I arrived home from work at about 6PM and turned on the television. Just as the news of some activity at Florence and Normandie flashed across the screen, my pager went off.

18:10 hours

Mayor Tom.Bradley appeared live on television, expressing his outrage at the verdict. A riot had started.

Heading back out the door, I stopped to say goodbye to my wife, Dolly, who stood chatting with some neighbors outside.

"I'm going back downtown. I don't know when I'll be back."

"What are you talking about?" she asked, apparently frightened by the look on my face.

"Something's getting started. I have to go," I said, as I kissed her and turned to get in my car. It was the last normal moment I would have for days.

When the King verdict was announced, I knew in my heart there would be a problem. This was the spark that would make it happen. A race riot hadn't occurred in Los Angeles since 1965, but there was no question about how high emotions ran on the outcome of this trial. Within minutes, I would see the first evidence of that.

Heading toward the office downtown in my unmarked city car, I entered the freeway and pulled into the fast lane. A car pulled up next to me with an African-American man at the wheel. He looked at my car, which somewhat resembled a police vehicle, and then at me, and our eyes met. What happened next astounded me. He rolled down his window, stuck his head.out and spat at my car. Saliva spread across my windshield as he drove away.

This symbolic attack stunned me. Turning on the windshield wipers to clear away the glob of spit did little to wipe away the shock. That lone individual, by his actions, represented to me the anger that African-Americans must have felt at that verdict. Tragically, this small personal incident foreshadowed catastrophic things to come.

I spent the next 30 to 40 minutes in traffic, not arriving at headquarters until about 7PM. Upon my arrival, I learned of the following events:

At **18:04 hours** our dispatchers were already having difficulty getting through to the Police Department via telephone and computer, even though they were physically just down the hall. At one point, communications deteriorated so much that runners literally carried messages back and forth.

We're ringing LAPD and we're getting no answer.

One minute later, the first reported assault against the Fire Department occurred at 71st and Normandie. Someone threw a brick, hitting engine 46. I later learned this call came across our radio at 18:54 hours:

Light Force 64: "OCD from Light Force 64, I'd like you to send LAPD to 93rd and Hoover. We're being pelted by rocks en route."

OCD: "Light Force 64, Roger. We're ringing LAPD, and we're getting no answer."

When our dispatchers did get through, they were often told that there were no units to escort our ambulances in. We were unprotected going in to highly volatile situations to treat patients and wanted police support, but the LAPD could not continue to spare police officers. This created a serious problem for Fire Department administration which would not be resolved for another day. When it became evident that police escorts were in short supply, we held a meeting the next morning with the highest levels of the LAPD, California Highway Patrol, and military representatives.

But routine escorts weren't available yet. We continued to handle emergencies within the riot area with limited assistance from the LAPD.

Orders for the complete activation of the EOC were given at 18:13 hours. Just 17 minutes later, a demonstration began at Parker Center, Los Angeles Police Department Headquarters. I would witness it firsthand within the hour.

I was nearing headquarters downtown at 18:46 hours, oblivious to the fact that rioters had pulled Reginald Denny from his gravel truck at Florence and Normandie. Denny happened to be at the wrong place at the wrong time and had no way of knowing that a physical disturbance had started.

Denny was on his way to deliver sand to an Inglewood cement-mixing plant when about five men surrounded his rig, one of them pulling him from the truck's red cab. Live news coverage from a helicopter directly above televised the actions of rioters who mercilessly beat and kicked him. At one point, one of the rioters struck Denny in the side of the head with a brick as the world witnessed the ruthless brutality of this attack.

Somehow, two men and two women came through the crowd to Denny's aid and drove him to the hospital. After being admitted to Daniel Freeman Memorial Hospital, Denny underwent three hours of emergency brain surgery, miraculously surviving his wounds. Sadly, violence began to spread after this event.

At **18:51 hours** Captain Edward Carlson from OCD (Operations Control Division) walked down to the EOC where he began to coordinate efforts between the police and Fire Departments. At this time, Assistant Chief Ed Allen requested Police Department escorts for Fire Department resources entering the riot area. He didn't get them.

Ambulances continued to go in to the riot area without an escort, facing extreme danger. Calls kept coming in and we kept taking them. We didn't refuse to go, but we were learning how dangerous it was. Recommendations made a year later would keep us from going into a riot area if this happened again.

Aerial view of the city's unrest - structure fire as a result of the riots.

OCD directed all available Fire Department resources to report to the command.post at 54th and Arlington, the Rapid Transit District bus yard. This was to become Arlington IC (Incident Command).

1900 hours

After more than 30 minutes in traffic, I had exited the 101 Freeway at Los Angeles Street, made a right turn and immediately encountered a mass of about 1,000 people surrounding Parker Center, Los Angeles Police Headquarters.

Dozens of helmeted police officers stood between the crowd and the police facility with their batons out, ready to protect their headquarters. The assembled crowd consisted largely of African-Americans, some Hispanics and quite a few Anglos. Momentarily unable to drive forward, I watched their rampage with amazement and fear. I could clearly see many of the demonstrators' expressions and the look of rage on their faces overwhelmed me. Pure emotion spilled out, fueling their actions into focused destruction. In spite of the numbers of police, the mob was able to smash lobby windows and set fire to the guard shack in the parking lot.

Rocks and bottles sailed through the air, nearly hitting my car, as members of the crowd screamed angry insults. I wondered if I could safely get by because the situation looked so out of control. Visions of being pulled out of my car and killed actually entered my mind. What I didn't know was that minutes earlier, a few miles away, rioters had pulled Reginald Denny from his car. To my relief, I finally maneuvered by and made my way down into the underground parking area.

Within minutes, I was at headquarters, walking into OCD, located four floors beneath City Hall East. OCD became the department's dispatch center, which would also serve as our department's command center. From there, we would attempt to control the actions of our field resources.

Checking the monitors, I instantly saw on television what was still going on four floors above me. Outside, the mob was burning the lobby, breaking the windows, and starting fires in City Hall - right above our heads.

"There is nothing to prevent people from coming right down, the same way I had come down," I thought. There was nobody but unarmed guards to stop them. They could have come right in and killed everybody.

As Deputy Chief Donald Anthony began giving me a situation status update, I tried to orient myself to our circumstances. Almost 30 years after I began as an ambulance driver, a scared kid still figuring out what to do, I was in command of an overwhelming situation. In spite of my rank and experience, or perhaps because of it, I understood the inherent dangers we all faced. I suddenly felt fearful and all too mortal. Keeping my concentration and focus was the best defense I had. No number of office meetings could have prepared me for the next couple of days. Nothing could have.

I watched the rampage with amazement and fear.

19:01 hours
Battalion Chief Claude Creasey, commander of the dispatch section, reported that the Police Department had just declared a tactical alert whereby all on-duty police officers are informed that an unusual incident or disturbance has occurred within the city.

19:15 hours
Violence increased and spread westward. At Coliseum Street and Martin Luther King Boulevard a throng of some 100 people tossed concrete bus benches into the intersection. Rocks, bottles and chunks of concrete greeted innocent motorists as they passed. Like Reginald Denny, another unfortunate driver was yanked from his car and beaten senseless.

Within minutes the crowd swelled to nearly 300. Battalion 18, Battalion Chief Michael Bowers, contacted OCD with the urgent message that his firefighters at Fire station 94 needed immediate Police Department assistance due to mobs surrounding the station.

19:16 hours
I set to work, tuning out the feeling of dread I was fighting. Assuming medical command, I monitored EMS activity at the dispatch consoles and listened to Fire Department radio traffic. I placed phone calls to David Thompson, my Assistant Bureau Commander and Kevin Nida, my Staff Assistant, advising them to report immediately to the dispatch center. At this point in time we recalled additional chiefs as well as dispatchers.

19:18 hours
Police escorts began. Five Police Department vehicles escorted Engine Company 66 to a medical call on 56th Street. On scene, an angry crowd threw rocks and bottles at the apparatus causing both fire and police department personnel to flee the scene.

19:30 hours
Firefighters and paramedics weren't even safe in the confines of their own stations. When someone hurled a chunk of concrete against the door of Fire Station 14 and gunshots were fired, paramedics inside called the police. Upon arrival, officers encountered four suspects attempting to break into the station. The intruders turned their weapons on the police and opened fire. As a result, police shot one suspect who attempted to escape. We were quickly realizing our vulnerability, both in terms of possible harm and in our suddenly limited ability to take care of the public. By now, my head was pounding.

19:33 hours
So many calls came in on the 911 system that it froze up and simply failed. Pacific Bell reported a "system maximum overload" for the 911 system, which meant that we couldn't even accept all the calls that were coming in. This was the first time the 911 system had ever failed from the sheer volume of calls alone. We've had electrical problems, or momentary system failures involving our computer, but this happened due to the vast number of calls.

In Los Angeles, all 911 calls are routed to a Public Service Answering Point (PSAP), operated by the LAPD. Public Service Representatives (PSR's) answer all 911 calls. When a call comes in that is not a police problem, but rather a fire or medical problem, it is immediately routed to the Fire Department.

The attack demolished the windshield of Chief Manning's city vehicle as it approached Normandie and Florence, leaving the ax embedded in the sedan's roof.

On a normal day in 1992, the PSAP received slightly more than 12,000 emergency calls. On Wednesday, April 29, the PSAP received more than 35,000 calls, representing nearly a 200 percent increase in call volume. Of that number, the Fire Department typically responded to 32 structure fires and 747 EMS calls every 24 hours. On April 29, the department responded to 601 structure fires and 792 EMS calls.

That was just the beginning.

19:37 hours
Fires were being set faster than we could put them out and looting was out of control. Deputy Chief Anthony directed the commanders of Division 1 and Division 2 to fight fires using heavy streams of water in order to initiate quick knock-downs (control of fires) and move to the next fire as rapidly as possible. Chief Anthony ordered that only closed apparatus (vehicles with roofs) be used for move-ups (bringing additional fire engines into the target area from other districts). Enclosed fire apparatus minimized the possibility of firefighters being injured due to objects thrown at them.

19:38 hours
Rioters threw bottles and other debris, including a pick-headed ax at the vehicle of Battalion Chief Terry Manning, commander of Battalion 13. The attack demolished the windshield of Chief Manning's city vehicle as it approached Normandie and Florence, leaving the ax embedded in the sedan's roof. Although not seriously injured, Chief Manning suffered minor cuts from broken glass hitting his face. In my opinion, this was nothing less than attempted murder.

19:40 hours
Battalion Chief Terry Manning was attacked again. An African-American man in a white T-shirt, standing in the street, hurled a wine bottle at Chief Manning's vehicle striking the middle of the windshield.

19:46 hours
Deputy Chief Anthony established a tactical alert in Division 2, the South Central Los Angeles area. He requested a staff recall for all chief officers and dispatchers normally off duty to come in.

20:14 hours
Because of continued and increasing violence against firefighters, OCD ordered all companies to discontinue firefighting efforts and report to 54th and Arlington where police escorts were waiting.

20:15 hours
First civilian fatality. An 18-year-old male died of a gunshot head wound at a bus stop located at Vernon and Vermont Avenues.

20:18 hours
Two county strike teams, additional engine companies from the County of Los Angeles, arrived to assist the City of Los Angeles. OCD assigned one to the command post at 54th Street and Arlington and the other to fire station 3, located on Fremont Avenue in downtown L.A.

20:46 hours
Staging was also set up at fire station 3, near my office, in an effort to prepare for additional casualties.

The skeleton of a burned car sits at the intersection of Florence and Normandy.

20:50 hours
I received a most disturbing call.

A dispatcher yelled out "Chief Cowen, line 6185."

I picked up the phone and my blood turned cold at what I heard. Paramedic III Ron Myers frantically explained to me that he and his partner were holed up at Martin Luther King/Drew Medical Center on the fifth floor. "We're staying in a room for our own protection," he told me. Myers, Paramedic II Dave Boragine, and Paramedic Trainee Tom Jackson had been on the way to an assault call when their ambulance came under attack at 103rd Street and Avalon. Since they had already been pelted with rocks from rioters, Myers thought they had simply been bombarded with something heavier.

"It was like big cinder blocks hitting the rig, bouncing the rig all over the place," Myers remembers. The impact hit the ambulance so hard that he had to correct the steering to stay on course.

Immediately, the ambulance started losing power, chugging and whining from its damage. Once he knew the vehicle was in trouble, Myers abandoned the call and headed straight for the medical center.

Just at the ramp to the hospital, the engine died, but they had made it to their destination. Myers didn't realize what had hit the ambulance until they actually got out and looked at the holes in the vehicle. Somebody with a high powered rifle had shot the engine compartment of the ambulance. Bullets had come through the passenger door, the left turn signal, and the front grill. A bullet had also ripped through the radiator and damaged the engine. They were lucky to be alive.

Still, they weren't out of danger.

"Can you rescue us?" Myers and his partner asked me from their room on the fifth floor.

He said that from what he could see looking out the hospital window, the whole city below them looked as though it was on fire.

Essentially, they were trapped since there was so much gunfire in the surrounding area that they dared not leave.

"We're shut up in this room and most of the community that's rioting would like to kill us," he told me.

I told him we would send help as soon as we could, but we didn't have the resources at that minute to rescue them. There weren't enough LAPD officers to send help, so Myers and the others remained at the hospital until the early morning when escorts could lead them out.

20:50 hours
My staff assistant, Kevin Nida arrived. After briefing him, I directed him to respond to the Emergency Operating Center (EOC) at Los Angeles County USC Medical Center to act as liaison with our dispatch center.

Essentially, they were trapped since there was so much gunfire in the surrounding area that they dared not leave.

20:58 hours
Deputy Chief Dave Parsons assumed command at 54th and Arlington. Strike teams were requested through the Office of Emergency Services (OES). We began the process of requesting mutual aid from other fire jurisdictions. Ultimately more than 100 different Fire Departments, some from out of the state, came to our assistance.

We began staging additional ambulances at 54th and Arlington, creating a medical group to handle large numbers of patients for a multi-casualty incident.

I directed a second medical group to be established at Fire Station 3 in anticipation of increasing numbers of injuries and put Paramedic Supervisor Larry Mayer in charge of it. Each medical group received five additional rescue ambulances.

21:15 hours
We began air reconnaissance, sending up helicopters to spot fires. I was informed that pilots and co-pilots literally sat on body armor to protect themselves against rifle fire.

21:30 hours
At this point, we had 340 personnel working on 63 fire companies and 19 rescue ambulances from Slauson Avenue south. Between Manchester and Slauson, 18 structure fires burned; between Slauson and the Santa

Monica Freeway, another 15 fires burned wildly. Within the downtown area, three additional structure fires had started.

Between 21:30 and 22:00 hours
Amid the growing chaos, one of the floor captains yelled, "Chief Cowen, there's somebody from L.A. County USC Medical Center on the line. Can you handle, sir?"

I picked up the phone wondering what new crises this call was bringing. A woman at the other end told me she was a supervisor of nurses and she was calling on behalf of seven other nurses. They wanted us to drive them down into the riot area in order to volunteer their medical services!

My initial thought was that these nurses were mentally unbalanced and on some kind of a suicide mission. Our firefighters and paramedics are equipped with vests and have additional training. Neither the police nor Fire Department had the resources at that moment to coordinate their request. Nurses without escorts would be terribly vulnerable to attack. It was ridiculous, however well-intentioned.

"It's far too dangerous," I told her, expecting her to agree.

"We're not afraid. We're dedicated nurses," she said. "We're going down there."

"Excuse me," I said, growing perturbed and not believing what I was hearing. "You don't understand. This is an extremely dangerous and unpredictable area right now. It would not be wise nor safe for eight nurses to go into the riot area."

"Well then we'll drive ourselves."

Now, my patience was growing thin. "You will do so at your own risk. We will not assist you and, in fact, I'm telling you that you cannot go down there. Do not go! You will not get in and you will be turned away."

After I hung up the phone, I realized I had been less than courteous to these nurses. Despite the fact that they had every good intention in the world, we couldn't allow it. Had they heard the next bone chilling call for help, they would have understood.

21:48 hours
Scott Miller was shot. Minutes later, we would receive a similar distress call.

21:56 hours
The OCD radio crackled with the following transmission: "OCD from Light Force 50, we need help! We have shots fired!" Again, our firefighters and paramedics were under siege.

Members of Light Force 50, comprised of two engines, had been split apart to handle different fires. The unit dispatched to a fire at Vernon and Vermont came under life-threatening attack. Several armed hooligans carrying AK-47 assault weapons threatened the crew. Faced with the threat of death, firefighters traded two $3,000 hand-held radios for their lives. Against all odds, Engineer Kelly Kilmartin found a way to send a help call from the engine company so at least OCD knew what had happened.

Having had their rig captured, the crew was then forced to flee the scene under attack by gunfire. Members of Light Force 50 scattered to save themselves, while listening to automatic weapons fire at their truck. Worse yet, they became separated from each other and from their lifeline at Fire Department headquarters. Thank God they found safety with a family in an apartment across the street.

Street view of the city's unrest.

22:30 hours

The Los Angeles Police Department called OCD indicating that their SWAT team had found and secured Light Force 50. In spite of their ordeal, the firefighters returned to their rig and to duty, fighting the fire they had been trying to put out when they were forced to flee. This time, though, they had police protection. The other unit from Light Force 50 had been working to fight a blaze at a mini-mall. To their horror, they noticed a contingency of half a dozen men nearby carrying two-foot machetes. As it turned out, the men were neighbors who wanted to help the firefighters; they were there to protect the firefighters and stood guard as the crew worked.

22:31 hours

Nearly 200 incidents per hour continued to pour in to our dispatch center. The vast number of incoming calls overwhelmed the communications center. At the same time, the safety of firefighting and paramedic personnel at the 54th and Arlington command post remained the highest of priorities.

22:45 hours
We had 31active structure fires, 122 companies and 25 rescue ambulances committed, for a total of 570 personnel working. My headache had moved to the pounding stage.

DAY TWO, April 30
Looking up at the clock following a planning meeting after midnight, I realized that it was the next day. As physically exhausted as I was, I couldn't sleep and was wide awake. And scared to death. I speculated about what further challenges would await us as a department and as a city. The call volume had seemed enormous the first day. We hadn't seen anything yet.

The next 24 hours literally brought me to my knees. Listening to radio traffic throughout the night, I realized that the turmoil would continue. Violence had escalated overnight as fires and looting continued unabated. From midnight on, fires continued out of control with 15 to 20 incidents reported at a time. More than 160 fire companies fought to keep up with ever-increasing structure fires. At the same time, looting and gunfire kept pace with the flames.

The second day brought more of everything: more fires, more looting, more trauma. To make matters worse, we had logistical nightmares recalling off-duty personnel. Many exhausted firefighters were already working in their 36th hour waiting to be relieved. Chief officers who came on duty had to find a staff assistant, emergency vehicles, and body armor.

Regrettably the need for body armor in the form of bullet-resistant vests increased dramatically because firefighters had become victims. Rocks, bricks, bottles, concrete fragments and anything else readily attainable was used against department personnel. Scott Miller's shooting had indelibly imprinted the level of danger in everyone's mind. Fewer than half of all on-duty firefighters had been issued vests prior to this civil disturbance. Only fire companies assigned to high incident locations had received vests; paramedics assigned to rescue ambulances had been issued vests for several years due to the high risks they faced.

It was 1989 when the department first purchased body armor as personal safety equipment. Initially only paramedics were issued body armor. In 1992, fewer than 500 vests had been issued to department personnel. The vests were rated at 2-A which meant they could potentially stop a 9 millimeter or 357 magnum round.

Given the increased hostilities from snipers, as well as gunfire from passing motorists, Arlington Incident Command (IC) had notified our Supply and Maintenance Division to deliver all available body armor to the command post at 54th and Arlington before midnight. Battalion Chief Jimmy Hill, working through the EOC, set up the acquisition of additional body armor on loan from the Army National Guard's Reserve Base in San Luis Obispo.

At 30 minutes past midnight we sent a lone red and white LAFD helicopter to northern California to bring back 175 flack vests for the protection of Los Angeles firefighters. Mutual aid strike teams were required to wait at the command post staging area until the vests arrived. Later in the day, another LAFD helicopter flew to Los Alamitos Air Force Reserve Center to retrieve 250 additional pieces of body armor. Our department's efforts to ensure body armor for all firefighters and paramedics never ceased.

The signs and symptoms of violence could be seen and felt long before the civil disturbance. In 1989, the department first purchased body armor as part of personal safety equipment. It is most unfortunate that body armor had not been issued to each and every member of the department long before this major disturbance occurred. (Within 60 days, the LAFD had purchased body armor for each on-duty member; 635 were ordered at a cost exceeding $300,000).

0100 hours

California Governor Pete Wilson proclaimed a State of Emergency at the request of Los Angeles City Mayor Tom Bradley. Just 45 minutes earlier, the Mayor had also issued a "dusk to dawn" curfew in South Central L.A. Not only did the curfew limit the time residents could be on the street, it also prohibited the sale of gasoline, except for vehicle fill-ups within the area. By 3:55 that afternoon, the curfew extended to the entire city of Los Angeles.

The sheer number of reported emergencies peaked between 01:00 and 02:00 hours. In one hour, 253 new incidents were reported, among them 24 new fires.

Standing at a wall map, I traced the reports of new fires with my finger and confirmed looting at the same locations. This meant that people stole merchandise and torched the building to cover their trails. There were times I could forecast where the next looting and fire would occur. It seemed almost like a pattern. Loot and burn, loot and burn, loot and burn.

All through the night firefighters responded to burning structures only to be fired upon time and time again. Listening to two-way communication between the firefighters both comforted and tormented me. It helped to hear their voices which meant they were okay, but the constant threat of violence toward them hung over me.

Toward dawn, for some quiet time and personal reflection, I retreated to my 10th floor City Hall East office. From there, I watched the first strands of light reflect off the City Hall tower across the street. "At least it's still standing and we're still alive", I thought. I had barely eaten. I closed my eyes for brief moments at my desk from time to time. I was aware that sleep deprivation was beginning to take its toll as evidenced by the constant low level headache I couldn't seem to shake. Nevertheless, it was my responsibility to be alert and ready for our next planning meeting. The executive staff, approximately 10 staff members, tried to hold meetings every four hours in the fire chief's office. Sleep would have to wait.

The Los Angeles County Office of the Coroner attributed 53 deaths to the civil unrest.

08:00 hours

I directed David Thompson, my Assistant Bureau Commander, to report to the command post at 54th and Arlington and take command of the medical group. Captain Thompson responded to Dodger Stadium staging where he obtained a police escort en route to 54th and Arlington. It was Captain Thompson who maintained control over all medical operations at Arlington command post.

Shortly after noon, the first contingency of National Guard troops hit the streets of South Central L.A.

Approximately 14:30 hours

Brigadier General James D. Delk met with LAPD Chief Daryl Gates, Sheriff Sherman Block, Highway Patrol Commissioner Maurice Hannigan, Undersheriff Robert Edmonds, and three senior CHP commanders. At this meeting, Commissioner Hannigan agreed to provide protection for firefighters at the request of Chief Gates.

By evening, CHP officers replaced LAPD personnel in providing escorts. Although I was not present at the meeting earlier in the day, Donald O. Manning, the Fire Chief, told me that it was Chief Ed Gomez of the California Highway Patrol who came to our rescue. Through Chief Gomez's efforts, Los Angeles became saturated with highway patrol officers whose duty and responsibility was to protect firefighters and paramedics as well as fire stations.

At Vermont Avenue and 27th Street, Tom Sedry and Arturo Pallacios were among those helping to clean up a building shared by a discount store and the Exposition Park Church of the Nazarene. Many were members of the congregation, but many others simply wanted to help.

By nightfall, the California Highway Patrol had nearly 2,400 officers assigned to the Los Angeles area, some coming from distant locations. Chief Gomez had arranged to provide 300 officers and 100 vehicles who provided escorts for LAFD and other Fire Departments who came in to assist us. We received 3,244 structure fire calls and 1,025 EMS calls that day.

LAFD firefighters will not soon forget the camaraderie that we shared with officers of the California Highway Patrol during those difficult days. I still hold the highest respect for them.

23:00 hours

That night, I was alone in my office drawing up some plans. For hours, I had worked at fighting off the panic I felt. It wasn't just exhaustion. So much hatred and destruction had been unleashed in our midst that nothing we did could keep up. My feelings turned to utter despair.

Getting down on my hands and knees, I knelt beside my desk. In that moment I prayed to God the rioting would stop because nothing human was going to halt this thing. I have struggled with my beliefs since childhood, always weighing the good and the evil of what God commanded. That night, my theological questions didn't matter because something more powerful than mere man was needed, and I needed somewhere to turn.

I was down to sleeping in my office on the floor. We slept when and where we could. Adrenalin had taken the place of hunger for me and I kept drinking coffee to stay up. I was up for two or three days straight with naps, and felt lucky to get three hours sleep one morning from 2AM to 5AM.

I showered in the gym facilities on the 9th floor. Fortunately, I had a locker there stocked with towels and shaving gear. On that third morning I took the time to shave because I looked like hell. Beyond a weak attempt at good hygiene, I wasn't showering to get clean, but using cold water to stay awake. Heading into the third day, I felt weary. My headache had numbed into a dull throb. Something had to give.

DAY THREE, May 1

Several large fires still burned but few new fires were being set. As the day wore on, the end to the turmoil was in sight. By afternoon, the LAFD began to release fire agencies who had come to our aid. We had experienced the worst United States civil disturbance of this century.

I felt as though we had been through a battle.

Damage assessments were astounding. Overall, in a 105 square mile radius within the boundaries of L.A.'s 464 square miles, more than 1,000 structures were fire damaged; buildings and contents damage totaled more than $567 million.

Due to differing statistics, there is no definitive total for the numbers of injuries. The Los Angeles County Office of the Coroner attributed 53 deaths to the civil unrest. In addition, Los Angeles County hospital emergency rooms data revealed that more than 2,300 people suffered injuries between April 29 and May 3; more than 225 people required hospital admission. The Emergency Medical Services State Authority (EMSA) has estimated that pre-hospital care providers treated an estimated 179-238 injuries in the field setting.

Despite more than a dozen verified accounts of attempts to murder firefighters and paramedics, no Fire Department members died during the riot. Law enforcement agencies, including the California National Guard, reported 66 injuries to their personnel. Regretfully, 59 firefighters suffered injuries, four from gunshot wounds. Apparatus Operator Scott Miller's were the most critical. The bravery of the men and women of the Los Angeles City Fire Department, as well as other Fire Departments, continued to amaze me.

When it was all over I sat at my desk, humbled by this experience, and grieved for our city. I thought about the fires, the deaths and injuries, and prayed for Scott Miller. I frequently obtained updates on Miller who remained in critical condition following surgery.

In the years it took him to recover, Miller worked in the Bureau of Fire Prevention and Public safety in a light duty capacity. In spite of his life threatening injuries, Miller made it through. I'm pleased to say he was promoted to Fire Captain on June 28, 1992.

In the days and weeks following the riot, I kept questioning whether we could look back on this and learn something from it. I wonder still.

Post Script

Thinking back on the Los Angeles Civil Disturbance (L.A. Riots) that occurred in April, 1992, I remembered some things:

First, the Los Angeles Civil Disturbance was the largest and most devastating civil disturbance to occur in the 1990s in the United States. It ignited quickly following the announcement of the Rodney King trial verdict on Wednesday, April 29. The four LAPD officers were acquitted after being charged with unreasonable force in the arrest of Rodney King. The riot, or rebellion as some call it, lasted four days.

The more than 100 agenices that responded overall did very well in terms of meeting the medical needs of the victims. Pre-hospital providers cared for and transported a significant number of the injured. Hospitals were able to triage, treat and otherwise care for the injured that were transported to them. On November 19, 1992, at the request of the Emergency Medical Authority's Director, the Governor officially recognized the EMTs, public service agencies, private ambulance companies, and hospitals for their heroic action taken by them and their employees to save lives and care for the injured.

Initial hospital emergency department data indicates that 2383 persons were injured between April 29 and May 3. Of the total, 227 were admitted. Interestingly, based upon preliminary findings from a Centers for Disease Control study, hospital estimates of the number of injured, directly related to the disturbance, may be overstated by as much as 763 (32%). If the correction is accurate, then hospitals treated between 1620 and 2383 patients whose injuries were directly caused by the civil disturbance. The California State EMS Authority

A police patrol vehicle is set on fire and overturned by a roving crowd which was originally protesting outside Parker Center.

Rioters at Florence and Normandy.

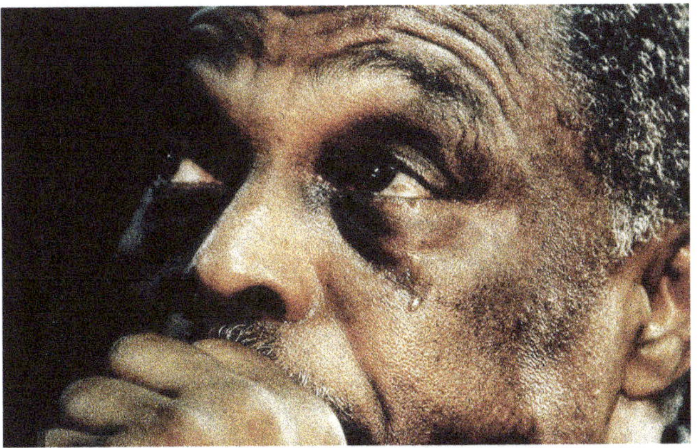

A tear gave witness to the reaction by Rev Cecil L Murray, pastor of the 8,000-member First African Methodist Episcopal Church of Los Angeles, as the verdicts were announced.

estimates that pre-hospital care providers treated an estimated 179 to 238 injured persons in the field.

The Fire Services and EMS providers sustained three or four injuries depending on the source of the information. The Los Angeles Police Department, California National Guard and other law enforcement agencies reported 66 injuries. These are included in the above total numbers.

After careful examination of the causes of death, the Los Angeles County Medical Examiner determined that, as of August 11, 1992, 51 deaths occurred during the Los Angeles Civil Disturbance. A few year's later, during the demolition of some structures in the South Central area of Los Angeles, at least one decendent was found whose death was believed to be a direct result of the civil disturbance.

UPDATE ON FIREFIGHTER SCOTT MILLER

The shooter was caught by excellent police work four months after the riots. He received 16 years in prison and pleaded no contest. Then Chief of Police Willie L. Williams announced that officers have arrested a man and suspected gang member on suspicion of shooting firefighter Scott Miller in the face as Miller rushed to the scene of a fire on April 29, the first night of the Los Angeles riots. The 22-year-old was arrested without incident at 2:30PM on a street corner in South Central Los Angeles. Police detectives had been contacted by witnesses to the incident, which left the firefighter in critical condition. The Police Chief indicated that the shooter would be charged with attempted murder and prosecutors will ask that he will be held without bail. Additionally, the individual was also charged with being an ex-convict and possessing a weapon.

The bullet struck firefighter Miller in the neck and mandible which severed his carotid artery causing Miller to have a stroke and become temporarily paralyzed. He spent 7 weeks in Intensive Care and 6 months in recovery. He ultimately returned to the Los Angeles Fire Department on restricted duty and was later promoted to Captain assigned to the Fire Prevention Bureau.

At the time of the shooting the engine company was traveling north on Western Avenue near Adams to a fire caused by the riots. A dark colored vehicle attempted to pass the fire truck on the right but backed off before turning off its lights then accelerated past the fire truck. As the vehicle drove along side the fire truck, the driver of the vehicle extended his arm from the window and fired a handgun striking firefighter Miller. Miller was 33 years of age at the time of the incident. Fire Chief Donald O. Manning said of the arrest, "I certainly want to thank the top quality work by the LAPD in bringing about his arrest."

Twenty-five years after the L.A. riots, Captain Miller stated, "I have been able to enjoy a long career with the Los Angeles Fire Department." In an interview in 2017, Miller stated, "I am celebrating my 36th year on the department. I have a grandchild that I have been able to watch grow up and that is just the fruits of happiness. I had a bad day. I got shot! But I had a really good day from the standpoint of having a severed carotid artery and stroke and survived it."

M E M O R A N D U M

May 11, 1992

TO: File

FROM: A. R. Cowen, Commander
Bureau of Emergency Medical Services

SUBJECT: CIVIL DISTURBANCE COMMITTEE

The first meeting of the Civil Disturbance Committee will be conducted at 0830 hours, on Monday, May 11, 1992 at In-Service Training.

A. R. COWEN, Chief Paramedic
Commander,
Bureau of Emergency Medical Services

ARC:cmc:4345T

May 13, 1992

TO: Members, Civil Disturbance Committee

FROM: James P. Denney, Committee Member

SUBJECT: MINUTES OF MEETING, MAY 11, 1992

PRESENT:
Chief Paramedic Cowen, BEMS
P.S. Joe Martin, Chairman, EMS 5-A
P.S. Art Morin, EMS 6-C
P.S. Marc Segal, EMS 5-C
P.S. Larry Mayer, EMS 1-B
P.S. Don Lee, Resource, Inservice Training
P.S. Jim Denney, EMS 6-A

The meeting was opened by Chief Paramedic Cowen at 0900 Hrs. Chief Cowen laid the foundation, parameters, and goals of the committee. It is his intent that the committee arrive at both long and short range goals. The EMS bureaus budget relative to "V" hours was discussed.

Chief Cowen instructed the committee to have a preliminary report completed and submitted by May 29, 1992, and that the report address items for paramedic risk reduction that could be implemented immediately. Chief Cowen exited the meeting at 0930.

Joe Martin gave an overview of the problems encountered during the early phase of the riot. Specific areas of concern were lack of resources, lack of protection for paramedics, lack of assistance on the part of the command staff, and lack of cooperation on the part of the L.A.P.D.

Martin then further defined the parameters and goals of the committee. A discussion ensued wherein all relative topics regarding the recent civil disturbance were discussed.

10 specific areas of concern emerged from the discussion:

1. Disaster V. Normal operation
2. Tactical operations
3. Private Ambulances
4. Hospital operations
5. Recall
6. Law enforcement
7. Public relations
8. Communications
9. Safety
10. Equipment

Assignment of these areas were made to each member to investigate and report back at the next meeting. The next meeting was scheduled for May 15, 1992, at 0900. The meeting was adjourned at 1200 Hrs.

James P. Denney

LOS ANGELES FIRE DEPARTMENT

DONALD O. MANNING
CHIEF ENGINEER AND GENERAL MANAGER

June 12, 1992

TO: Commander, Bureau of Emergency Medical Services

FROM: Civil Disturbance Committee

SUBJECT: OPERATIONAL RECOMMENDATIONS FOR IMMEDIATE IMPLEMENTATION DURING LARGE SCALE CIVIL DISOBEDIENCE

SUMMARY
As directed by you, the Committee on Civil Disturbance has developed the following recommendations for immediate implementation during large scale violent civil disturbances such as the recent riot.

RECOMMENDATIONS

1. Dispatch: EMS dispatch protocols, during a civil disturbance, should be modified to exclude the A category calls and instructions should be given to the caller regarding alternate methods of obtaining assistance.

2. Response: Rescues should respond emergency both to and from incidents, thereby limiting their exposure time in hostile, dangerous environments.

   All patients that are transported should go to the closest ER regardless of that ERs' status. All criteria regarding catchment, service, or pediatric concerns should be suspended for the duration of peak violent periods, or at any time the system becomes overwhelmed due to civil disturbance.

3. Patient Care: During civil disturbance, or widespread catastrophe, paramedics should function on standing orders based on reference 806 of the PHCM.

4. Private Ambulance: The utilization of private ambulances should be considered in uninvolved areas of the city. This procedure has been developed during the private ambulance study. Private ambulances routinely handle non emergency calls. They carry their own liability insurance and workers compensation. All private ambulance personnel meet minimum state and county requirements and standards for emergency care at the EMT/BLS level. This would immediately free up department resources for relief in the riot area.

Private ambulance companies, by law, maintain incident logs that record the time, address, and nature of response in addition to patient information, transportation, and destination information.

5. Hert Teams: Hert Teams should be utilized by the command post in casualty collection points, or where ambulances are staged. Patients with minor injuries would then be triaged by them which would result in less crowding of E.R.s' and a quicker turn around time for rescues. Any patients requiring further treatment could be loaded into private ambulances or buses and transported to more distant facilities outside the riot zone.

6. Dead Bodies: Dead bodies should be collected and returned to the command post/staging area where a temporary morgue could be set up and supervised.

7. Full Arrest: Patients in cardio-pulmonary arrest, unless witnessed by the paramedics, should be pronounced dead.

8. Family Members: Unless necessary, family members should not be transported with patients.

9. Kidnap Warning Devices: External kidnap warning/help devices similar to those used by taxis and other private enterprises should be mounted to rescue ambulances.

10. All members should be issued ballistic vests.

11. Uniforms: Badges should be removed from uniforms during civil disturbances. The designated uniform for paramedics should be jumpsuits with embroidered insignia, including non-reflective badges.

12. Radios: Radios should be modified so that the emergency locator button is functional.

13. Food and Water: A 3 day supply of food and water should be available for each member on all apparatus.

14. Medical Cache: An R/A should be equipped with command equipment and a medical supply cache for use during any major incident, including civil disturbance.

15. Documentation: The only documentation of patient care should be the F-902M. Journals should reflect only the members on duty, significant incidents, and state of equipment.

16. Female Paramedics: Female paramedics should not be separated during civil disturbances (unless specifically requested by them). As long as police/nat'l guard escorts are provided, they are in no more danger than their male counterparts.

17. Air Ambulances: Air ambulances present significant hazards to those members working them. They are also vulnerable to gunfire. They should not be utilized for civilian patient transportation. However, if the patient is a member of the fire, police, or other emergency service organization the use of the Air Ambulance should be a consideration.

18. Universal Precautions: The practice of universal precautions should be strictly enforced during civil disturbances.

19. Recall: Recall during civil disturbance should include all light duty personnel, and a proportionate number of EMS Supervisors to maintain the normal ratio of supervision. Supervisors should also be considered when forming medical groups.

20. EMT Rescues: Firefighter EMT staffed rescues, when assigned to a medical group, should not be drafted or volunteering for firefighting duties while in the staging area.

21. Rotating Resources: Rescues from uninvolved areas should be considered for rotation to affected areas in order to provide relief to other members. This rotation should be for a segment at a time. This would help to alleviate cumulative stress during peak periods of civil unrest.

22. CISD: CISD and stress monitoring should be accomplished at staging areas and command post in affected areas.

23. A pre determined response plan should be developed by the Department, and incorporated into the ICS, that identifies actions to be taken during a tactical alert.

    The plan should include safe locations, tactical policies and procedures, logistics, police/nat'l guard coordination, mission goals and objectives, and specific assignments for key personnel.

    After action reports should be an integral part of this plan. The after action reports should be in a narrative V. technical format for easier analysis by lay persons.

    Training under this plan, such as that used for other scenarios by the Department, should be conducted on a regular basis.

24. Protection for Emergency Rooms must be considered both for the safety of Department personnel and patients transported to them (On April 29, 1992, armed gang members gathered in the emergency parking area of Holy Cross Hospital and blocked the exit).

Emergency Room personnel should receive Incident Command System familiarization training (they are currently considering adopting this format through the PCC organization).

25. Paramedic Supervisors are the only Department resource that responds alone. Consideration should be given to double staffing of EMS Districts during peak periods of civil unrest. This would also serve to enhance supervision at large scale incidents.

James P. Denney

Joe D. Martin, Chairman,
Civil Disturbance Committee

JDM:JPD

LOS ANGELES FIRE DEPARTMENT

DONALD O. MANNING
CHIEF ENGINEER AND GENERAL MANAGER

June 17, 1992

TO: Chief Engineer and General Manager, THROUGH CHANNELS

FROM: A. R. Cowen, Bureau Commander
Bureau of Emergency Medical Services

SUBJECT: OPERATIONAL RECOMMENDATIONS DURING CIVIL DISTURBANCES

SUMMARY

At the last All EMS Supervisors Meeting held on May 6, 1992, one of the items for discussion was the Civil Disturbance. A long discussion was held and resulted in a Bureau Committee being formulated in order to make recommendations to the Chief Engineer. The Committee consisted of the following Paramedic Supervisors:

Joe Martin, EMS 5, "A" Platoon, Chairperson
James Denney, Bureau of Emergency Medical Services
Larry Mayer, EMS 6, "A" Platoon
Arthur Morin, EMS 6, "C" Platoon
Don Lee, Training Division

The group was directed to come up with <u>short term</u> recommendations, at no or very minimal cost to the Department. It was pointed out that any such recommendations must be approved by the Chief Engineer.

The attached document represents short term operational recommendations that could, if approved, be implemented immediately at no cost or minimal cost to our Department.

I am available, at your convenience, to meet with you to discuss the group's recommendations.

RECOMMENDATIONS

1. That the attached document be reviewed for possible implementation.

2. If some or all of the recommendations are approved, the group would be directed to work out the mechanics of each point.

A. R. COWEN, Chief Paramedic
Bureau Commander,
Bureau of Emergency Medical Services

ARC:cmc:4443T

Attachment

Racial Inequities/Discrimination

The long slow march for progress and a better department

Driver Given 'Silent' Treatment

Ambulance Driver Cold-Shouldered

Our City's diversity is one of our greatest strengths.

As our City and the nation still grapple with race, LAFD continues to be an exemplary leader in the country's largest department. An organization seeking to be one of mutual respect, cultural tolerance and professionalism.

ENGINE No 30 · L·A·F·D · TRUCK No 11

Ambulance Driver Cold-Shouldered

1957 article from *Los Angeles "Eagle"* illustrates the systemic racism of that era in the Los Angeles Fire Department

The first Negro ambulance driver to be hired by the City of Los Angeles since World War II is being given the same type of nerve-shattering "silent treatment" as that meted out to Negro firemen under the John F. Alderson regime, the Eagle was informed this week.

There are two important differences, however. One is that not everyone in the department is ready to go along with the cold-shouldering. The other difference is that a lot of people are talking about what is happening.

Going To Extremes

The Eagle checked these reports with Robert Roberts, supervisor of the Ambulance Service of the City. Roberts gave the name of the driver as Donald Smith, who, he said, has been with the department for about two months.

"I don't know what we can do about the 'silent treatment,'" said Roberts. "I'm going to extremes," he continued, "to see that he gets more than a fair break. We took him from the station where he seemed to be having trouble, but I'll say this, if he'd been white, I would have fired him."

Accident Reported

Roberts said the department had received a complaint that Smith had backed into an automobile while he was driving an ambulance, and that he had not reported the accident. The woman whose car had been hit, he said, reported the incident, and it is now under investigation. He said also that there had been another complaint against Smith, accusing him of "reckless driving" while he was transporting an obstetrics patient to the hospital.

Wouldn't Talk

Smith, when approached by the Eagle, was reluctant to discuss the treatment to which he is being subjected. He said he's only interested in doing a good job.

"I have a wife and three children—the oldest is six—and I left the County General Hospital because I thought the city job offered me more opportunity."

Rough Time

From various sources, however, the Eagle obtained information that the young ambulance driver is having what one person called, "an awfully rough time."

Smith was referred to the City Ambulance Dept. by Civil Service authorities, after he had passed the exams. He was told there was an opening, but when he applied he was informed that there had apparently been some mistake and that the opening available was for a man on a temporary emergency basis.

Smith reportedly checked again with the Civil Service Dept., and subsequently the Ambulance Dept. got in touch with him and advised that there was a permanent job available, and that he could have it if he so desired.

Perfect Record

Smith was a clinic driver at General Hospital for two years, but had worked at the hospital for about five years. He had a perfect driving record while he was there. He resigned that job and began serving on his present job May 11.

According to reports going the rounds about 80 percent of the city ambulance drivers and attendants are determined "to get Smith out of the department." The word has also been passed around that "it was the NAACP" that got Smith the job, though apparently the NAACP was in no way involved.

Driver Given 'Silent' Treatment

The accident in which Smith was reportedly involved occured May 28, but it was not until early in July that any queries were made about it.

Supervisor Roberts said that Smith denied that he hit any car. Attendant Hiries, who was with Smith at the time, at first said he wasn't sure whether Smith had hit any vehicle or not, but later said that there had been a collision, according to Roberts.

Smith has now served two months of his six months probationary period. If he lasts six months, the job is his, but it looks as if there are four long, hard months ahead.

African American Firefighter Museum

Engine No. 30 LAFD
Truck No. 11

LOS ANGELES FIRE DEPARTMENT

ENGINE COMPANY Nº 30

CHARLIE M. DEAN

EDWARD FREEMAN

BENNIE T. HOOKS

CLINTON L. McDANIEL

THEODORE R. WEBB

WILLIAM E. HALL
CAPTAIN

JACKSON L. TAYLOR
CAPTAIN

JOSEPH F. WILSON

L. E. WASHINGTON

OTIS BROWN

WALTER R. BROWN

HOWARD W. JEFFERS

PAUL J. McCARTY

FRANK MILTON

HARRY A. YOUNG

Security Pacific National Bank Collection, Los Angeles Public Library

RACIAL INEQUITIES

Our historical stain and the silent treatment

I do not want to skip a rather deep tear in the fabric of the Receiving Hospital System and I am referencing the way minorities were treated by fellow workers in an earlier time. At the time I was hired by the City of Los Angeles in March of 1967, it was a time of radical change that was overtaking the country.

After being hired I became aware of only four African American Ambulance personnel: Donald Smith, Fred Hicks, Albert Stuckey and Edmond McDaniels, all of whom turned out to be excellent ambulance attendants and ambulance drivers.

The first one to be hired was Donald Smith and he had to endure the "silent treatment" when he began working. Fred Hicks suffered some of the same treatment, as did Albert Stuckey and Edmond McDaniels. These individuals were part of the transition to the Fire Department on July 1, 1970.

In 1968 I worked with Fred Hicks and I recall him being exceptionally nice to me and I never forgot him. Even today, when I think about all of my past partners when working as an ambulance driver, Fred Hicks comes into my thoughts. He was highly intelligent and we treated each other with respect. I would have gladly been his permanent partner if possible.

Don Smith became a paramedic and was highly successful in paramedic training. Paramedic Fred Hicks received a disability pension on August 25, 1979 after more than 20 years of service, while paramedic Smith resigned his position on November 19, 1979 to accept a position with UCLA in the Prehospital Care Office. Albert Stuckey received a disability pension on June 28, 1973 having served the City of Los Angeles for 5 years. Edmond McDaniels received a disability pension on January 1, 1976.

I got to know Don Smith quite well while on the Los Angeles Fire Department and he was a personable individual, friendly and professional. He died a few years later while working at UCLA and was honored by many people at his funeral. Thereafter he was honored by an annual event.

Upon being transferred to the Fire Department, the entire Ambulance Corp. were in for significant and life-altering changes. Some personnel accepted the changes, some did not. Regardless, change was in the air and inevitable.

While working on the Los Angeles Fire Department I became friends with numerous African American members to include some Chief Officers. One that I was assigned to work with was Battalion Chief Paul Orduna. It was through Chief Orduna that I learned about "The Old Stentorians." This dealt with the manner in which African Americans were treated within the Fire Department by the administration.

In working with Fire Chief Donald O. Manning and Fire Chief William R. Bamattre I can say, without any reservations, that neither of them used any racial terms, slurs or derogatory stereotypes at any Staff meetings, Operations meetings or Bureau Staff meetings during my tenure with the Los Angeles Fire Department.

Much of this chapter on Racial Inequities within Central Receiving Hospital and the Los Angeles Fire Department is taken from actual documents of that time in our shared history.

I had a choice in assembling this chapter to either white-wash out the speech of that time or leave it intact as a time capsule. Currently in regions of our country some states are mandating a white-washing of our rocky history and failures as a nation out of our public school's history books. It's within this deeply concerning backdrop of our continued struggles that this choice to let the speech of the day be historically accurate. Although we have come a long way in our department and as a nation, we are clearly still struggling with race and the dream of equality for all men and women.

Courtesy of AAFFM

Sam Haskins was the first black man hired by the Los Angeles Fire Dept.

Excerpts from "***THE OLD STENTORIANS***"
Dedicated to the memory of Arnett B. Hartsfield (Fireman) and Billy G. Mills (L.A. City Councilman)

A group of black firefighters formed a group called "The Stentorians", a name selected for its appropriateness and definition: from Stentor, a Greek herald celebrated for his powerful voice. Extremely loud or powerful (a stentorian voice; able to utter a very loud sound).

The Stentorians adopted the motto: "We only fight the Department on integration." Their pledge was to support the Department on every other occasion such as bond issues, pension, benefits and salaries. Their hope: To, in the end, maintain the respect of every fireman. They did not expect the ferocity that came.

The history of the black firemen is fascinating. Call Fireman Sam Haskin is the first known black man to work on the Los Angeles Fire Department. He came to Los Angeles around 1880 and began working as a "Call Fireman" in 1892. It was a paid part-time position that was needed so he could cover for members who were off on vacation or sick. It was a time of the horse-drawn Hose Wagon.

On November 19, 1895 Engine Company 2 received an alarm at the station which was located at 2127 East First Street. The Engine Company responded with the Hose Wagon leading the way, with the steam engine following. Fireman Haskins climbed on the rear tailboard of the engine next to the engineer. When they hit rough pavement on Main Street, Sam Haskins lost his balance and fell into the large wheel on the left side of the boiler. Sam Haskins died a short while later at the Engine House. He was well-liked and had many friends around town. He was the first member of the Fire Department to die in the line of duty and his funeral was attended by Chief Walter S. Moore, his assistant Ed R. Smith, and Ira J. Francis, the electrician.

A large detail of 30 men from the Fire Department as well as members of the police department attended. The funeral procession was headed by a band and Chief Moore delivered a grave-side address.

The death of Fireman Haskins prompted Councilman Ashman to direct the Fire Commission to organize an Engine Company to be composed of colored men. A motion was put forward to the Fire Commission on November 26, 1895.

Courtesy of AAFFM

(l to r): Fireman Bill Cotterell, Capt. James Akers, Fireman Sanford Jones and Fireman Herb Spragin.

Lieutenant George W. Bright was hired in October 1897 and was the first black member of the Los Angeles Fire Department. Appointed by the Fire Commission and assigned as a Call Man and assigned to Engine Company No. 6. In less than a month on November 1, 1897 Bright was promoted to a full-time horseman and assigned to Engine Company No. 1. On January 31, 1900 he was promoted to Driver Third Class and assigned to Chemical Engine Company No. 1.

On August 1, 1902 George Bright was promoted to Lieutenant. In those early days Chief Officers made the promotions. However, before the Fire Commission would certify his promotion, Bright, being the first colored to express desires for such advancement was required to go to the Second Baptist Church and obtain an endorsement from his Minister and congregation.

This is where Segregation began. The Department, to avoid Bright from commanding white firemen, gathered up all of the colored and Mexican-American firemen and formed the city's first all-black fire company: Chemical Company No. 1, located at 137 S. Belmont (or 129 Loma Drive) across the street from the present site of Belmont High School.

At the turn of the century, the demographics of Los Angeles were changing. It was decided to move the black firemen from Hose Company No. 4 (in an all-white area) and move them to Fire Station 30, an emerging mixed-race neighborhood. In 1924, Hose Company No. 4 was closed and Engine Company 58 opened in the same building. The black firemen were transferred to Engine Company 30.

On September 4, 1917 the City Council directed the Fire Commission to remove the white firemen from Fire Station 30 at 1401 S. Central Avenue and replace them with the black firemen from Hose Company No. 4. Then Acting Chief Engineer O'Donnell resented the City Council's interference of internal Fire Department affairs and refused - only he had the authority to assign personnel. In addition, Engine 30 required an engineer and the city's Engineering Department had a policy of refusing to certify blacks. Blacks were only trained to operate chemical hose companies.

The black firemen and their community leaders had mixed feelings. Many of the old black firefighters preferred the system as it stood. Some saw it as an advantage, as an easier chance for their individual advancement. Shift trading was informal, but even more the blacks feared the probable hostility they could encounter if transferred to a white company. Another proposal was put forward by the black community and many black firefighters: convert Engine 21 and 22 to all black companies which would open up promotional opportunities for more captains and enable the department to form a battalion of all black companies led by black chiefs on each platoon.

A third approach was the one primarily espoused by the younger black firefighters who felt that the existing system was blocking them from promotions, even within their own stations. With all the positions their own two companies already filled they had no place to go. They planned to make the LAFD their career and wanted immediate and total integration of the blacks at Fire Station 14 and 30 into stations throughout the city. They found strong 14th Amendment Constitutional support for their ideas as well as the backing of the National Association for the Advancement of Colored People (NAACP) and Los Angeles' black-owned newspapers.

Flash forward to Chief John H. Alderson who was appointed Chief Engineer (today called Fire Chief) on March 7, 1940. He was welcomed aboard as a member of the LAFD on September 2, 1923, promoted to Captain in 6 years and then Battalion Chief on October 16, 1935. He was assigned to Battalion 9.

Alderson and Integration is an interesting chapter in the history of the Los Angeles Fire Department. The Old Stentorians called it Alderson vs Integration. As written in the documents of the "Old Stentorians" the years between 1937 and 1946 might well be termed even less eventful in the lives of Negroes in the department than the years before, but for two events; a force and an object which would clash with the violence of thunder and flash with the searing strength of lightening. The object was to integrate the Negro members of the department into firstly higher ranks and secondly into all other stations which had remained all white since Bright became a Lieutenant in 1902. The force was Chief Engineer John Alderson and the resistance which he generated within the Fire Department itself, the Civil Service Department, and the general Los Angeles community as a whole. The first period of history then was dominated by segregation; the second was clearly spotlighted by "integration."

John Alderson was a Rhodes Scholar who also studied for the ministry, a brilliant firefighter who introduced the "academy concept" for fire training, including the drill tower. It had been rumored that the specifications for the Chief Engineer position were especially written for him in late 1939. His rank at that time was that of a Battalion Chief, and up to that point in time only Assistant Chiefs qualified for the position of Chief Engineer. However, his abilities were undisputed and it seemed to all concerned that the mere technicality of a "spec" requirement should not be permitted to deny the city the services of such a man as its Fire Chief. Many of the black firemen believed that the Civil Service specifications were changed so that he could meet the qualifications - an interesting fact, in light of the anti-standard-lowering statements he would make nearly a decade and a half later, in arguing against the cause of integration.

The early Alderson years, 1940-1946, was a period during which both the idea of restricting Negro members to two stations and limiting the number of such stations thoroughly crystalized. It occurred to some members of the Negro community that there just might be a way to increase the number of promotional opportunities available to their firemen. They came up with the idea that it was time to have two more all

Negro stations, based on the premise that a couple of things would result. First, it would not be anything negative to the Chief's position to keep them out of the white stations. Next, it would create a complete Negro Battalion, and thereby allow growing room for some of the bright young men in the department to promote. They considered some men as potential Battalion Chiefs. Other positions in lesser ranks would be automatically created, since each new station would require new men in all classes.

This group, under the leadership of Mrs. Charlotta Bass, publisher of the *California Eagle Newspaper*, approached Chief Alderson. His reactions clearly reflected his attitude concerning increasing the number of Negro openings, though the language he used must have confused some, as they heard and read more of his position statements. "Are you asking for segregation?" he inquired. "I am unalterably opposed to and will never approve another segregated station." The effect of his position, though laudable on the surface, was to eliminate expansion potential in one direction.

In the mid 1980s I, as Assistant EMS Bureau Commander, was assigned from the EMS Bureau to Operations for several Internal Affairs investigations. This was not unusual as EMS expertise was needed in those cases involving EMS Bureau personnel. The first case was one involving a Firefighter/Paramedic who had several complaints lodged against him from community members. I was to partner up with Battalion Chief Paul Orduna, one of the few African American Chief Officers at the time.

We hit it off immediately. Chief Orduna introduced me to "The Old Stentorians", a manuscript concerning the history of the black firefighters of the past. I began reading the document at home with great interest and found it to be sometimes unbelievable as to what pranks and insults would be perpetrated upon the black firefighers. One of the Fire Commissioners indicated that the Fire Commission had decided to pass over Orduna because he looked "too good" or "too pat". They decided he was not a "bonifide applicant" and there had been some organized effort to produce the most impressive young Negro that could be found. Then convince him to take the firefighter examination for the singular purpose of causing trouble. At that time it was apparent that none of the commissioners viewed this situation as improper. Somehow this man named Orduna must be stopped from making it to the "drill tower" for training. Somehow, they thought, he needed to be stopped.

The Commissioner indicated further that when Orduna drove to Los Angeles all the way from Omaha the second time (he had driven out a previous time to take the Fireman's test) it was decided that it was perhaps that he was serious about the job. Even getting to the tower, after his second try, gave him little confidence that he would get through. Orduna was very sensitive to everything in the wind. The rumor was overheard and passed on by a friendly white fireman that Orduna was to be "taken care of" at the tower. It was decided that great effort had to be made to save his job before the discharge actually took place.

At the time this occurred Deputy Chief Bahme was working as the Department Personnel Officer and was as friendly as a white fireman could be in those days. He was a gifted fireman and had written the Dangerous Chemical Code. He was much respected throughout the department. It was decided that Arnett Hartsfield (one of the authors of "The Old Stentorians") would contact Bahme and plead with him to investigate the Orduna rumors, and to consider very carefully the anti-integration attitudes of the Tower personnel. It should be pointed out that Bahme was a lawyer as well. It was determined that the County Law Library would be a safe and inconspicuous place for two lawyers to have a casual conversation. The Deputy Chief promised to look into it, but he never reported back.

Within three or four days of the clandestine meeting, a related incident was unfolding. Fireman Rey Lopez was upset that he was being transferred from Fire Station 84 to another company. He thought it was just another series of hassles that he had gone through in the last couple of shifts. Hartsfield, somewhat concerned that he had heard nothing from Chief Bahme, had confidence in the Personnel Officer's commitment and what his looking into the matter would produce. He had also been informed that Orduna had done very well in training having been given excellent ratings from his "house mother", Station Captain. By all indications he was going to shortly conclude his probationary period. He suggested to fireman Lopez that it was quite possible he was being moved to make room for Orduna in the Negro spot at Fire Station 84. At that point Lopez became accepting of his transfer: Lopez then stated, "If that is why it is happening, then I will go along with it. I thought they were just picking on me again."

Orduna passed and was indeed assigned to Fire Station 84. Deputy Chief Bahme had delivered. Paul Orduna would later test for Captain and ultimately became a Battalion Chief.

Now deceased, I reflect on my time working with Chief Paul Orduna, who was a very intelligent and hard-working Chief Officer. Together, when assigned to Operations on several Internal Affairs investigations, we worked well and shared many stories about tough times on the Los Angeles Fire Department. I am saddened that he had to go through such deplorable treatment.

Courtesy L.A. Public Library

Los Angeles firefighter in uniform in 1910.

The integration fight went on for many years and involved the City Council, various mayors and the NAACP. In 1938 a new Mayor of Los Angeles was elected. Fletcher Bowron brought further improvements in city government including formal elimination of segregation in most departments. During the years 1949 to 1953 the Negro community, led primarily by the NAACP, attacked the "vestige" remaining in the Fire Department. Under Bowron, and, incidentally, under the policy of locating Negro firemen in stations strictly on the basis of color in 1953, their numbers reached 74, and the following year broke the all-time high of 81. This included 55 firemen out of 1721, 9 Auto Firemen out of 252, four engineers out of 181 and 6 captains out of 287. Despite the improvement, there were none who had reached any of the ranks beyond captain - the highest rank within an engine house (fire station).

Both Mayor Fletcher Bowron and Norris Poulson who followed, stated they would fight segregation. Success went to Norris Poulson.

Mayor Norris Poulson had a meeting in his office with Chief Engineer Alderson and the fire commissioners on January 7, 1954 and released the following statement to the press, "In an effort to conform with my firm

USC Library Collection

Referred to as "The Hill", Chemical Co. No. 1 was closed in 1907 and Hose Company No. 4 went into service in the same station with the same all-black crew.

policy of securing fair and equal treatment for all, the Board of Fire Commissioners has decided that there should be, commencing within the next six months, a gradual correction of these practices. In the interest of unity and my overall responsibility to all our citizens of whatever racial origin, I have acceded to this program of gradual correction of these policies." But several of the Commissioners and Chief Alderson disagreed with the Mayor, the Fire Chief denying that he agreed to do such a thing, "in six months, or in two months, or in one year."

In the meantime, the NAACP was tiring of the bickering between the Mayor, the Fire Chief and the Commissioners. The rhetoric continued but nothing was happening so the NAACP went to Superior Court. A petition was filed and approved, forcing Chief Alderson and the Commissioners to speak on the issues they had raised.

In court the drama continued to unfold as the Chief was called as the first witness. His testimony explains, though by no means justifies, earlier statements that he made when addressing the disparity between the number of Negroes in the city and the number in the Fire Department (10% vs. 3 % respectively). Alderson felt that "the Negro cannot compete, principally because of requirements for a high school diploma. The Negro population of Los Angeles consists in the main of an influx from the deep south which started during World War II. Most of these people are not high school graduates."

"In cross examination by NAACP attorneys, Alderson was quoted by the *Herald-Express* as saying that he believed in racial segregation. Other specific questions and answers recorded by the newspapers during the two-day session follow: Q: "Is it by accident or design that only Negros have been assigned to the two stations in question?" A: "It is not an accident. The practice has my complete consent and approval, and no one has imposed this policy on me."

Two of the Fire Commissioners stated they approved of the segregation policy and saw no change coming out of the Fire Commission. One of them stated, "From the information I have obtained and the people I have talked to, it appears that the firemen at stations 14 and 30 (the Negro Stations) do a fine job as a team and are well-trained...for that reason, I must go along with the policy-making officers of the Fire Department in their decision, until I'm convinced that I am wrong."

The Fire Commission, nevertheless, voted to answer the City Attorney's question in the affirmative. "Yes, assignments were made on the basis of race." The attorney, faced with this clear contradiction between the Chief and the Commission, passes the buck by advising that the problem was one that could only be solved by "administrative decision."

Both the State Attorney General and the United States Supreme Court condemns the policies. In a later interview, Chief Alderson implied he would quit the Department if the Commission persisted, "I will not remain to see it torn down to a second, third and fourth-rate Department", he stressed.

Ultimately, the Mayor directed the Fire Commission to end segregation; in a letter he placed responsibility for resolving the problem squarely upon them. They had the job of setting policy, while it was the Chief's job to carry out that policy. He also demanded in the toughest language to come from him that the Chief be fired if he does not go along, and "replace him with a man who does not regard himself as above the laws of our City, State and Nation.

There was tremendous support for the Chief throughout the Department. It should be noted that Chief Alderson was credited with making the Fire Department not only efficient, but among the top in the Nation. This reputation brought him immediate expressions of empathy from many different groups. It was viewed by many that the Chief was the victim of a vicious attack by the Mayor, the Fire Commission and the NAACP. After all it was the City Council that adopted a resolution early on praising him for his leadership and skills in building the City's fire-fighting techniques and fire-prevention methods.

Some local newspapers supported the Fire Chief, but *The Mirror News* graphically and visually set forth a majority editorial opinion in one of its cartoons. A giant snail with "L.A. Fire Dept. Integration" written upon its shell. A fireman on top labeled "Chief Alderson"; three hands each pulling a Fire Alarm Box lever; one labeled Public", another "Fire Comm.", and a third, "Mayor".

Cartoon from *The Mirror News*, circa 1955.

In its editorial of July 25, the same newspaper said, "Over the years, Fire Chief Alderson has done an outstanding job of building the Los Angeles Fire Department into one of the best in the nation." In view of his administrative ability it is difficult to understand how and why the Chief has been bogged down in what should have been a relatively simple task of integrating a few Negro firemen through a Department numbering 2,500 men.

On May 17, 1954 the United States Supreme Court handed out opinions in the cases of Brown vs Board of Education. They indicated "Classifications based solely on race must be scrutinized with particular care, since they are contrary to our traditions and hence constitutionally suspect. As long ago as 1896 this court declared the principle that the Constitution of the United States, in its present form, forbids, so far as civil and political rights are concerned, discrimination by the General Government or by the states, against any

Courtesy of AAFFM

Company-30, historic photo of Fire Station Engine No. 30, circa 1947.

citizen." Chief Justice Earl Warren, former Governor of California, significantly, delivered them.

Despite the fact that Alderson categorically denied that he made his assignments based on race, he pointed out that Negroes had been assigned to work in other capacities other than Fire Stations 14 and 30. He named Fire Prevention as one location. "Every transfer and assignment which I have made during my term of office has been based not on race but what in my considered opinion was best for the morale of the Department, the efficiency of the Department and the benefit to the people of the City that the Department serves."

Assemblyman William Byrum Rumford, a Negro from San Francisco, had asked the State Attorney general to study the question based on the statement of facts prepared by the Los Angeles Branch of the NAACP. The opinion came down in July 1954. It supported the position of the applicant in the following language: "If Negro firemen have been systemically assigned only to fire houses already entirely manned by Negro firemen and regularly have been denied transfers to other fire houses, the courts will conclude that the administrative officer is acting upon assumptions concerning the racial group characteristics of Negroes. Such action is not permitted. State opinion was prepared under the direction of Attorney General Edmund G. Brown, later to become California Governor.

Based on the U.S Supreme Court, not to forget the NAACP, Chief Alderson was to be fired by the Fire Commission. As the Mayor had pointed out to the Commission earlier, they had the power to deal with the many refusals of the Chief. The Mayor wanted quick action. A secret meeting was called by Mayor Poulson, inviting the Commissioners and the City Attorney, Roger Arnebergh, to discuss the matter. He had decided to force the dismissal.

On December 15, 1955, Alderson was ordered relieved of duty by the Fire Commission on the charge of insubordination in that:

1. He refused to sign a Fire Commission order directing all personnel to cooperate with a private investigator hired to probe the problems of integration in the Fire Department.
2. He defied the Fire Commission by transferring integrated men back to all Negro stations.
3. He refused to discipline white firemen for alleged acts inimical to the integration of Negroes into white stations.

The Fire Commission Board immediately appointed Deputy Chief Rothermell to the position of Acting Fire Chief. He had come into the Department in 1912 and he and Alderson had been friends through the years. When asked by a reporter if he planned any transfers of personnel, he replied "absolutely not!" He indicated further that he would not do anything that would upset Alderson's integration program. The latter comment added much confusion in light of his predecessor's most recent actions.

In a short time, Chief Rothermell wavered on his earlier comments and eased back on his pro-Alderson statements he had made. Meanwhile Alderson continued in the limelight, though dimly, protesting his dismissal, claiming he had not been insubordinate, but instead had fallen victim to the whole integration war which had been mapped and commanded by Mayor Poulson for political reasons. His age was not the only thing that Rothermell's appointment as Acting Chief Engineer (age 65) look like a temporary arrangement. Within hours the Fire Commission asked for an examination to fill the permanent position. Battalion Chief Charles Bahme was the only applicant. Later, others applied. One was Assistant Chief William L. Miller, a Lt. Commander in the United States Naval Reserves. He had been relatively quiet during the integration fight; his name did not show up on any of the literature, news stories, or interviews covering this very difficult time. In fact, it gave him a considerable advantage.

Rothermell had clearly lined up with the pro-Alderson forces, and applicant Bahme was considered a "good guy" by the pro-integration personnel within the Department.

Courtesy of AAFFM

At the turn of the century the demographics of Los Angeles were changing. It was decided to move the black firemen from Hose Co. 4 and its all-white area, to Fire Station 30, an emerging mixed-race neighborhood.

HOW DOES IT ALL END?

Chief Engineer John Alderson announced his intention to retire effective December 29, 1955. Meanwhile, the integration pressure cooker was reaching the point of boiler. Years of steadily burning tensions spilled into the fire stations. Alderson was growing physically and emotionally ill. The firefighters still called him "Big John" - but not to his face. It is clear that he was delaying action until full integration occurred with or without him as Chief Engineer.

Years of steadily burning tensions, frustrations, hate, rumors, propaganda and attacks upon Alderson by organizations and people who were perceived by the firefighters as knowing nothing about life in the fire stations, provided all of the necessary ingredients for turmoil.

Alderson retired on schedule. On January 17, 1956 William L. Miller was appointed Chief Engineer. The first order of business was a solution to the integration problem. Miller asked for time to do it and by then the combatants were so weary that they agreed to give it to him. Two weeks into his administration, Miller transferred eight black firefighters unopposed to integration to Fire Station 7 at 2824 S. Main Street. Miller said he intended it as an experiment. The experiment at Fire Station 7 worked.

In September 1956 with little difficulty, all black firefighters were transferred into 17 of the City's 91 fire stations. Hazing did continue intermittently, but the long agony was essentially over. All black fire stations 14 and 30 were no longer segregated. They became integrated too.

If Alderson is to be faulted, the criticism must stem from his failure to take definitive action when he realized integration was inevitable. He could and should have taken the action before the problem got beyond his control. Those who knew him best say that Alderson's charisma among members of the department and his leadership strengths were such that the firefighters would have accepted integration, however unhappily, if only he had acted sooner.

History demonstrates that valuable lessons can be learned from events of the past. With the integration horrors over, there were long-standing and positive fallouts. For starters, it helped propel one of the most outstanding black officers who ever served the department, Jim Stern, to become LAFD's first Battalion Chief on February 6, 1968. Chief Stern, thoroughly imbued with the LAFD's high standards of fire prevention and fire protection, went on to become Chief of the Pasadena Fire Department and one of the few blacks ever elected President of the International Association of Fire Chiefs.

The hard and bitter lessons learned during the integration period surely had a helpful impact upon the entrance of women and other minorities into the uniformed ranks of the LAFD.

Another upside of the integration aftermath was that it reminded everyone of the fact that traditions die hard in the fire service. More than half-a-century of segregation tradition was broken in the relatively short period of time it was, without creating permanent rifts in the department, and testifies to the resilience of the LAFD and its members.

The hard and bitter lessons learned during the integration period surely had a helpful impact upon the entrance of women and other other minorities into the uniformed ranks of the LAFD.

If in Los Angeles, I recommend everyone stop and check out the **African American Firefighter Museum**. It is located at 1401 S. Central Avenue, Los Angeles, CA 90021. Phone number is (213) 744-1730. It opened in 1997, has brought the past alive and is a chance for all visitors to see it. The building is listed with the National Registry of Historical places and is a cultural landmark in and for the City of Los Angeles.

Paul Ditzel

1926 – 2005

A friend to me, the Department, and our City

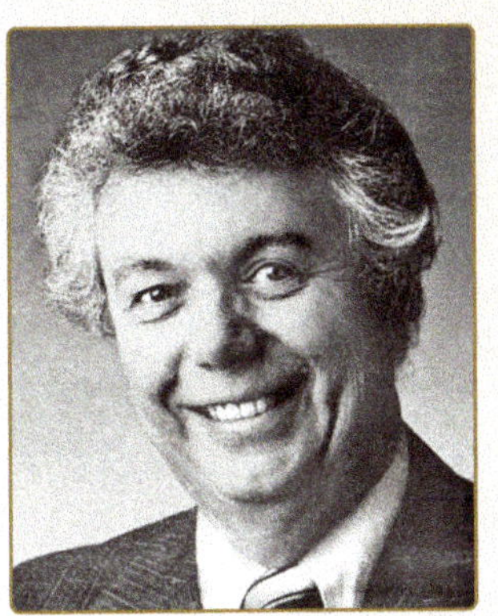

Many of the facts and history contained in this book are sited directly from Paul's numerous works on the subject of the LAFD during his long and storied career.

The City's first civilian Fire Inspector
Appointed March 1, 1967 by Chief Raymond Hill

Author – "A Century of Service"

Author – "Fire Engines, Firefighters"
Submitted by his publisher for a Pulitzer Prize in American History

Editor – "LAFD Centennial 1886-1986"

Bowker Award Winner (for "Railroad Yard")

Newspaper and Wire Service, reporter and columnist

A proactive associate of LAFD for more than 36 years

Chairman of Mayor Tom Bradley's Arson Task Force and multiple public awareness committees

Paul was a trusted adviser to the Honorable Mayor Tom Bradley

Paul knowingly put his professional livelihood at risk when he took a deliberate and controversial stand against the racially-motivated hurdles facing African Americans within the LAFD. As predicted, this stand against the inherent biases of the time within the Department hierarchy did indeed cause Paul to be suspended from his staff writing position for a major publication.

My dear friend Paul will be remembered fondly for what he brought to the broader conversation on multiple fronts and actions he took seeking a better Fire Department and a better City - the stand Paul took for so many of us living in the City of Angels.

WILLIAM R. BAMATTRE
CHIEF ENGINEER AND GENERAL MANAGER

December 29, 1997

TO: All Members, Bureau of Human Resources
THROUGH CHANNELS

FROM: Alan R. Cowen, Deputy Chief
Bureau of Human Resources

SUBJECT: **HUMAN RESOURCES STATEMENT-ZERO TOLERANCE**

The Los Angeles City Fire Department is committed to providing a professional work atmosphere in which employees at all levels are viewed as integral components of the overall management team of the Department. The people in any organization are the most valuable resource of that organization and as such must be accorded the respect and dignity due any member of the community whom we serve. The above is not only the philosophy of the Los Angeles City Fire Department, but serves as my personal leadership vision of the Bureau of Human Resources. It is essential that every employee within the Human Resources Bureau understand my commitment to this philosophy.

In support of my vision, I will not tolerate any ethnic, gender or any type of discrimination in the workplace whatsoever. Additionally, as the Commander of the Bureau of Human Resources, it is my charge to ensure that zero tolerance for any act of discrimination is maintained in the workplace. Furthermore, I will personally hold all officers and supervisors accountable for their actions and those of their subordinates relative to the absolute policy of zero tolerance of any act of discrimination, hostility, harassment or unprofessionalism within the workplace.

Not only is differential treatment that could result in discrimination based on race, gender, or national origin unlawful, but activity of this nature disrupts the morale and performance of an organization; it is wrong.

Dignity, respect and fairness are not only employee rights; they are human rights as well.

ALAN R. COWEN, Deputy Chief
Bureau of Human Resources

ARC:ann

BEE-WARE 911

African Honey Bees

In early 1993 I began to be concerned about the Africanized honey bee due to reading about the dangers they may cause if a person is stung. The media gave this subject considerable attention following confirmation of their arrival in Arizona and the first death in the United States. The victim was an elderly Texas man.

Special training session to deal with a new threat to LAFD, the "Africanized honey bees".

Africanized honey bees have been blamed for 151 deaths in Mexico since 1987 and more than 1000 deaths in the 36 years since they were released accidentally in Brazil (as of 1993). The bees that were reported in Arizona were expected in Southern California in the summer of 1994. Traps were set along the Arizona border in order to alert agricultural personnel when the swarms arrived.

I put this entire subject on a Bureau Commander's meeting in 1993 in order to present this startling information and hopefully be ready for the possibility of LAFD personnel being stung while on emergencies. In addition, I was prepared to order any equipment and supplies that may be needed to meet this potential crisis. At the meeting I presented the facts as I knew them and was careful to not make this a bigger issue than it was; my reception by the other Bureau Commanders was lukewarm to cold.

Of the four Bureau Commanders, two thought I had been drinking "fire water" just to suggest that this would affect firefighters. The other two (myself included) were open to the fact that firefighters may well run into these nasty bees when in the wooded areas of Los Angeles or where people who are beekeepers may experience them. One Deputy Chief thought it was absolutely ridiculous. Upon the completion of my presentation, the Fire Chief, Donald O. Manning, told a personal story to the staff. In short, while he did not experience any Africanized honey bees, he did have a swarm of bees that took up occupancy in his home within a wall. He indicated that the wall was taken out and thousands of honey bees had invaded the inner sanctum at his home.

Firefighter dons the necessary protection.

Duct tape: pride and proven method in the emergency responder's tool kit helps keep the bees outside protective gear.

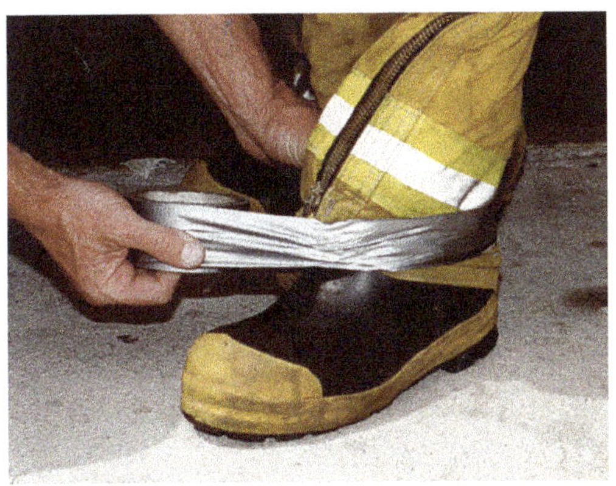

Needless to say, he asked me to give him my original F-225 (red letterhead formal request) and stamped it APPROVED and signed it. I kept my grin to myself and watched the two deputy chiefs who had poo-poo'd my idea give me a strange look.

I went to work right away and had my staff begin working on obtaining the necessary equipment to include bee hoods, videos for each of the then 102 Fire Stations in the City of Los Angeles, and other "indestructible veils" for use by firefighters and paramedics. I also went to meetings of the Los Angeles County Beekeepers Associations where I met Mr. C. R. (Charlie) Duncan, the President of that organization. His business card had his name, address and phone number plus a caricature of a honeybee, with the inscription under his name that simply stated, "Counselor to Her Majesty". His organization was well aware of the Africanized honey bee and totally agreed that Fire Departments everywhere should be cognizant of these angry bees and be prepared (or should we say BEE PREPARED).

Our Training Division prepared a training bulletin entitled, "Africanized Honey Bees". It contained various sections: Introduction, Characteristics and Behavior, Public Health Impact, Personnel Safety and Considerations, Controlling Measures, Emergency Medical Treatment and Bee Hoods (nets).

Soon after, every fire station in the City of Los Angeles was now prepared for any bee emergency. A short video was obtained from the A. I. Root Company, in conjunction with the Erhart, Ohio Volunteer Fire Department. The video is short but covers everything one would need to know to handle a bee emergency.

As Chair of the EMS Committee of the California State Firefighters Association at that time, we organized a presentation of the Africanized honey bees that was hosted by Northridge Hospital Medical and Trauma Center. Our speaker was Mr. C. R. "Charlie" Duncan, President of the Los Angeles County Beekeepers Association, as one of our featured speakers, an expert in the field. Firefighters from all over the area attended the seminar in 1994 and came away with a greater knowledge on how to handle bee emergencies.

The Bureau of Emergency Medical Services received nearly a hundred calls about our program, some from other agencies out of California. Today, 30 years later, the LAFD still is ready for any bee incidents.

SHOOTING
USC Medical Center

On February 9, 1993, I responded to Los Angeles County USC Medical Center for a shooting of three doctors by an armed gunman. Additionally, two women were held hostage for several hours before the gunman surrendered to police. Police identified the individual as a disgruntled former patient who was irritated over what he described as poor medical treatment. Hospital officials indicated that the gunman did not know the doctors he shot nor the two people he held hostage. The suspect was quoted as saying, "I feel like I am a victim of a medical conspiracy", as police led the handcuffed man to the police vehicle.

One witness said the shooter said nothing, but just opened fire and everyone was screaming "Run! Run! Run!"

One doctor received gunshot wounds to the abdomen and head and was in extremely critical condition, another was shot in the upper body and suffered a collapsed lung, while the third was shot in the upper arm and scalp and was in serious condition. One witness said the shooter said nothing, but just opened fire and everyone was screaming "Run, Run, Run!"

After shooting the doctors, the suspect went into an office and came back with a hostage who was struggling, her head locked in his arm. Chased by several security guards, the suspect barricaded himself in an X-ray area. Two hostages were ultimately released after several hours of negotiations. One of the hostages was a female physician and the other a receptionist, who was on her first day of work at the hospital. Both were quite upset after the incident.

A 44-caliber magnum revolver, a 38-caliber automatic pistol, a sawed-off rifle and a hunting knife were recovered from the shooter according to Los Angeles Deputy Police Chief Robert Gil. It should be noted that the incident did not force the entire hospital to evacuate. However, the then busiest emergency room in the nation interrupted care for thousands of patients. LA County USC Medical Center at that time had 2045 beds and served as many as 15,000 patients a day and is the largest of the six public hospitals and the cornerstone of the County's trauma care network.

The shooting renewed concerns about safety in Los Angeles County Hospitals. Workers at hospitals have been concerned about their safety for years but efforts to improve security have been cut by tight budgets. Many doctors and health care workers have been frustrated because they work in dangerous environments. One of the physicians stated, "It's a common occurrence that we take weapons from patients after they have already been on our tables" said Dr. Paul Wallace, then President of the union representing resident physicians and interns at county hospitals. Wallace said his organization has pushed for additional security

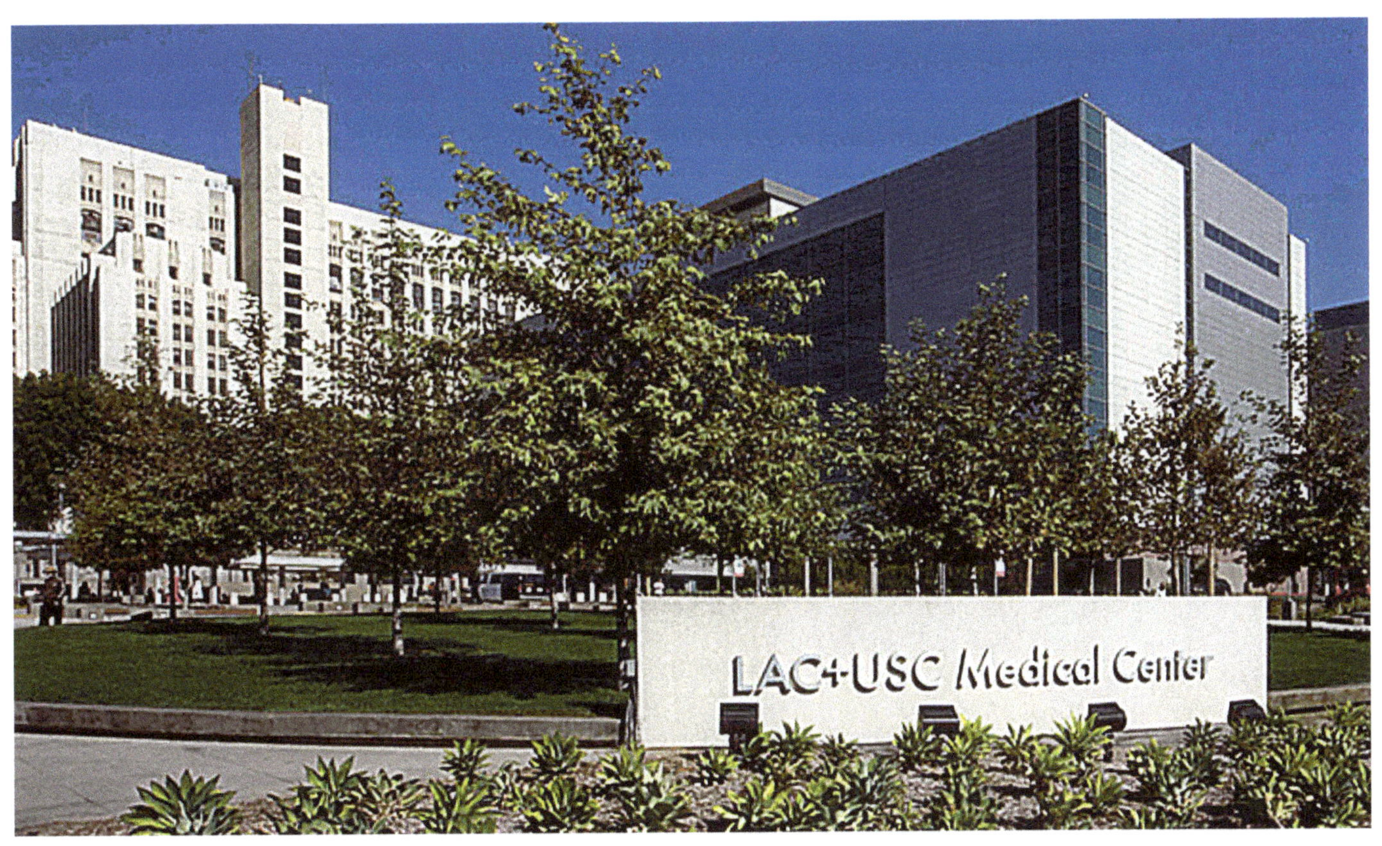

measures to be taken for two years, but repeatedly has been told that the county has little money to invest in additional improvements.

Los Angeles Hospitals remain a potential for violence to this day. Virginia Price Hastings, Los Angeles County Emergency Services Director at that time stated, "The area hospitals, both private and county-owned, have been increasing targets of violence in recent years particularly in emergency rooms and trauma centers where stress, frustration, gang members and violent or drugged patients combine to cause problems. Literally every hospital has armed guards," stated Hastings. "The fear is not so much the victim but what comes with the victim."

VIOLENCE
in Emergency Departments

As the result of three physicians being shot in the Emergency Department of the Los Angeles County/USC Medical Center on February 9. 1993, a task force was established to study the problem. The task force was initiated by the Los Angeles Emergency Medical Director's Association and the Healthcare Association of Southern California that included participation by the Los Angeles City Fire Department, Emergency Nurses Association, Los Angeles County Department of Health Services, Los Angeles County Medical Association and hospital and non-municipal security representatives. The subject matter was the problem of emergency department violence in Los Angeles County.

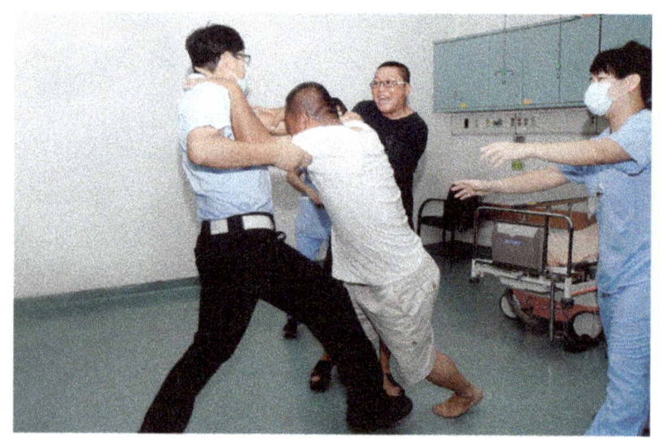

Without a doubt, violence in the workplace is on the rise in our country. Post offices, courthouses and hospitals are seeing more and more violence, episodes that seem to be increasing. This is no secret to those who are employed in emergency departments; it is more violent and more dangerous than ever before.

This select task force desired to collect factual data and thus developed a survey instrument to obtain not only data but perceptions and beliefs about emergency department violence. Most of the questions were directed to hospital emergency department managers, but some were specifically designed for security staff. The survey was sent out to 85 receiving hospitals that comprised Los Angeles County's Emergency Medical System (EMS) at the time; 77 responded, a 91% response return. The 4,082-square-mile county was divided into five districts based on pre-established Hospital Council criteria. The collected responses were representative of these districts and entire county.

It is unknown why 8 hospitals failed to respond to the survey, but it is highly unlikely that their responses would have differed from the 77 that did respond, or would have changed the outcome. This survey remains the first emergency department violence study to successfully gather data from a defined geographical area. Conclusions, therefore, are applicable to Los Angeles County only and should not be assumed to be accurate in other metropolitan areas.

Observations and Conclusions from the Survey

The results of the survey reflect an increase in the frequency of violent incidents in emergency departments. Verbal abuse from patients and their visitors, which occurs daily or weekly in 95% of the emergency departments, has become a way of life for emergency department staff. Threats of physical violence occurs weekly or monthly in 55% of them, with 19% reporting staff time lost due to related injuries.

While emergency department violence involving gangs is more likely to be publicized, drugs and alcohol - especially the latter - most often play a role. Patients and their visitors frequently carry weapons into the hospital. Knives are identified by survey respondents as the most common weapon encountered and guns run a close second. These facts suggest a troubling escalation in the deadliness of the armaments involved in these situations.

Violence in the workplace is on the rise in our country.

It is no surprise that the emergency department is a very stressful place to work. Considering this data, the emergency department is the place within the hospital that most of the assault/violent behavior occurs. The consistency of the data reiterates the need for upgrading hospital security measures. Security personnel are called upon almost daily to respond to the emergency department. Most hospitals report acceptable response times, but there is clearly a need for improved training and staffing of security personnel and for more solid policies and procedures. Whether or not security personnel should be armed is complex. Most of the survey respondents do not believe it is the answer for their institutions. Almost all of their security officers wear uniforms but most are unarmed. Only 11% carry firearms; at least one-third are armed with other types of devices.

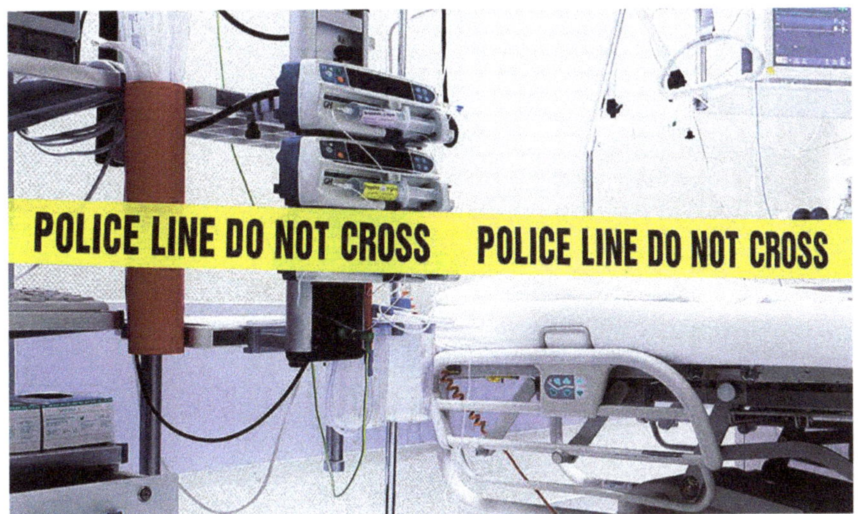

Based on survey results, the following task force recommendations, in large part, mirror the then new California Health and Safety Code sections 1257.7 and 1257.8 (formerly AB-508) which had a July 1, 1995 deadline for hospital compliance. Since violence in the emergency department appears to be inevitable, all hospitals should have developed appropriate and adequate security plans. Emergency department and security staff should have received training that equipped them to handle violent patients and situations. Communication between emergency department management, the hospital's security department and local law enforcement is essential in developing comprehensive response and contingency plans. Perhaps the single most important physical modification that a hospital can make is controlled access to the emergency department.

This survey was exploratory, a snapshot of existing conditions. As with most surveys it has raised many, many questions. The optics of emergency department violence is not a pretty one; much work is still needed to make our ERs safe.

In recent years prior to this event, hospital violence was quite apparent in the country. Examples include:

1991 - In Los Angeles four nurses were eating breakfast in the hospital cafeteria at Los Angeles USC Medical Center, when an individual sank a pair of scissors into the neck of one of the nurses.

In Salt Lake City, a 39-year-old Utah man, angry because doctors performed sterilization surgery on his wife, stormed a suburban hospital, armed with dynamite and two weapons. He killed a nurse and held 8 people hostage before surrendering.

In Costa Mesa, California, at Fairview Developmental Center, an employee who was angry at administrators for ignoring tensions in his division, shot and killed a facilities supervisor and injured two others.

In Los Angeles, gang gunfire tore through the windows at White Memorial Hospital in Boyle Heights and shotgun pellets struck a pregnant woman in the face.

1990 - In San Diego, California, a distraught man over the death of his father walked into Mission Bay Memorial Hospital and fired a barrage of bullets that killed a nurse and a hospital trainee as well as wounding a doctor and a visitor.

In Los Angeles at UCLA Medical Center, an assailant killed one woman and shot another several times.

In Los Angeles at LA County USC Medical Center, an 18-year-old gang member was shot in the face during an altercation involving about 20 youths who were visiting patients.

1989 - In New York at Bellevue Hospital Center, a 23-year-old homeless man with a history of psychiatric problems who had been living for weeks in a closet and roaming the hallways in a stolen lab coat, was charged with the rape and strangulation of a woman physician.

1988 - In Los Angeles, five carloads of gang members put Martin Luther King Jr./Drew Medical Center in Watts under virtual siege, converging on the lobby of the emergency room, terrorizing people.

1985 - In Chicago, a 32-year-old food service supervisor at Rush-Presbyterian, St. Luke's Medical Center, was assaulted and left bound and gagged on a hospital stairwell.

1984 - In Los Angeles at LA County USC Medical Center, a patient was shot to death by a security guard in the emergency room after he allegedly reached up from his gurney, grabbed another guard's gun and opened fire.

1982 - In Chicago, a woman being treated at the University of Chicago Medical Center in Hyde Park was raped in her hospital room.

In Chicago, a security guard was found beaten to death in a hallway of the Loyola University Medical Center near Maywood.

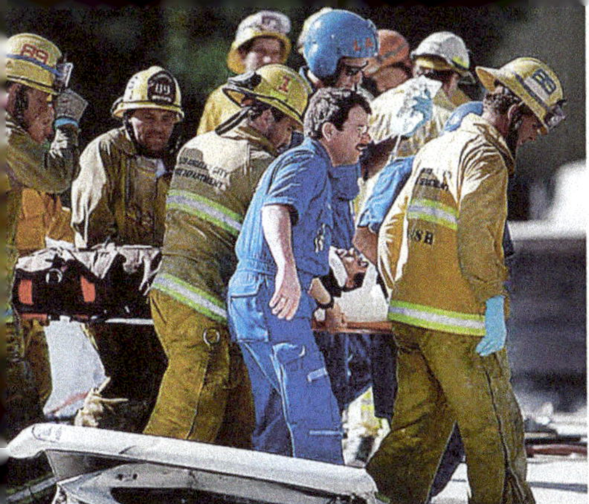

1994 Northridge Earthquake

Monday, January 17, 1994 - 4:30AM Everything was calm and quiet in Southern California. One minute later it wasn't! Southern California had a violently rude awakening.

1994 Northridge Earthquake

On Monday, 4:30AM, January 17, 1994, everything was calm and quiet in Southern California. One minute later it wasn't! Southern California had a rude awakening.

It was 4:31AM when a recently upgraded 6.7 magnitude earthquake rocked and rolled Southern California triggering dozens of fires, leaving thousands of people homeless and killing 57 people.

Called the Northridge Earthquake, it has been determined that in actuality, the epicenter was in Reseda, slightly south of Northridge.

The 6.7 magnitude shaker lasted a full 10 seconds as a mainshock followed by a full 30 seconds of rolling and rocking. Felt from Las Vegas to San Diego, it stands indelibly implanted in the minds, bodies and hearts of millions of Californians. Hundreds were injured, and hospitals scrambled to handle the onslaught, with 18 hospitals temporarily closing their doors, unable to function as emergency centers - themselves becoming casualties in need of aid.

Unquestionably, this quake was the largest to hit Los Angeles in anyone's memory. The 6.4 Sylmar quake in 1971 was a drop in the bucket compared to this monster. The only thing that didn't make this the "Big One" was that it struck on a legal holiday at 4:31AM. The same quake at 4:31PM on Friday would have probably killed thousands of people.

As it was, the quake caused major damage on three freeways, bringing to a halt the busiest freeway in the United States - the Santa Monica Freeway.

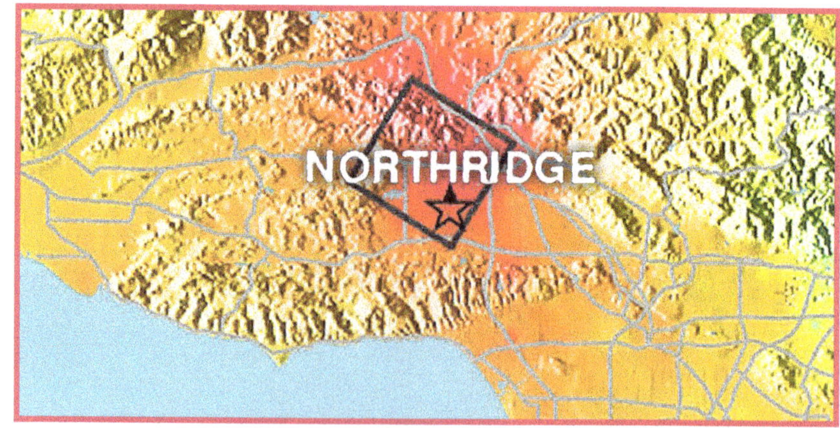

The 1994 Northridge earthquake was a moment magnitude 6.7 "blind thrust earthquake" that occurred on January 17, 1994 at 4:30:55 a.m. in the San Fernando Valley region of the City of Los Angeles. Casualties: 57 killed and 8,700 injured.

In Northridge, the worst case scenario came true - 16 people died when the Northridge Meadows apartment complex collapsed. The second and third stories literally collapsed on the sleeping. The three-story apartment suddenly was transformed into a two-story, with tons of concrete on top of the first floor. At the same time, LAPD Motor Officer Clarence Dean was flying off the freeway overpass that had suddenly, without warning, fallen away from the freeway. He died instantly.

California State University suffered major damage and fires. A four-level parking structure collapsed like a house of cards; a 64-car freight train derailed at Tampa and Nordhoff.

Kaiser Permanente's Medical office building on Balboa, north of Devonshire, fell to pieces in an instant, saving scores of women and children that would have been entombed had it occurred on a non-holiday during daytime hours.

The Wherehouse Music store, and many other businesses, was a total loss.

In comparison, nearly 23 years earlier, the San Fernando Valley awoke at 6:01AM on February 9, 1971 when a 6.4 magnitude quake killed 58 people. It became known throughout California as the Sylmar quake, having left over 1,000 injuries and damaging over 30,000 homes, 62 freeway bridges, 5 dams and four hospitals. Over 80,000 people were evacuated from their homes. Centered about 10 miles north of the small City of San Fernando, the Sylmar quake caused the temporary closure of many hospitals, including Olive View Medical Center, the Veteran Administration, Holy Cross Hospital, and Pacoima Memorial Hospital. Over 35% of the buildings in San Fernando were damaged.

The Sylmar quake also occurred early in the morning. This surely saved thousands of lives that would have otherwise been lost. It also was the impetus for the development of early earthquake preparedness. As it turned out, the Sylmar quake became the test for "earthquake safe" buildings, which were the result of stricter codes after the 1933 Long Beach quake. After the 1971 quake, L.A. passed a new reinforcement program which targeted over 8,000 hazardous unreinforced brick and masonry buildings.

Actions Taken By The LAFD

Kaiser Permanente Hospital was severely damaged that morning.

Within a minute of the Northridge earthquake, the Los Angeles City Fire Department went into the earthquake emergency operational mode, a pre-planned degraded dispatch that is implemented to conserve resources. Instead of sending usual assignments of companies, including rescue ambulances, a more conservative approach is utilized, wherein a single unit is dispatched, thereby making available scarce resources to handle the expected additional flood of calls for service.

Four floors under City Hall, the Emergency Operations Center (EOC) is made functional.

Each of the three Divisions that the City is divided into begin to conduct a roll call to determine whether any fire stations/apparatus are non-functional or damaged, as well as any injuries reported. Fire companies have immediately vacated all fire stations and moved to designated "safe areas".

Companies quickly report by radio to Battalion Commanders, who in turn do radio reports to Division Commanders. A time-tested system that works well is put through the test yet again! Following an assessment of damage, engine companies begin the task of doing drive-thru's within their Districts.

About the same time, early information received at the Emergency Operations Center revealed that more than 50 fires were burning, flooding in buildings occurred and power outages were reported. Fire and police stations are reported damaged, and due to generator failures, the computer system at the Department's Dispatch center failed and required "manual mode" dispatching. Luckily no 911 calls were lost. Serious consideration is given to evacuate the Emergency Operations Center and set up Department Command at Dodger Stadium, the pre-designated alternate site.

Department command took the following steps within an hour

1. L.A. City Department top staff was recalled.
2. The off-going platoon was held over to double routine staffing.
3. Fire Station 88 was established as Valley Command.
4. Dispatchers activated back-up dispatch systems at remote fire station.
5. 26 companies are sent to the San Fernando Valley as additional resources.
6. Additional Urban Search and Rescue Teams (USAR) are requested in anticipation of trapped people.

Hospital Status: six Valley hospitals are closed

Holy Cross Hospital
Olive View Medical Center
Northridge Hospital Medical Center
Granada Hills Community Hospital
Kaiser Hospital Panorama City
West Hills Regional Medical Center

Hospitals are closed due to "Internal Disaster," a category that fits in rather adequately as to the condition of the emergency department. While the desire on the part of most hospitals is to open, many find it physically impossible due to flooding, chemical spills resulting in hazmat incidents, and structural damage. Electrical failures result in inadequate/non-operative equipment. An EMS mess exists.

Damaged Fire Stations

Fire Station 70 is closed due to being unsafe for habitation. Major cracks in support columns have appeared. It is apparent that No. 70, located at 9861 Reseda, will need major renovation prior to being occupied. Fire Station 93, located at 19059 Ventura Boulevard, sustained serious damage. Brick plaster anchor supports came loose, and plaster has cracked.

Fire Station 78, located at 4230 Coldwater Canyon, had its hose tower torn away from the station. Plaster cracking was noted throughout the station, and 120 feet of exterior brick wall fell like rain. Ultimately, it was closed due to its unsafe condition. Engine 78 relocated to Fire Station 86, where it will remain until a new station is built.

Medical Branch Operations

As the EMS Bureau Commander, I went to my assigned Department vehicle and attempted to monitor radio traffic, but it was virtually impossible. Static was pronounced, and with the exception of a few words, legible communication was nill.

I responded to Fire Station 88, where I expected Department command to be organizing. Upon arrival, I assumed command of the EMS Branch of Valley Command. Deputy Chief Dave Parsons arrived simultaneously and became Incident Command. The Medical Branch was physically set up adjacent to the Department's Command Vehicle at Fire Station 88, just west of the station - tables and chairs were available.

Seven EMS Captains, including the EMS Assistant Bureau Commander, Dave Thompson, made up the Medical Branch at Valley Incident Command. While en route to Valley Command, Captain Thompson was re-routed to the Northridge Meadows apartments to supervise EMS activities. Captain Wade Jones, Commander, EMS District 3, "B" Platoon, assisted Thompson at what was to become a tragedy in itself - the death of 16 people due to a collapse. The Medical Group consisted of Captain Jones, (held over from the day before platoon), Captain Steve Johnson, EMS District 3, "C" Platoon, as well as Rescues 27, 39, 81, 93, 827, 818 (reserve) and a private ambulance. Dr. Palmer, LAFD's Medical Director, was also on scene.

Photo: LAFD

Thousands were injured, 18 hospitals temporarily closed and were in need of emergency aid.

Ultimately, 14 patients were seen and released at the treatment area, which was located in the parking lot of the post office directly across the street from the Meadows apartments. Seven more patients in all would be transported to area hospitals, three of which had been extricated from their entombment in first floor apartments by fire suppression personnel.

One of the first requests I received at Medical Branch was from Captain Thompson for a Department Chaplain. As it happened, Father Christian van Liefde had been talking with me only one minute earlier making himself available if needed. "Father Chris" as he is affectionately known, responded immediately.

At 10:30 hours, the Medical Branch determined that all ALS units operating in the San Fernando Valley would implement Communication Failure Protocols. This action was taken as Northridge Hospital and Holy Cross Hospital base stations were non-operational, having closed to internal disaster. The Department's use

Photo: LAFD

Over 112,000 structures were damaged in the earthquake.

of Communication Failure Protocols was announced on all rescue ambulance channels, and reaffirmed later via Department teletype and EMS District Captains.

The L.A. City Fire Department had regionally used Communication Failure Protocols in 1992 during the Civil Disturbances, and their use was without a single problem. Numerous hospitals appreciated their use, and subsequent newspaper articles chronicled their use. The Department of Health Services was notified of their implementation shortly thereafter and concurred with their use.

The use of failure protocols was discontinued on January 24, at 16:33 hours, seven days later. Paramedic units began to utilize their assigned base stations consistent with Reference No. 808, Base Hospital Contact. Although Northridge and Holy Cross Hospitals returned to normal base station operation, Holy Cross remained closed to ambulance traffic.

The Department of Health Services eliminated the ability of hospitals to go on diversion status to paramedic traffic with only "internal disaster" as the exception. This action enabled easier movement of patients to various hospitals.

Captain Kevin R. Nida organized the HAM radio operators (Amateur Radio Emergency Services), known as ARES, then responded to Valley Medical Branch. It was decided to send a HAM radio operator to as many hospitals as possible, thereby maintaining direct contact to maximize reliable and accurate information. Captain Nida would remain in charge of the ARES Communication Van at Fire Station 88 supervising amateur radio operation. This link between the Medical Branch and hospitals would prove to be invaluable, and facilitated radio traffic between the Medical Branch and the Los Angeles County Emergency Operations Center.

Amateur radio operators were the link at:

Olive View Medical Center	Granada Hills Hospital
Northridge Medical Center	UCLA Medical Center
Holy Cross Hospital	

Captain Harry Rich, Commander, EMS District 1, "C" Platoon, visited various hospitals to obtain specific and accurate information. His first-hand information, while bleak, was much needed.

Captain Allen Norman, Commander, EMS District 6, "B" Platoon, assisted early on with Medical Branch Operations, and oversaw communication with the L.A. County Emergency Operations Center, dispatch of resources from the Medical Branch and development of Casualty Collection Points, should they be required. Captain Larry Mayer, Commander, EMS District 6, "A" Platoon, supervised the Fire Department and private ambulance resources assigned to the Medical Branch. Captain Mayer would remain throughout the day and night at Fire Station 88 and ultimately was designated as the Medical Group Commander after I left Valley Command.

Captain James P. Denney, the EMS Bureau's Staff Assistant, maintained a dispatch log of still alarms that originated at Medical Command. In addition, he monitored and updated San Fernando Valley Hospital status with specific liaison within the Department of Health Services.

Captain Robert Linnell, Commander, EMS 1, "A" Platoon, was assigned the responsibility of obtaining emergency room status, including damage control. Bob attempted to obtain first-hand knowledge of damage by first calling emergency rooms on the telephone where possible; evacuation needs and assessments were determined.

The total number of 14 ambulances were staged at Valley Command. In Los Angeles County, 2,500 beds were lost as a result of the earthquake. Most hospitals closed as the result of water lines being ruptured, oxygen lines disrupted, and elevator power failure.

At the height of activity, only 136 critical beds were available County-wide, a frightening but real thought. In all, 18 hospitals were closed temporarily in Los Angeles County.

A total of eight hospitals required patient evacuation

Olive View Medical Center
Holy Cross Hospital
Northridge Hospital Medical Center
Granada Hills Community Hospital
L.A. County/USC Medical Center
Pediatric Pavillion
Veteran's Administration Medical Center
St. John's Hospital

Disaster Medical Assistance Teams, or DMATs, arrived several days after the earthquake. DMATs consist of physicians, nurses and emergency medical technicians and are provided by the Federal Emergency Management Agency (FEMA). Ten teams responded and four were used in rotation. They arrived at March Air Force Base on Friday night, January 21, and were taken by bus to sites in the San Fernando Valley area where tents were erected. The four teams were designated CA-1 through CA-4, referring to California and the numbered team. The four teams originated from Seattle, San Francisco, San Bernardino and Mexico, under the direction of Dr. Joe Iser, a Federal physician, U.S. Public Health.

The DMATs consisted of teams of 25-41 members. The teams established units complete with generators and were fully self-sufficient. By hauling in their own food, water and equipment, they become part of the solution, not the problem.

These MASH-like units have functioned in the worst scenarios, from hurricane Hugo in the Virgin Islands to Iniki in Hawaii. They go anywhere without using the impacted area's food and water. Members do not rely on resources at a disaster site.

Medically, the teams can handle from colds and flus to chicken pox and cardiac emergencies. They can refill lost medications, as one of the team members is a pharmacist.

The teams are dispatched by Federal Health authorities and are part of the national disaster medical system. The units are composed of civilians who carry their own equipment, which will operate on solar power if need be.

Most of the patients served by the DMATs were living in the various parks and shelters established since the shaker. Some were pregnant, others had lacerations and bruises. One child had chicken pox, another had fever and sore throat.

DMATs were sent to four County Comprehensive Health Centers as follows:
Burk Comprehensive Health Center in Venice
Mid-Valley In Van Nuys
Canoga Park Comprehensive Health Center
Valencia Health Center

In addition, DMATs responded to two acute care facilities: Northridge Hospital Medical Center and Granada Hills Community Hospital. All DMATs were demobilized on Sunday, January 30. In addition to DMATs, the Department of Health Services placed 12 mobile health clinic vans into service which provided minor medical care needs to approximately 30 parks.

Additionally, other mobile health vehicles from Kaiser Permanente, Martin Luther King/Drew Health Center and Mental Health Services were placed into service.

On January 25, 1994, a week after the most devastating earthquake in Southern California history, the following status of hospitals was released by the Southern California Hospital Council.

928 patients evacuated from damaged hospitals
805 beds available (136 critical, 669 non-critical)
7,757 patients treated/released from emergency rooms
1,496 patients treated/admitted to hospitals
57 dead
9,309 total casualties

At two billion dollars a second and two lives a second, the Northridge earthquake was most devastating and costly in terms of lives and property.

While this earthquake was the most damaging in anyone's memory, it could have been worse. In no small way, the efforts of Los Angeles City Fire Chief Donald O. Manning cannot be understated. It was Chief Manning who not only maintained Department command of this disaster, but was directly responsible for implementing the Fire Department's Disaster Preparedness Section just after the Whittier Narrows Earthquake October 1, 1987.

Community volunteers are trained by the Disaster Preparedness Section and become CERTS (Community Emergency Response Teams). The citizens who make up CERTS are dispersed throughout the City and obtain training in groups of 50. They are trained in basic disaster response, including fire suppression, rescue and first aid. Many volunteers were thankful for the training they received - some fully cognizant that their training saved lives and families. It was 1988 when Councilman Hal Bernson, in conjunction with Fire Chief Donald O. Manning, began the program. Over 10,000 citizens had been trained to date with more than half living in the San Fernando Valley.

Through Chief Manning's leadership and ability to forecast consequences, the City of Los Angeles was better prepared than ever to cope with this horrendous earthquake. Credit must be given to Chief Manning and the men and women who are out there where the rubber meets the road on a daily basis.

Now what?

Now 29 years after the Sylmar earthquake, we are still preparing for the "Big One". Let's be ready when Mother Nature shakes, rattles, and rolls.

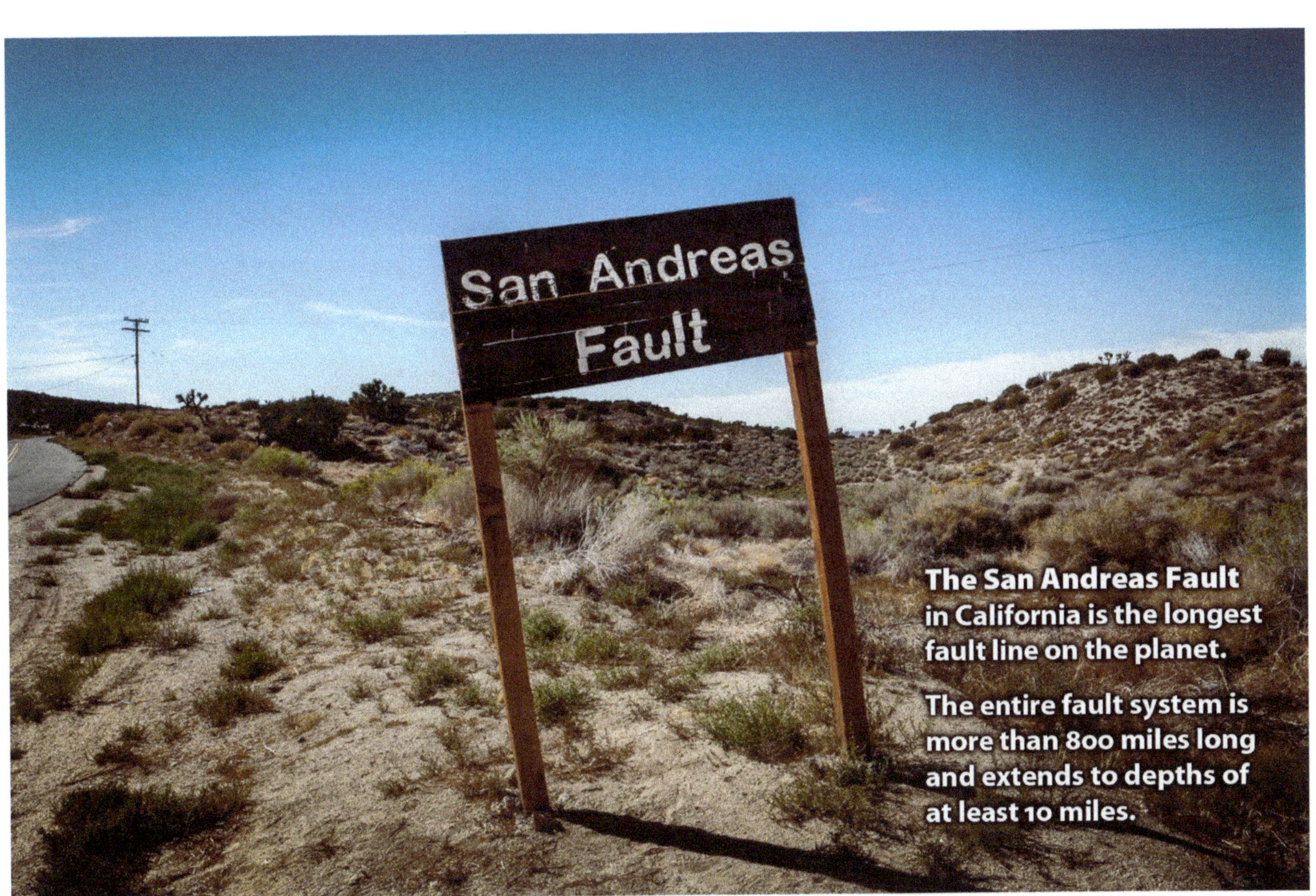

The San Andreas Fault in California is the longest fault line on the planet.

The entire fault system is more than 800 miles long and extends to depths of at least 10 miles.

FATALITIES: a sobering reality

Serving on the front lines of human tragedy

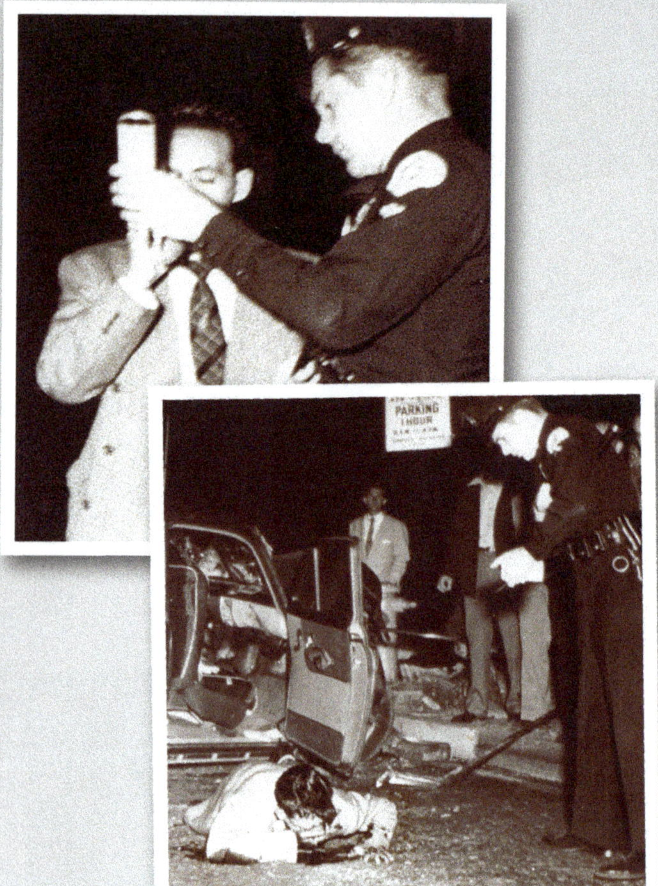

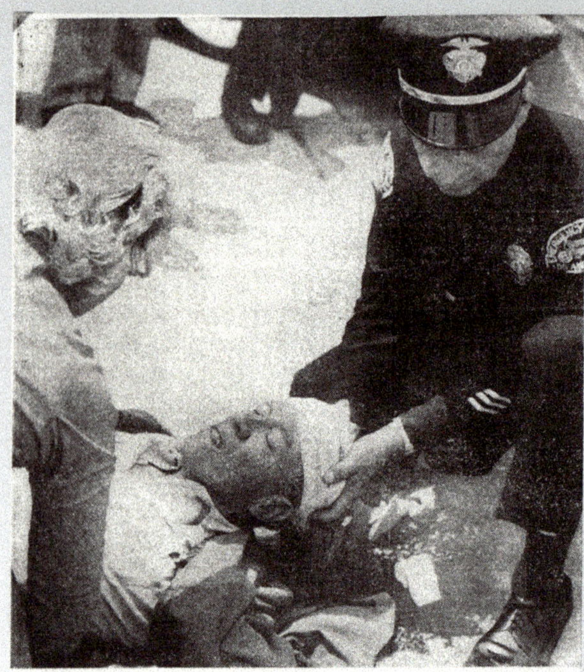

FIRST AID—Miss Leta Lamar, left, receptionist at Hollywood Memorial Park Cemetery, comforts Albert Tufts, organist, struck by auto while crossing street in front of cemetery entrance, while Ambulance Attendant D. V. Harris adminis-

Man on Way to Funeral Hit by Car at Cemetery

Albert Tufts, 74, Hollywood organist, was struck and critically injured yesterday afternoon on Santa

Witnesses said two cars stopped for Tufts but a third struck him. Driver of the third car was Richard Smy-

Hit And Run Victim

Authorities cover the body of a hit-and-run victim, Samuel L. Letterman, 62, of Santa Monica. Letterman was reportedly carried more than 300 feet by the auto.
—Evening Outlook Photo by Doug Andrews

SM Man, 70, Killed By Hit-Run Car

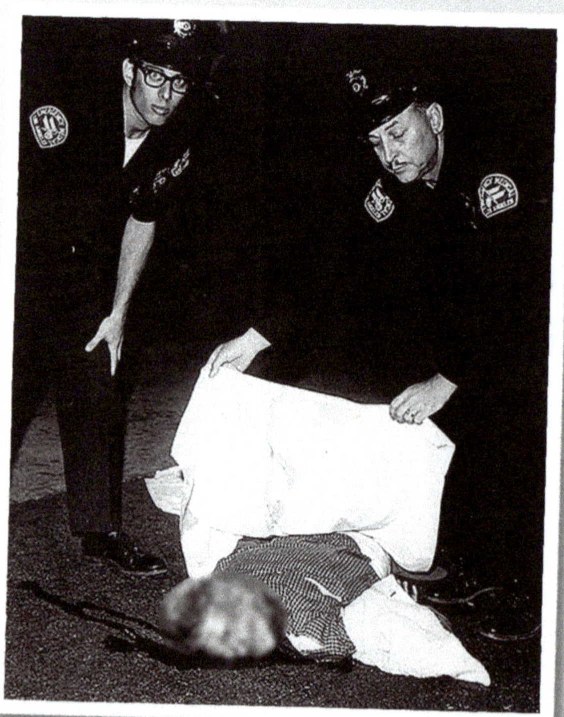

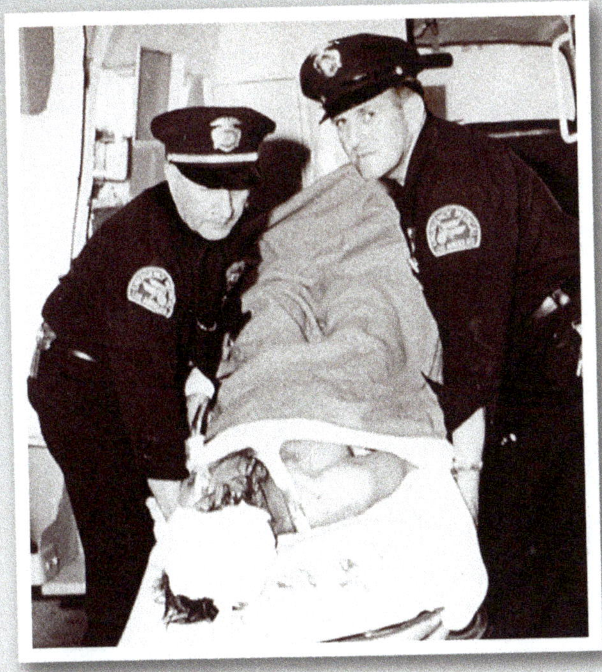

ADVERTISERS

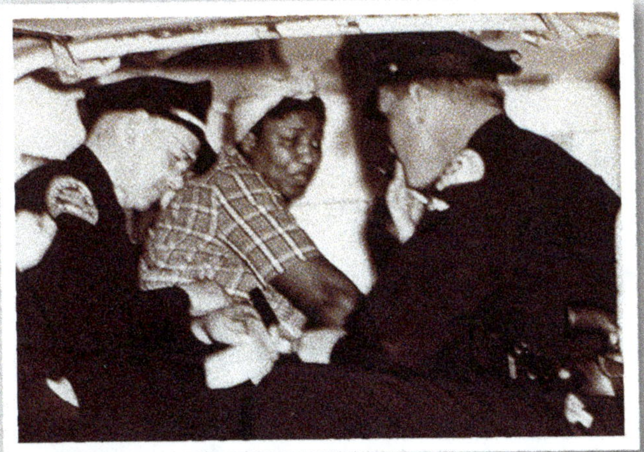

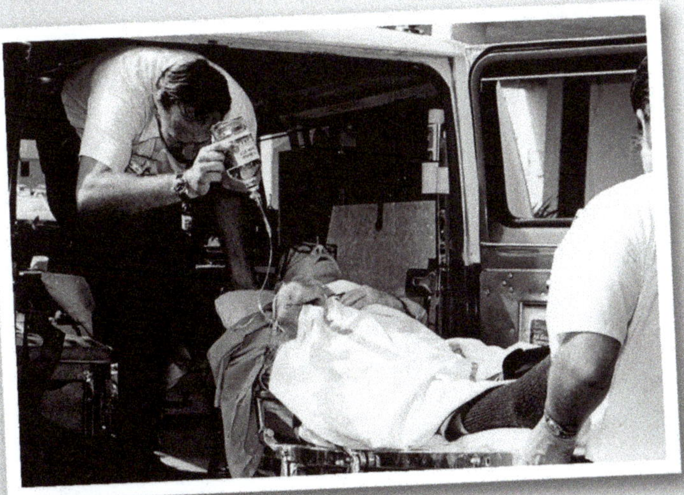

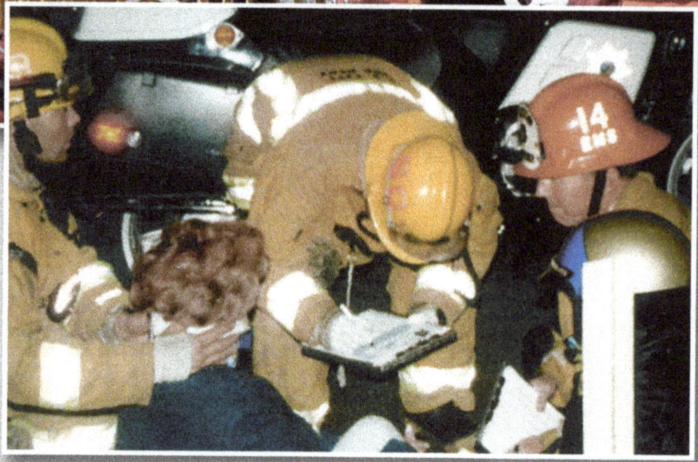

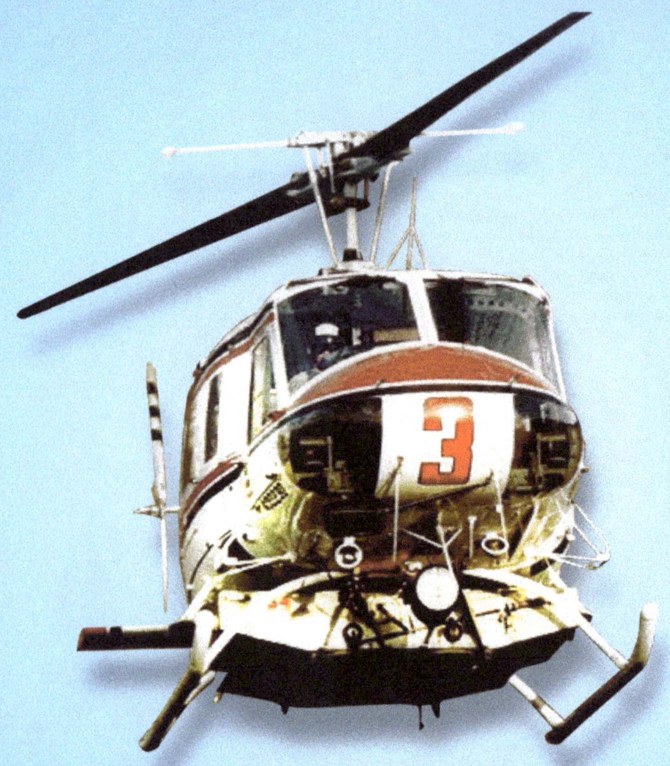

FOREVER REMEMBERED

FIRE 3

A traumatic day for the LAFD and all the families involved - arguably one of the saddest and most personally impactful days of my entire career.

FORCED LANDING
MARCH 23, 1998

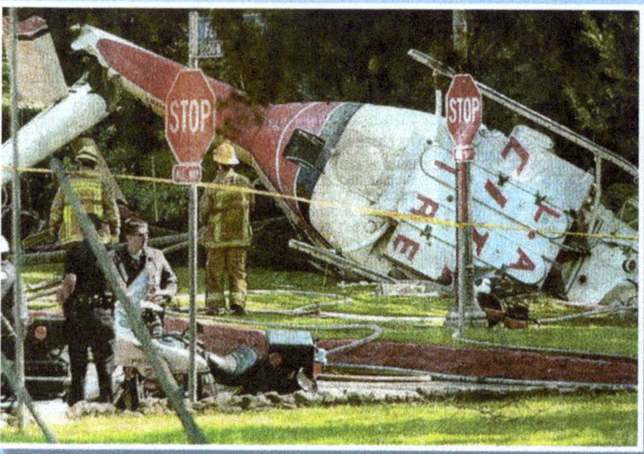

Ken Lubas, *Los Angeles Times*

Wreckage of Fire 3 helicopter rests in Griffith Park after crash that killed four people and injured two.

Early morning March 23, 1998 LAFD units responded to a tragic accident at Sunland and Wheatland in FS-24's District. They requested an air ambulance to transport a 12-year-old female patient to Children's Hospital. Fire 3 responded with a pilot and two HELITAC personnel from FS-90. Two firefighter paramedics from RA-81 were on board providing treatment. While rerouting to Children's Hospital, the helicopter crashed at Red Oak and Ferndell Drive in FS-82's District. Three department members and the young patient perished as a result of the accident. The two remaining department members were transported to County USC Medical Center in serious but stable condition.

Eric F. Riener
Firefighter
Lead Paramedic
Rescue Ambulance 81

Michael A. Butler
Firefighter
Paramedic
Rescue Ambulance 81

Michael D. McComb
Apparatus Operator
Fire Station 90

Partners

by Michael Butler

Side by side we race through the night
With blaring siren and flashing lights.
A life's at stake, a precious soul,
Perhaps too late, beyond our control.
Times like this have come before.
Never quite knowing just what's in store
When we arrive, our actions as one.
No thoughts need be spoken, just simply done.
To soothe a child's cry, to ease the pain
Knowing times like this will come again.
Though it's done many days a week
The bond between us is quite unique.
Different than that of a man and wife
For we can say we've saved a life.
To some it may just seem routine
The things we've done, the sights we've seen.
But you and I know it's changed our hearts
The ways we've seen life torn apart
And seen life begin new and fresh.
All the while praying we've done our best.
Some day another will take our place
A youthful still unknown face.
But never will time cloud my view
Of all the things I've shared with you
for we are Partners.

REFLECTIONS ON DEATH

As I grew older, books about death caught my eye. I memorized the great poem, *Thanatopsis*, by William Cullen Bryant after the first reading in high school and hundreds more poems with the same theme thereafter. Whenever I met a person who seemed truly happy in life, it was as though they had conquered a fear that I continued to grapple with. I would seek these people out and pick their brains in order to find out their secret.

No matter how hard I tried it was impossible to kick the death habit. Although I was able to sometimes put the death thoughts on hold for weeks or months at a time, it never disappeared completely; it was always in the shadows. Psychologist Carl Jung said he never met a patient, after more than 40 years in practice, whose unhappiness did not have its roots in the fear of ending, parting and the dark unknown of death.

Death thoughts cause most of us some level of fear and suffering in our daily lives. Kahlil Gibran states in *The Prophet*, "For life and death are one, even as the river and the sea are one."

Death has, more or less, been a daily companion to me. I have been able to control its influence, but it remains a strong and constant knapsack in my life. In recent years some activities abate my concerns about death, at least temporarily. My large telescope enables me to scan far out of this world into the expanses of space. I can see billions of light years away, almost an incomprehensible distance. This simple action of looking through an eyepiece into deep space allows me relief in the feelings of terror that death evokes and fills me with hope and lack of worry about earthly things. The solar systems have been in place long before I came along and will continue long after my departure. The idea of "me" and "I" being gone somehow seems acceptable to my mind when compared to the universe. When viewing the heavens, the idea of death and dying seems bearable, particularly when I view the constancy of the planets, our solar system, our Milky Way Galaxy and billions and billions of stars. I acknowledge that they will remain forever, no matter what.

Some people think that by studying about death and dying, or having a career in which death is everywhere (paramedic), we can become overrun with deep depression and misery. I disagree. I try to confront my fears and anxieties about death, and, through that process lessen the fear and despair. Only from being immersed in death have I begun to find peace and some tranquility surrounding the greatest of our fears. I was not aware of myself before birth and therefore it is quite likely that my awareness will disappear after death.

In paramedic training we learn that there is clinical death and biological death. Clinical is the absence of breathing and pulse, and the brain begins to die. The next four to six minutes are critical, because if no one begins CPR, the brain is permanently harmed. After 10 minutes or so, brain damage is imminent. Biological death is when the brain cells die and cannot return. Biological death is permanent. New advances are continuous and CPR changes every few years, but dead is dead.

Once you die, decomposition occurs, and we all acknowledge that. This is not the part that renders fear in me. I accept death in that simple explanation. The "process" of dying is where some of the fear arises from. I have seen literally hundreds of people die and have been with many at the exact time of death. In both medical and trauma cases, I have witnessed the time of death and continued resuscitation and airway management, defibrillated and administered drugs, solutions and medications.

Occasionally, my partner and I have been able to change the course of death. I recall patients with stab wounds to the heart and lungs who we worked on with great care and speed and rapidly transported to a trauma center with amazing results. The technical skills of trauma surgeons can be fantastic. Some patients lived to see another day and this was beyond belief. These are significant challenges for trauma surgeons and some cases, when I think about them, leave me in awe.

Sometimes it is what appears to be insignificant injuries that kill people. It still surprises me when someone bumps their head or has what initially appear to be very minor injuries and then end up dying. This is one reason that in my own career I learned early on to transport cases where other paramedics might have chosen to leave on scene. I have personally seen surgeons crack a chest in the ER on patients who appeared normal all the way to the hospital, only to have a cardiac arrest in the ER. The symptoms were none to minimal, but sudden hypotension and respiratory arrest occurred. I always had pride in my ability to assess patients, but it took years to develop those skills.

"For life and death are one, even as the river and the sea are one."

–Kahlil Gibran

It becomes a challenge personally to try and cheat death in the field setting. Traumatic cardiac arrests have a very low success rate in attempting to save them. But it is those cases specifically that make for the gratifying feeling that only EMTs in the field know about. It is clearly the period between clinical and biological death that lives can be saved and death can be defeated, at least temporarily.

As I eluded to earlier, the "process" of dying brings on images of suffering, shortness of breath and the inability to catch one's breath. Or the typical crushing chest pain of myocardial infarction sometimes evokes images of terror in me. I have had a dozen or so patients in my nearly 60 years in EMS who clearly articulated to me, "I am going to die" or "I will not make it to the hospital," and most died just as they said they would. I recall one elderly man telling me that without any emotion and even a rather curious calmness about him. Naturally, I began resuscitation immediately when the electrocardiogram showed asystole and my assessment verified it. Nevertheless, the man was pronounced dead in the ER.

Somehow, some people know when their time is up and they accept it. Others are full of fear and fight to the end. Some we are able to save and others we are not. The process can be frightening for the patient and the rescuer. I have been successful in assuaging some of the fear away for patients, but not for myself. Sometimes I realized after a death that it was me who was anxious, even though the patient accepted the reality of death.

There have been times during resuscitation that I have brought family members in who have requested to say goodbye to their loved one. I have always been cognizant of their ability to withstand seeing and hearing the sounds of the scene at a cardiac arrest: the drugs being verbalized, tubes being placed in their throats, CPR being administered and defibrillation occurring. But the ability to say goodbye is paramount to the grieving that will follow. I have always tried to show compassion in all cases.

The forever and ever is also disturbing to me. Even as a child, that concept was hard to swallow and bothers me to this day. When my own mother and father died, I knew it was forever. One minute they were alive and the next they were forever just a memory. Upon realizing this concept of never again seeing my parents alive sent me into instant tears and sorrow. We sometimes intellectualize death, but the stark reality is ever present that death is permanent and we will all die.

The memories and photos of our loved ones are left behind when they die. I can still see, feel and smell my father and mother before they died. Those are memories I will carry within me for the rest of my days.

When children die, it is worse than anything else for both the family and EMS providers. As uncomfortable as I am, I was able to try and calm families during this horrific time. In fact, nothing I or anyone can say or do can stop the pain of a parent at the loss of a child. I have unfortunately seen this all too often at swimming pool drownings, traffic collisions, shootings, stabbings, sports events, and even in kids with terminal illness. Even expected deaths are shocking when they occur.

This will serve as a continuation of my thoughts about death and dying based upon my own experience as a human being and paramedic. My background has been shrouded in death having been a Los Angeles Fire Department Paramedic for many years. Additionally, one of the reasons that I first began to work on an ambulance (1963) was to try and get closer to my greatest fear - death. I wanted to embrace death by being near it and trying to save people's lives. I might in some way better understand the workings of the how and why of death - perhaps in some way even abate some of my fears and trepidations concerning the subject.

Albert Alagava, my wife's brother, was having a terrible headache about 20 years ago. He was living in an apartment in a small community called West Hills - and I should point out that he was into hard drugs for many years. Nevertheless, my wife, Dolly, had promised her father that she would take care of Albert to the best of her ability. Dolly paid for his room and board for about 25 years. He was an off-and-on addict, mostly on. Despite his repeated attempts to get off of narcotics, including crack cocaine, he never did.

He described his headache as intractable and the "worst headache" he ever experienced. I suggested that he call 911 and be transported to a local emergency room. He ended up at West Hills Hospital in the Canoga Park area of the San Fernando Valley, where he was examined and given Tylenol and sent home. He stated that he walked the two miles to his apartment at 2:00AM. The next night he again was plagued with an unusually horrible headache and he again called Dolly. He was taken by Los Angeles City Paramedics to the local hospital but this time it was Northridge Hospital. It was there that a CT Scan was ordered and a large mass was seen in the frontal lobe of his brain. He was referred to Los Angeles County USC Medical Center, a facility that handles the poor and needy.

Within two days additional tests, scans and MRIs were obtained which showed a huge malignant and rapidly growing tumor spreading its tentacles down into the brain stem. Immediate surgery was arranged and brain surgery occurred within the week.

The Glioma was partially removed as some of the mass could not be fully excised due to it being in vital regions of the brain and would have ended his life. Recovery was rather rapid and Albert was able to go home with a giant scar and little hair left on his head. His ability to think and remember was not affected and he continued to heal but also needed chemotherapy and radiation. It was no secret that his brain cancer was terminal - not if but when it would kill him.

Dolly, to her credit, interrupted her life as a psychotherapist and took on the responsibility of care for her brother. She balanced her private practice with day after day doctors appointments, radiation visits and chemotherapy. She did everything for Albert with love and devotion that one only reads about. Her dedication and continued love for her brother continued for the last two years of his life. We were both present for the final hours, minutes and seconds when Albert finally left his earthly presence.

It is the last few hours that I will explore now. We arrived at the retirement facility (care facility or, really, final location of life) about 30 minutes after Dolly received the call that Albert was having some difficulty breathing. We had watched him deteriorate during the previous year; a slow but steady downward spiraling of his life, from walking normally to needing a cane, then wheelchair despite his continued resistance to using it. Eating had become difficult, communication and memory declined quickly, and the end could easily be forecasted.

He had a loyal pal, a cat he had rescued several years before. We arrived at this room and he was lying supine in bed, his cat at his feet. He was no longer conscious, but occasionally would ever so slightly seem to acknowledge his name and even recognize his sister and myself. I immediately noticed his irregular breathing and he appeared to be somewhat agitated, perhaps in pain. Dolly had arranged for Hospice care for Albert and they were exceptionally excellent. The nurse was concerned that he was agitated and administered Morphine to ensure that Albert was comfortable and out of pain. Several injections were administered over the next hour or so and we stayed with Albert during this period. Dolly was quietly talking to him and telling him how much we loved him and comforting him as best she could. I spoke to him close to his ear and told him how much I loved him and that it was OK to let himself drift off. I remember fighting tears and trying to articulate my words but not let Albert hear me cry. I don't know why this occurred within me; I only know that for some reason I did not want to cause fear in him if he could hear me. It was my own fear that I was experiencing and I did not want it to spill over to Albert. The sadness was overwhelming.

Within an hour, extra Morphine was needed to what appeared to be Albert somewhat agitated and beginning to thrash around a bit. After the Morphine, Albert settled down and appeared to relax significantly. Dolly stepped out of the room for a few minutes and I remained with Albert.

A few minutes later Albert's breathing became loud and more labored with periods of apnea. I realized that he was Cheyne-Stokes breathing, irregular followed by periods of apnea. I knew that the end was coming soon so I called for Dolly.

Dolly walked into the room just prior to Albert suddenly opening both of his eyes widely, as if looking at something across the room. He then took a very deep breath and slowly let it out . A period of apnea was evident and then another breath, all the while looking straight ahead with his eyes fully opened. I said to Dolly, we can now say goodbye, and each of us told Albert we loved him and it was now OK to go. A final breath occurred and it was his last breath on earth.

How does one confront their own fears and anxieties about death? It is a thought process that was slow for me and ultimately diminished my fear and despair. Only through immersion into death have I been able to find some peace and tranquility surrounding the greatest of our fears and terrors.

It is quite likely that my awareness of my own death will vanish after death itself. Since I do not remember being born, it follows that after death there will be no memory of the process of dying. My experience with a very old man in his late nineties revealed much to me when he exclaimed, "Why is it taking so long. I am ready to die but it is not happening". I learned so much from this giant of a man; his bravery in facing the loss of himself did not scare him one bit. He lived a very long time and saw his 24-year old daughter die of cancer and he could do nothing to save her life. He also survived the holocaust and lost his entire family. How could I not admire such a great and honorable man. He was in no fear of death and even welcomed it.

My fear of death abated dramatically after I began to read the words and philosophy of Epicurus, the famous Greek philosopher. He was born in 341 BC in Samos, Greece and died in 270 BC in Athens, Greece. Epicurus practiced "Medical Philosophy" wherein he treated the "soul". He believed in eliminating human misery which was caused by the fear of death. He believed that the terror of thinking about our own death short circuits our enjoyment of life and our joys.

**"Why should I fear death?
If I am, then death is not. If death is, then I am not.
Why should I fear that which can only exist when I do not?"**

It is through contemplation of Epicurus that relief from the fear of death is possible. Death is inevitable and all that breathe will share the same destiny. Whether we accept this reality or not, death will come to all living things. It seems to me in a logical way that we should not dwell on something we cannot control. Rather, we should act accordingly to things we can control.

Some thoughts I have had make up this chapter. It is obvious to me that most people have a dysthymia, or mild depression that is long-term. And that dysthymia is death. It is ever present in our lives and some people can't seem to stop thinking about the inevitable. This constant low level death dysthymia is a common theme in some pre-hospital and hospital personnel. EMT's whom I have talked with have acknowledged this malady; some have even needed medication to try and eliminate this culprit.

In my career, I have seen horrific and unspeakable injuries, many perpetrated by other people. Some are results of accidents, whether traffic collisions, aircraft crashes or gunshots, others by burns, murders with resultant decapitations, etc. I have resuscitated hundreds, if not thousands, of human beingjs in my career, many of which were clinically dead and some who were biologically dead.

These things were done because it was in the best interest of my patients since there were no other options except to pronounce them dead. But we were taught to give everyone the benefit of the doubt; to especially try and resuscitate the very young to the best of our ability. EMTs and Paramedics have done so for more than 60 or so years. It is what all of us were taught to do. When newly graduates of EMT or Paramedic training hit the streets, it used to be the philosophy to "resuscitate a lizard if you could".

It was another way to show you had the training to save lives and would do so under any circumstances. As time went on and medicine became more advanced, it was realized that we could prolong death to some extent but in the end the patient would die anyway. I can remember resuscitating people that by today's standard would be pronounced dead at the scene of an incident. Of course I exclude cases in which not transporting could have resulted in a riot or other civil disturbance.

The point is that I believe in assisted death. Let me be crystal clear: I do not believe in assisted suicide due to deep depression, which is very treatable. I have seen people die peacefully in the presence of their family and friends and I have seen death which was miserably painful. Most pre-hospital providers will attest to this fact - that some deaths are absolutely devastating and with intractable severe pain that even heavy drugs won't totally eliminate.

Death itself cannot be prevented - in the end is in no way treatable. Therefore, in the end we all must accept the inevitable, as hard as it is to do so, especially if it is our own family member. Faith plays a major role in this arena, and if one's belief gives hope and relief then that is good.

Many times in my life I have seen an animal so severely injured that there was no hope for recovery - dogs being run over by the wheels of an automobile or a deer struck on the highway or a huge majestic whale caught in the propellers of a large ocean-going ship. When I see the pain and excruciating agony of an animal there have been times that l have considered ending the life of that creature to stop the agony and lancinating pain. The moral issues shot into my brain at the times and I took no action because of guilt or the inability to carry out my thoughts into action. One major argument is that animals are not people, and animals don't think and reason like people. That may be true but they feel pain and agony and it breaks my heart to see anyone / anything in severe pain. We, as rescuers, want to stop pain and agony. lt is in our sense of being a rescuer, in our essence.

One of the items that has never left my mind when I was a field medic back in the 1970s was that we were constantly told to not medicate too much, just enough to take the edge off the pain. Some of this was valid; narcotics could mask abdominal pain and chest pain. Thankfully, that argument has abated since the advent of CT and MRI scans, where clear visuals of what is going on inside someone can be determined, and they can be adequately sedated. However, this old thinking even involved patients who were suffering with pain beyond belief from cancer. Most of the time this thinking was the result of religious beliefs and convictions. At the time, no amount of agony was justified to interfere with the natural progression of death.

Thankfully, rational thinking has come of age. It is for this reason that I support the mercy and dignity of assisted death. Of course only the individual can make that decision; if a person by his or her own belief desires no medication or pain reducing drugs then they have that right. On the other hand, pain is quite subjective in that some people can tolerate incredible degrees of pain while others beg for medication. During childbirth, I have seen many women insist they will have a natural birth without any mind-altering drugs and medications. This frequently changes when the level of pain increases several fold. Sometimes the patient suddenly changes her mind and requests pain medication simply because it too difficult to endure the suffering that can accompany childbirth.

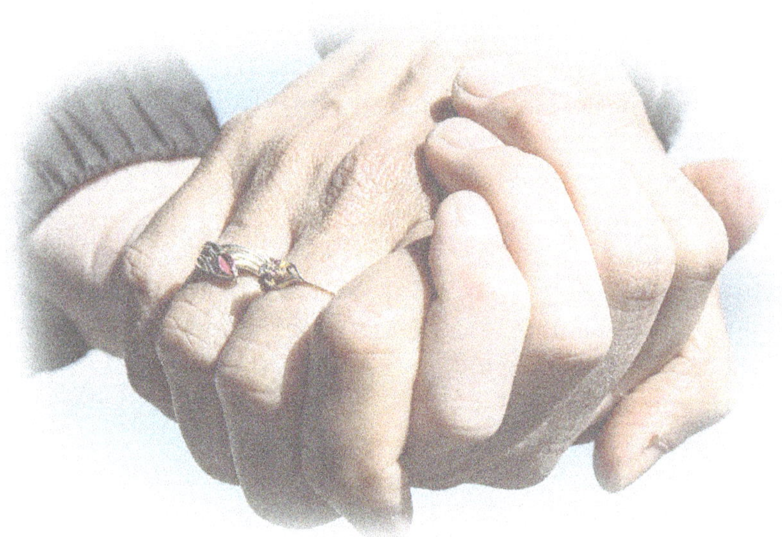

DEATH WITH DIGNITY

We must respect the patient's rights whether religious or otherwise when addressing end of life issues. But I must also profess that in my own view a dying individual should not have to endure the agony and prolonged misery that can accompany death. It can not only affect the patient but also family members who are present at the time of the approach of death. Having been present many times at this juncture of a person's life, I can attest to the various thoughts and comments by families at this most difficult time.

My conclusion to all of this, despite the fact that most states in our country do not allow assisted death is that it is a shame and must be corrected. A few states have been bold enough to enact Death with Dignity regulations.

Oregon's ground-breaking law was the first of its kind in the United States. In 1997 the State of Oregon enacted the Oregon Death with Dignity Act whereby the population voted this into law. It states that a resident of Oregon diagnosed with a terminal illness by at least two medical physicians who will probably die within a 6 month period and is mentally competent and not depressed, may be given a prescription for an oral medication that is lethal. The individual must self-adminster the substance.

We need to pass legislation on a national level similar to what has been done in Oregon and, of course, this must always be a personal choice that meets the standards of the Oregon Death with Dignity Act.

UPDATES

As early as 1976 the Natural Death Act passes, protecting physicians from being sued for failing to treat incurable illnesses at the request of the patient.

Pre-1990, Death with Dignity was pondered in California. It should be noted that California joined the ranks of having the option on June 9, 2016. It was former Governor Jerry Brown who would sign the End of Life Option Act into law in 2015 in California, which took effect in June of 2016. More than 40 million Californians join the other states.

At present the following states also have current Death with Dignity laws on the books:

Oregon has Death with Dignity Act 1997
Montana has Death with Dignity Act 2009
Washington has Death with Dignity Act 2009
Vermont has Patient Choice and Control at End of Life Act 2013
Colorado has End of Life Options Act 2016
California has End of Life Options Act 2016
District of Columbia has Death with Dignity 2017
Hawai'i has Our Care, Our Choice Act 2018
Maine has Death with Dignity Act 2019
New Jersey has Aid in Dying for the Terminally Ill Act 2019
New Mexico has End of Life Options Act 2021

TEACHING EMT

In 2000, I received a phone call from the Chair of the Emergency Services Department of Los Angeles Valley College asking if I might be interested in teaching a college level EMT course. Mr. Carl Smith had been the Chair of the Department for some time and I asked where he got my name and who had recommended me for the instructor's position. He said it was Ron Reis. Ron was my neighbor who happened to be employed by the Los Angeles Community College District.

I asked Carl when the class would be starting and he told me it was in two days. My response was "What?" What about time to prepare for the class, and a thousand other questions. He told me he would assist as best he could. He invited me to meet with him the next day and do some paperwork, such as an application, fingerprinting, and lots of other needed requirements. While part of my mind was thinking how fun this might be and a nice transition into retirement, the other part of my mind was churning away with thoughts of every possible problem that might come up. I was not worried about the subject matter as much as preparation of notes, attendance sheets, rules and regulations of the college and a host of other rather important issues. Why in the world would I be hired in two days to teach a class that was full (40 students) in a bungalow with no air conditioning without so much as an interview.

The interview would occur the next day with the Department Chair. I arrived 30 minutes early and headed for Bungalow 1 where the administration office for the department was located. I knocked at the door, Carl answered it and I entered. There were two desks in the small office and it was very obvious that an argument was taking place as I walked in. Carl was in a heated discussion with another instructor - of Administration of Justice - and they were yelling at one another.

I stated to Carl, "Maybe I can come back later?" He said, "No, let's talk now". I sat down thinking that at any moment these two were going to be in hand-to-hand combat. I could see twisted faces and red cheeks as these two were about to get physical. I stood up to leave and the instructor said to Carl, "We'II finish this later", and stormed out. Carl simply said, "Welcome to Los Angeles Valley College".

I was somewhat concerned as Carl appeared to be not feeling well, pale and sweating. I asked him if he wanted to postpone our discussion and he said no. Carl reaIly turned out to be a very nice fellow, but I could not help but think that this altercation had taken its toll on him.

Carl invited me to sit at the desk next to his which was to be mine beginning that day. I did not ask him about the battle that nearly occurred just prior, but rather concentrated on what I was getting into. He merely told me there had been a disagreement with his fuIl-time faculty member and left it at that.

My first semester at Los Angeles Valley College went well and about 30 of the 40 students went on to be successful Emergency Medical Technicians, having passed the Los Angeles County EMS Agency Examination.

So much had happened in one day that I could not wrap my head around it. A part-time job at a local college, teaching a class that I Ioved and being paid for it. It seemed too good to be true.

Little did I know that a year later, I would be a full-time faculty member and then Department Chair for the next 12 years. Sometimes opportunities knock at your door, and if you're eating - stop - and if you're sleeping - wake up. Opportunity and chance came together on that day and changed my life in so many ways.

My first semester at Los Angeles Valley College went well and about 30 of the 40 students went on to be successful Emergency Medical Technicians having passed the Los Angeles County EMS Agency Examination. That was 22 years ago and still today occasionally I will be on the freeway and an ambulance will be next to me and suddenly a siren will sound and one or both EMTs will be waving from the ambulance to me. I naturally will wave back and give a thumbs up sign to the crew. It is times like these that make teaching worthwhile. The backbone of our EMS within this country are EMTs who are not paid enough and who dedicate themselves to taking care of the sick and injured. It pleases me beyond words to see them working in a field setting and know that our team at Los Angeles Valley College played a role in their success.

The second semester was far easier since I knew my way around the campus and made many contacts within various departments. The staff at personnel and reprographics are top-notch and can be extremely helpful. I implemented many changes once I began to get the swing of things at the college. The textbook (which has been updated many times and seems to have gotten better and better) and the use of PowerPoint presentations, made teaching easier and far more effective. Teaching was fun and exciting but I was considered a strict teacher by most of the students. I instituted several new programs within the EMS class: group discussions, teams, and tried to make learning easier and worked on motivating students. This was not an easy task as I found out. Some students were not ready for a college class, with poor study habits, inability to critically think and excessive absences and tardies.

A syllabus was created that allowed only three absences throughout the entire semester; the prohibition of cell phones that seemed to be an addiction. The first day I would clearly articulate what was required to be successful, give out a copy of the syllabus with the rules of the class, and have them sign and date a document that they had received the syllabus and were aware of what was required to be successful.

It worked very well the second semester, but about 40% of the class did not make it. Each person who was not successful was interviewed personally and I reviewed the scores of the quizzes and examinations with them. Nearly 95% of those who did not pass admitted to not taking the class seriously and not reading the chapters nor participating in classroom discussions. I always thanked students for their honesty and rarely did a student leave mad. In fact, many came back the next semester and were successful. It was a wake-up call to many students that what was needed for success was dedication and commitment. They needed to let EMS become part of them, to eat and drink EMS, and dedicate themselves to once and for all learning the information. Many did just that.

Carl Smith, the Chair of the Emergency Services Department, retired after my first year and another full-time instructor became the chair. I could vividly remember the verbal altercation between the two a year earlier and now that instructor was my chair. I suspected that no matter what occurred, a collision between us was bound to happen; I did not have to wait very long.

It was not long before an incident occurred involving myself and the other instructor. I happened to be in the Office of Academic Affairs and the instructor, who was then department chair, asked me to follow him as he made some copies of a document. The room was where the Vice President of Academic Affairs' secretary was located as well as other female workers. Additionally a few students were at the counter when it happened.

I was near the door when he, trying to be funny, made an off-color joke directed at me. He had asked me a medical question that was totally inappropriate and not funny. I looked at him in disbelief and knowing the potential of a series of complaints, simply turned around and walked out of the office. I did not utter a word back to the instructor.

Knowing I was still on probation it irked me that I was being investigated for something that was beyond my control.

About a week later I received in my mailbox a notice that a hearing was to be held for inappropriate comments made within the Vice President's Office. Knowing I was still on probation it irked me that I was being investigated for something that was beyond my control. My hearing date with the Vice President was a week later at 10:00AM in her office. I was absolutely innocent of any wrong-doing yet needed to answer to this inquiry. I had not spoken to the instructor since the incident but was prepared to go before the Vice President and be interrogated.

I was early for my appointment and had dressed in a coat and tie in preparation for what was to happen. I told the secretary of my appointment and she indicated I should take a seat. In less than five minutes the door opened and out came Susan Carleo, the Vice President of Academic Affairs. She invited me in and asked me to have a seat. While nervous internally, I was calm outwardly since being innocent gives one a sense of well-being. She reiterated the complaint involved and it was no surprise to me; three letters had been written concerning the statements made to me by him and they were accurate. Dr. Carleo asked me to explain what had transpired.

I related specifically and concisely what was directed to me by the instructor and that I had merely walked out without answering his question. I related what the question was and the reason why it was not answered. Further, I related that it was purposeful that no comment was returned in that I was well aware that complaints would likely be generated by such a comment. As such, by not responding to his comment (in the form of a question), I was innocent of having anything to do with his comment.

I informed Dr. Carleo that at the moment of the comment, I turned and walked out, thus not becoming a part of his dialogue. In fact, by my silence at the time, I should not even be in her office answering anything having to do with the comment. By not commenting back to him, I had eliminated myself from the entire episode.

Dr. Carleo then stated that my response was exactly what each of the three complainants had written, thus eliminating me from the one-way conversation. My lack of response cleared me totally of the charges that truly belonged to the instructor.

Dr. Carleo tore up the document she had prepared and declared me innocent of any wrong-doing. I thanked her and turned toward the door but she stopped me and stated that his appointment was at 9:00AM but he was a no-show.

After leaving and heading toward my office, he approached me and asked, "Did you burn me?" I looked him in the eyes and said "No", and further stated, "I just told the truth". He walked away and did not return to the office for several hours. When he entered he said, "I gave you this office and I can take it away", whereupon I answered by saying, "I didn't have an office when I came to the college and I don't need one now".

In a few months I was off probation and earned tenure. Finally, I did not have to worry about being harassed by him and thus concentrated on being the best instructor I could be and following the policies and procedures of the college.

Several more issues arose involving this instructor but I was not involved. In fact, he became involved in more serious situations and within a year was terminated from the college. As fate would have it, I was called into court to testify against him and he ultimately lost his appeal from being terminated.

Again fate stepped in and I was voted by my peers to be the Emergency Service Department Chair, a position I would hold for 12 years until I retired in July 2015.

The Return

After nearly 15 years of teaching EMT at Los Angeles Valley College, which equates to nearly 60 classes over that period, I can appreciate that some of these students we teach will quite possibly, someday, treat us. As we all wax older on this island we call planet earth, it occurs to me that many of our students will go on to become excellent EMTs and Paramedics, not to mention nurses, physicians and other medical professionals. Some students articulated that they desired to be physician assistants, X-Ray technologists, physical therapists and nurse practitioners. Yet others mentioned mid-wives as their goal, chiropractors and

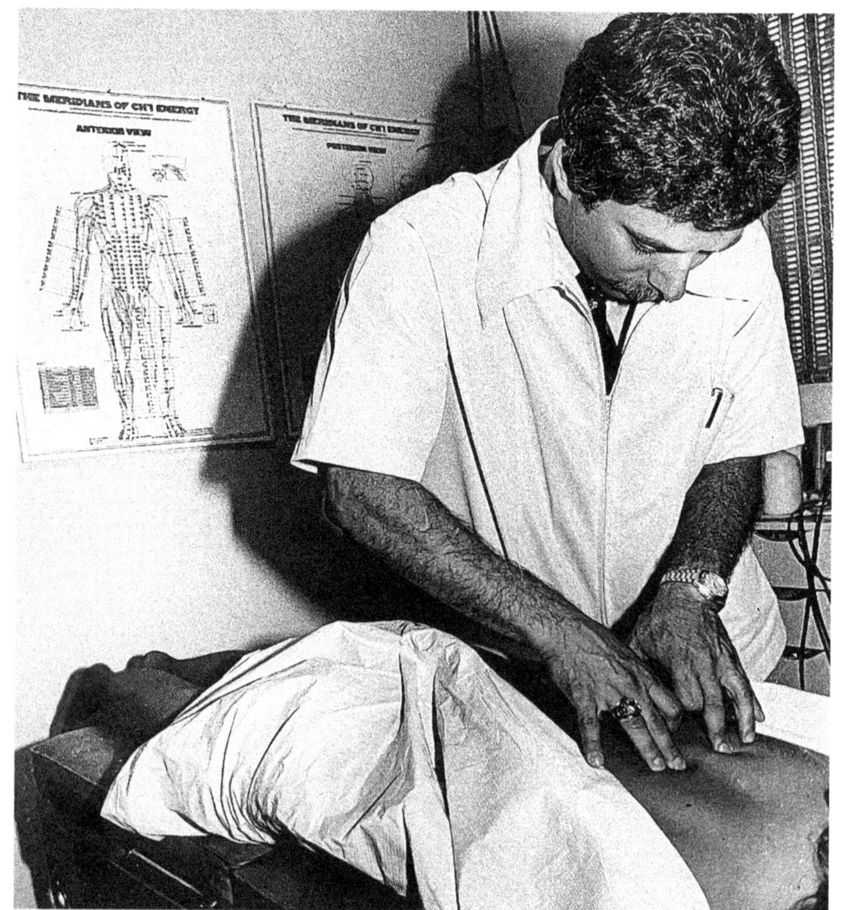

Treating a patient during my years as a Doctor of Chiropractic.

podiatrists. So many choices by so many students.

For reasons yet unknown, I decided that upon reaching my 70th birthday I would retire from teaching and perhaps return to my old profession as a Doctor of Chiropractic. I had, for the past year, been practicing two to three days a week and enjoyed it tremendously. I had a relationship with an X-Ray and MRI facility nearby as well as a lab within our building. All was going well and yet when I received a phone call it all began to change.

The call was from the new chair of the Emergency Services Department at the college, my replacement. We have an excellent relationship and I was even on his interview board when he came to the college. He requested that I come back to the college for next semester and that the instructor who was hired for the afternoon class was leaving and not returning after his current semester was over. At first I was stunned and then something deep down inside of me, like a voice, reached out to me and said, think about this. I had settled back to retirement and now a calling deep inside of me, like a long lost well, had set off some water flowing inside of me.

My contract stated that after 180 days I could return to the college as an Adjunct Instructor and teach up to 67% of my full-time load, which is slightly over 10 units. The EMT course of study is 8 units. Was this really happening? Should I return to teaching part-time? My head was swirling around like a tornado as to whether I should retire from practice as a chiropractor and teach once again. I retired in July 2015 so the Spring semester begins in February, 2016 which is slightly more than the required 180 days.

As my mind raced, I needed to decide to either practice or teach. As I write these words today, I can truly say I have thoroughly given this serious thought and accepted the offer from the college to return. I teach the same class that I previously taught from 1:00PM until 4:25PM on Monday, Tuesday and Wednesday. This was a real paradox for me as I thought my career as a college professor was over. Not so!

When I spoke to Yasmin in Personnel, she welcomed me back on the telephone and indicated she had spoken to several members of the Emergency Services Department and they supported the decision. While she could not see it over the phone, I had a huge smile on my face. This smile represented not only being back on staff in our department, but more so because of the family I was returning too. My colleagues have become so important to me that we are like family. To see them and work with them give me a joy that can only be found when you work alongside fellow instructors for a decade or more. So this change in my life is even a surprise to me; unexpected and joyous.

The future seems a bit brighter and I feel a sense of mirth throughout my body. I returned to Los Angeles Valley College in 2016. So fast forward to 2023, I'm still here teaching.

"What seems to be the problem?"

With all of the things that EMS providers are supposed to be aware of, it is no wonder that patient approach needs some work. Before one even steps out of the ambulance, one's eyes need to be scanning the visible area for lurking dangers, safety hazards, and about a thousand other concerns. Naturally, the EMS providers need to be set up in gloves and be cognizant of body substance isolation and universal precautions as well. We are all aware of blood borne pathogens and communicable diseases. In fact I teach my EMT students to treat each patient (in terms of blood borne pathogens) as if they have every disease you have ever heard of or read about. This is not to cause fear, although it may, but rather to ensure that students don't ever forget to use every available safety tool. Self-protection is a vital part of EMS.

We are talking about communication when we speak about patient contact. The first or initial contact with an EMS provider will remain with the patient for a long time, maybe as long as they live. So do what you can given the circumstances to make it right. Your facial expression, verbal and non-verbal communication and eye contact are vitally important when you first contact the patient. Even your body position is significant. Just imagine towering over a child who is sick or injured. Dropping to one knee to maintain eye contact with the patient at their level is important. The non-verbal can be as important as the verbal initially. The power of eye contact cannot be overestimated as you begin patient contact. Imagine if the patient is angry and you are interpreted as giving them an "evil eye" look. It may not be your intent but they may interpret your eye contact as curt. It takes practice to get good at patient contact.

**I had a dream and woke up startled;
sat up and began to remember some of the highlights
of the thoughts within the dream.**

Verbal communication is an essential part of solid patient care. One of the most important things to do is say hello and tell them who you are. If you don't know their medical problem, then it is essential for the EMS provider to say, "What seems to be the problem?" This reflects your desire to help the patient and allows for them to hear and see that and then articulate their response to you. The rest will come naturally.

There is far more to this subject than just a greeting and what's wrong with the patient, but this is the first contact with your sick or injured individual. Start out correctly and your experience, as well as your patient, will benefit.

I was being replaced with other people on the Fire Department. They were younger, newer and youthful; they were being promoted to positions I held, and I was leaving. I realized somehow that they were taking our places. All of us old timers were being replaced by "newtimers". Kevin Nida was in my dream. I brought him out of the field setting to be my staff assistant at the EMS Bureau Office in about 1985. I was at that time the Assistant Bureau Commander of EMS. Although I originally brought him up to assist the Chief Paramedic, within a year or so, I found myself being promoted to that very position when my boss left. I recall tears in my eyes; tears of sorrow that I was leaving and also tears of joy that he was getting a promotion to Captain and being sent out to a fire station. And it was me who was causing the tears. He was ready to move on after 6 or 7 years as my assistant. I knew this day would come and somewhere back in my mind's recesses, I dreaded it.

I had come to enjoy my time having him in the office; there had been several others over the years but Kevin stood out. He was smart, capable and had the knack of truly participating in the management process of operating the largest pre-hospital care Fire Department-operated system in the country. My dream flooded me with emotion, enough to awaken me startled with the realization that this not only was happening but that it was supposed too. The older personnel, at some time, must move over and let the new breed take over. It is not a simple transition for those who stand before the new to take the throttles from the old. Oh yes, I thought, the new were certainly capable, but what about me? I am still capable as well. At the same time, I had to acknowledge my own "stepping aside" for the new group coming. Yes, I kept saying to myself, my replacement is coming soon. The new must replace the old.

Somehow, some way, I knew my time was going to overtake me. I had been the Paramedic Chief for 9 years, and then a couple more as Deputy Fire Chief. Now it was time to move on. That reservoir of power we all contain within us was telling me "it is time". After nearly 32 years, I knew it was time to retire. Yes, time to be replaced, but also turn the page to the next chapter my life.

There is joy (and sorrow) in knowing that your organization is set up to continue without you. In fact, it is set up with that in mind. When a firefighter, captain, or Chief moves on, the system is like a heart beat; it doesn't even skip a beat. The new come in and take the reins to steer the department for the next 10 or 20 years. That is how it has been and will be in the future. There is joy in knowing that you participated in the running of the department and can rest assured that others will follow you, so as to allow the ship to continue in the proper direction. The transition, in fact, while emotional, is designed to operate that way. And so it was with me.

The transition from active duty to retired is both wonderful and sad. It is anticipated soon after one has joined the organization. But part of the acceptance must include the acknowledgement of old age, and the ability to step aside and allow your successors to take over. Then thoughts of one's self being obsolete, driver's licenses being in jeopardy. I admit that age is creeping up on me, that I am progressing in my life, that I must move aside. It is both wonderful and fearful for me. I welcomed retirement but had the feeling sometimes that I was a relic to be appreciated by those, who, in their turn, have taken up the fight to take over the ship.

I am retired after my many years on the LAFD, many of which I loved and dreamed about. I am proud of my achievements but now a part of me wants to relax with the days I have left to live. I still have all of my memories and bask in them. Is it now unusual for me to sit back and remember how it was, my history with the fire service? This surely must be a natural thing - with tears sometimes, but all in appreciation to having been able to make the journey. I know that I helped others as a paramedic, but my memory clouds some of it now, although it still comes through.

I still can remember almost every aspect of my career and be comfortable in the fact that I did my best. It was indeed my great honor to have served the good people of Los Angeles.

Acting Fire Chief Tim DeLuca (far left) presenting me to the Fire Commission in early 1987, with my family: my wife, Dolly, and daughter, Kate, and my parents, Pauline and Joseph Cowen. Fire Commissioner Harold Kwalwasser (far right) looks on.

Fire Chiefs I was honored to work for during my 30 years with the Los Angeles Fire Department

CHIEF RAYMOND M. HILL
April 25, 1966 to May 31, 1975

CHIEF KENNETH R. LONG
June 1, 1975 to June 29, 1977

CHIEF JOHN C. GERARD
June 30, 1977 to June 6, 1982

CHIEF DONALD O. MANNING
January 20, 1983 to 1995

CHIEF WILLIAM R. BAMATTRE
April 4, 1996 to January 1, 2007

Some of the Fire Chiefs from 2007 to present

CHIEF DOUGLAS R. BARRY
September 18, 2007 to August 30, 2009

CHIEF MILLAGE PEAKS
September 10, 2009 to June 2011

CHIEF BRIAN CUMMINGS
to Oct 2013

CHIEF RALPH TERRAZAS
August 8, 2014 to March 25, 2022

CHIEF KRISTIN M. CROWLEY
March 25, 2022 to present

City of San Fernando Police Department

Since my Dad was a Culver City Reserve Police Officer from 1939-1955, I always wondered what it would be like to be a police officer myself. My younger brother, David, was a Los Angeles Deputy Sheriff for 34 years. He joined the Sheriff's Department in 1969 and was promoted to Sergeant in 1989 and finally retired in July of 2003, his career having spanned 34 years.

In 1982 while on duty as an EMS Captain, I responded to the San Fernando Police Department for an incident and was asked by the then Chief of Police if I ever considered becoming a Reserve Police Officer. After two meetings with the Police Chief, and then graduating from the Police Academy, I was sworn in as a Level 1 Reserve Police Officer. After a one year probation was completed with a FTO (field training officer), I was able to go on patrol solo. In 1987 I was promoted to Reserve Sergeant and then in 1990 to Reserve Police Lieutenant. I worked patrol, Internal Affairs and Administration during my career and retired in 2001. I fully realized my childhood dreams of functioning in the capacity of a police officer. I treated the public with respect and was very cognizant of the difference in uniforms. When in my LAFD uniform the public was very appreciative of the fire service and often came to our fire stations with pies, cookies and other treats. When in my police department uniform, it was not unusual to get less than appreciated looks and occasional comments by some people. Yet during holidays the Police Department received lovely cards and pies as well. The police officers, nevertheless, are very dedicated professionals. Their job duties and responsibilities are very different than those of the fire service. I had the opportunity to wear both uniforms and felt proud of each.

One of my proudest moments was approved by Chief of Police Dominick Rivetti in the 1980s, when he approved my plan to place defibrillators on police vehicles in order to save lives. That program still exists and is maintained by dedicated professional police officers who respond very rapidly to cardiac arrest patients whose hearts are too good to die. I remain the coordinator of that program to this day.

City of San Fernando
Police Department
Exemplary Service
from 1983–2001
Alan Cowen
served as
Officer
Sergeant
Lieutenant
POLICE

I hope you have enjoyed reading this book as much as I enjoyed writing it.

For all the future first responders who may read this, you are embarking on a most exciting profession, to be respected by all of society. There can be no greater chosen job than helping others in their greatest time of need. When someone's life is in the balance and you are the one to intervene, you will be doing what most people cannot do: responding to their immediate needs and trying to save their life. It is a stressful occupation, without a doubt, but when your tour of duty is over you will be filled with gratitude that you gave your best effort to help.

For all of the Paramedics, Firefighters and EMTs who are out there right now, doing your job duties and responsibilities, where the rubber meets the road - I commend you and please stay safe. You are giving of yourself when you care for another person. Your skills and expertise will lead you to save many lives in your time as a first responder. Stay safe and be careful.

I want to request of you a favor: please don't put this book on a shelf and forget it. Instead, leave it on a desk or table where you can open it and remember how great each of you are, how important your career is, and how you can treat your next patient...whether it is 2:00PM or 2:00AM.

Thanks!

Fraternally,

Chief Alan R. Cowen, Deputy Chief (Ret.)
Former Paramedic Chief
Los Angeles Fire Department

I want to take this opportunity to express my gratitude and thanks to Patrick and Crystal McCoppin of McMac Publications for their industry expertise in making sure all the elements of this book were compiled accurately and professionally. Both Patrick and Crystal have been in the graphics and publishing trade for over four decades and made many unique suggestions that were incorporated into this final product. They both are passionately invested in the end product.

If that's not enough, they invited me to start this project with a visit to their home in Mammoth Lakes, California - a long working weekend to review all the materials I collected over the past few decades for the book you are now holding. Their generosity is appreciated, which I may add included some great meals throughout my time there. We've made many lasting memories and I wish to thank them both from the apex of my heart.

During this lengthy project I've learned that I'm their very last client after a long and successful career. I consider myself quite fortunate to have gotten this project in just prior to their retirement.

Alan R. Cowen
Thousand Oaks, CA
2023

Please consider a quiet moment of reflection for the
men, women and families who have paid the ultimate price
while in service to the people of the City of Los Angeles

www.ingramcontent.com/pod-product-compliance
Lightning Source LLC
Chambersburg PA
CBHW041509120626
46551CB00018B/2358

* 9 7 9 8 2 1 8 5 2 3 1 5 2 *